Sunburnt Cities

In recent years there has been a growing focus on urban and environmental studies and the skills and techniques to address the wider challenges of how to create sustainable communities. Central to that demand is the increasing urgency of addressing the issue of urban decline, and the response has almost always been to pursue growth policies to attempt to reverse that decline. The track record of growth policies has been mixed at best.

Until the first decade of the twenty-first century, decline was assumed to be an issue only for former industrial cities—the so-called Rustbelt. But the sudden reversal in growth in the major cities of the American Sunbelt has shown that urban decline can be a much wider issue. Justin B. Hollander's research into urban decline in both the Sunbelt and Rustbelt draws lessons for planners and policymakers that can be applied universally.

Hollander addresses the reasons and statistics behind these "shrinking cities" with a positive outlook, arguing that growth for growth's sake is not beneficial for communities, suggesting instead that urban development could be achieved through shrinkage. Case studies on Phoenix, Flint, Orlando, and Fresno support the argument, and Hollander delves into the numbers, literature, and individual lives affected and how they have changed in response to the declining regions.

Written for urban scholars and to suit a wide range of courses focused on contemporary urban studies, this text forms a base for all study on shrinking cities for professionals, academics, and students in urban design, planning, public administration, and sociology.

Justin B. Hollander is an Assistant Professor of Urban and Environmental Policy and Planning at Tufts University, Massachusetts, USA and a Research Scientist at the George Perkins Marsh Institute at Clark University, Massachusetts, USA.

"[Justin Hollander] favors an idea called "smart decline" or "smart shrinkage" which boils down to a version of the old lemons/lemonade wisdom: If your city stops growing, can you do something positive with that? Can you manage shrinkage the way you once hoped to manage growth?"
Scott Dickensheets, *Las Vegas Sun, USA*

"Hollander takes on the dominant paradigm of cities attempting to grow out of decline and challenges the common assertion that Sunbelt cities will quickly bounce back from the foreclosure crisis. He combines solid scholarship with engaging narrative to make Sunburnt Cities a must read for planners, policymakers, scholars and anyone interested in the future of these boom-and-bust places."
Dan Immergluck, *Associate Professor, School of City and Regional Planning, Georgia Institute of Technology, USA*

"This is a useful analysis that will be a welcomed addition to the urban planning literature"
Prof Emily Talen, *School of Geographical Sciences and Urban Planning, Arizona State University, USA*

"Sunburnt Cities is a call to action for planners and policymakers to change course from "growth at all costs" to a development model that is green and economically sustainable. Hollander once again establishes intriguing connections that few have made as he eloquently describes how communities in the Sun and Rust Belt can learn from each other in addressing declining populations and increasing property vacancy. A must read for practitioners, policymakers, and researchers throughout all regions."
J.M. Schilling, *Associate Director, Metropolitan Institute, Virginia Polytechnic Institute and State University, USA*

"[Hollander] at Tufts is a rising star in planning research"
Lisa Schweitzer, *Associate Professor of Urban Planning, University of Southern California, USA*

Sunburnt Cities

The Great Recession, depopulation, and urban planning in the American Sunbelt

Justin B. Hollander

Foreword by Frank J. Popper

Routledge
Taylor & Francis Group

LONDON AND NEW YORK

First published 2011
by Routledge
2 Park Square, Milton Park, Abingdon, Oxon OX14 4RN

Simultaneously published in the USA and Canada
by Routledge
270 Madison Avenue, New York, NY 10016

Routledge is an imprint of the Taylor & Francis Group, an informa business

Typeset in Frutiger by
GreenGate Publishing Services, Tonbridge, Kent

Printed and bound in Great Britain by
TJ International Ltd, Padstow, Cornwall

British Library Cataloguing in Publication Data
A catalogue record for this book is available from the British Library

Library of Congress Cataloging-in-Publication Data
Hollander, Justin B.
Sunburnt Cities: the Great Recession, depopulation, and urban planning in the American Sunbelt / Justin B. Hollander.
p. cm.
Includes bibliographical references and index.
1. Cities and towns—Sunbelt States. 2. City planning—Sunbelt States. 3. Migration, Internal—Sunbelt States. 4. Sunbelt States—Economic conditions—21st century.
I. Title.
HT123.5.S86H65 2011
307.760973--dc22
2010026798

ISBN13: 978-0-415-59211-6 (hbk)
ISBN13: 978-0-415-59212-3 (pbk)
ISBN13: 978-0-203-83438-1 (ebk)

Contents

List of figures

List of tables

Acknowledgments

This book owes much to the support and encouragement of a broad network of friends, colleagues, and family members. First, there are my colleagues in the Department of Urban and Environmental Policy and Planning at Tufts University: Julian Agyeman, Rachel Bratt, Mary Davis, Laurie Goldman, Fran Jacobs, James Jennings, Shelly Krimsky, Clare McCallum, Maria Nicolau, Barbara Parmenter, Ann Rappaport, Rusty Russell, Ann Urosevich, and Jon Witten. Beyond UEP, I also enjoyed great support from colleagues across the Tufts campus, special thanks go to Andrew McClellan, Lynne Pepall, Durwood Marshall, Kent Portney, and Jeff Zabel. Graduate students at Tufts provided invaluable research assistance on this book, including Erin Heacock, Elizabeth Antin, Pete Kane, Erin Kizer, Sarah Spicer, Michelle Moon, Becky Gallagher, Jessica Soule, and Courtney Knapp. I am also deeply indebted to the scores of local officials, community leaders, and engaged residents who participated in this research.

My early interest in the topic of this book was supported by Peter Wissoker, Frank Popper, Jeremy Németh, Joe Schilling, Terry Schwarz, Niall Kirkwood, and Kristen Crossney and to them I am grateful. At the generous invitation of Edward Glaeser, an early version of this research was presented at the Taubman Center for Local and State Government at Harvard University in 2008. More advanced versions benefitted greatly from feedback received at the public talks I gave in 2009: the Association of Collegiate Schools of Planning Annual Conference, the Boston University School of Social Work Colloquium, and the Greening the Post-Industrial City: Innovative Reuse of Philadelphia's Idle Lands Conference at Drexel University.

The writing of this book would not have been possible without the financial support of the Tufts University Faculty Research Awards Committee and the Genesee Institute—thanks go to Christina Kelley—and Robert Johnson and Pamela Dunkle at the George Perkins Marsh Institute at Clark University. Thanks as well to Armando Carbonell at the Lincoln Institute of Land Policy for his ongoing support.

I am grateful to Susan Schulman for her efforts in finding a publisher in Routledge and acknowledge the patience and attention offered by Alex Hollingsworth and Louise Fox at Routledge. Thanks also go to *Plan Canada* for granting permission to use in this book portions of an article I co-authored with Frank Popper in 2007 (volume 47, issue 2). Portions of Chapter 7 were adapted from an article I wrote in *Cityscape* in 2010 (volume 12, issue 1).

Most of all I offer my deepest appreciation to my family for helping make this book a reality.

Foreword

Justin Hollander, my friend, co-author and former Rutgers city-planning student, treats an important subject. He explores the beginnings of what I suspect is the final phase of a long-term three-part global transformation in First World economies. The shift will probably hit Information Age American cities and suburbs hard, especially in the Sunbelt, his focus. He shows the initial turns—early, but unmistakable if the reader knows where to look—of one of the hinges of contemporary land and environmental history. It amounts to a breathtaking sight, one that will affect nearly all of us.

Hollander, a Tufts University professor with much practical experience, wrote an ambitious and well-received 2009 book, *Polluted and Dangerous: America's Worst Abandoned Properties and What Can Be Done About Them*. It offers a field guide to a nasty new set of large land-use amphibians, HI-TOADS (read the book) full of toxic waste and other hazards. He shows how and why these creatures are not about to go extinct. He traces their natural history, explores their ecology and describes how they can evolve—with help from their planner-keepers—into more benign animals. In 2010, he published *Principles of Brownfield Regeneration: Cleanup, Design, and Reuse of Derelict Land*, written with Niall Kirkwood and Julia Gold, applying this approach to the keystone species of HI-TOADS, urban brownfields.

In *Sunburnt Cities: The Great Recession, Depopulation, and Urban Planning in the American Sunbelt* he turns his imaginative eye to an even larger topic that could reach to the level of national destiny. The book seems to start innocently. It shows what planners, local governments, community activists, and other urbanists have traditionally thought about city depopulation: not much. They have mostly ignored the possibility and, when it did happen, the reality. Zoning is the standard local city-planning device for controlling land uses, and no American zoning ordinance explicitly or implicitly sees depopulation or shrinkage as even distant eventualities.

Yet big deindustrializing Northeast and Midwest cities of the U.S. Rustbelt, like Buffalo, Cleveland, Philadelphia, and St. Louis—plus the grand-slam case, Detroit—have steadily lost population since the middle of the last century. Their hardest-hit neighborhoods—already mostly poor and minority at the start—have become nearly deserted by all but the most wishful, desperate or immovable, such as the elderly, the prey of criminals. The same tragedy often overtook mid-sized Rustbelt cities: Camden, New Jersey; Cairo, Illinois; Waterbury, Connecticut, and their many counterparts. The depopulation makes much of a Boston–Baltimore Amtrak trip, say, or a drive through many Great Lakes cities dispiriting, journeys through American ruins. In 1900, Buffalo, New York, was the country's eighth largest city. Now downtown Buffalo, especially around its gigantic Late Victorian city hall, looks like a size-forty man in a size-sixty suit. Reputable community organizers talk of the failed state of Ohio.

Two or three generations of unmistakable urban shrinkage saw next to no serious local response, much less a national one. The typical results are neighborhoods or large parts of cities that are in some ways worse than slums. They are places from which civilization is withdrawing or has withdrawn. The outcomes are a national embarrassment, really an American disgrace. Such areas feature numerous empty lots, decaying houses and businesses, security grates everywhere and a sense that even the more prosperous-looking facades hide fearsome economic insecurity. Hollander's excellent analytic chapter on Flint, Michigan, the first home of General Motors and later Rivethead and Michael Moore, documents how the process plays out.

Then the book moves to the Sunbelt. It shows that in late 2006, the region's previous fast growth, which had partly sprung from the Rustbelt's depopulation, began to falter, soon giving way to actual neighborhood and city decline. Now the cause was not deindustrialization in the automobile or steel sectors, but real-estate collapse—mortgage foreclosures, underwater equity and homeowner walkaways. And now the locus was not old industrial cities, but the suburban or suburban-looking parts of new Information Age ones.

By June 2010, Nevada had the nation's highest foreclosure, bankruptcy, and unemployment rates, a rare triple play of financial and land-use misery. Big chunks of local Sunbelt economies had relied on home-building and real-estate transactions: growth that stopped. Hollander dissects the destruction in Fresno, Orlando, and Phoenix, where empty unsanitary swimming pools and collapsing multi-car garages symbolize middle-class and affluent despair. Interestingly, Texas has thus far mostly escaped this ordeal because it has tighter lending laws and a more diversified economy than other Sunbelt states, including oil. Meanwhile, of course, Detroit and its peers continued their depopulation, as the 2010 Census showed.

The book's mood, perhaps oddly, offers encouragement. In Flint, the three Sunbelt cities and elsewhere, Hollander finds the beginnings of a movement for smart decline. I and my wife Deborah Popper, a geographer at the College of Staten Island/City University of New York and Princeton University, coined the term in a July 2002 piece in *Planning*. We played off a familiar planning term, smart growth, which essentially means using environmental ideas to guide growth.

Hollander shows the tentative emergence of all kinds of smart-decline Sunbelt and Rustbelt devices: visioning exercises, land banks, rapid delinquency sales to neighbors, and aggressive strategies to maintain parcels unwillingly held by public agencies—even the demolition of unoccupied structures, as has happened in Flint or the promotion of urban farming, as has happened in Cleveland and Detroit. The Rustbelt has experienced depopulation for much longer than the Sunbelt, and has only in the last five years or so started to deal with it. I agree with Hollander that the Sunbelt will soon feel compelled to catch up.

What he wants from planners and other urbanists is a rethinking of the very idea of growth: should cities always seek it? They should, he argues, sometimes aim for smaller and better—certainly different—results than the unthinking quest for growth has yielded in Detroit or Tampa. They can invent new ways to evaluate growth and decline prospects before they are stuck with 2011's Youngstown or Phoenix; or—to take Southern but not formerly fast-growth Sunbelt examples— 2011's Memphis or pre- or post-Katrina New Orleans. They can find arguments to convince skeptical city politicians, business groups, and home- and landowners, all of whom have always seen growth as an unquestioned imperative, always lived in communities where local politics and local real estate were nearly the same activity. In short, Hollander says, an abstract and eminently opposable planning idea like smart decline can float in the stagnant vat of American urban and suburban politics. Again I agree with him, especially over the long run.

In fact the issues get even larger, reach more people, bigger land areas, longer historical spans, and deeper emotional trauma. Generations before huge chunks of Cleveland and Orlando began depopulating because of deindustrialization and foreclosures, vast rural regions faced shrinkage because of uncontrollable, often capricious national and international shifts in their agricultural and natural-resource markets—and also because their people fled the markets' uncertainties for the then-growing cities.

Thus Northern New England—parts of Maine, New Hampshire, Vermont, and by some definitions New York State's Adirondack Mountains—began shrinking in 1825, as the completion of New York's Erie Canal opened up competitive Midwest farmlands (and powered Buffalo's growth at the Western end of the canal). Northern New England's depopulation did not end until the early twentieth century, when new automobiles and their roads made the region more accessible to Boston, New York City, and other Eastern Seaboard tourists and second-home buyers. Similarly, parts of the rural South saw White and Black depopulation for generations after the Civil War.

Several large rural regions are now experiencing long-term shrinkage: for example, the Lower Mississippi Delta, stretching from Illinois, Kentucky, and Missouri in the North through Louisiana in the South; central Appalachia, consisting of parts of Kentucky, North Carolina, Tennessee, Virginia, and West Virginia; the northern Midwest, comprising parts of Michigan, Minnesota, and Wisconsin; and central Alaska, between the Brooks and Alaska Ranges.

The best-known current case of rural shrinkage is perhaps the Great Plains, the sixth of the Lower 48 that stretches from Montana and North Dakota in the North to New Mexico in the South. The region has parts of ten American states, plus parts of three Canadian provinces and of four Mexican ones. Less than two decades after white American settlers began homesteading the Plains, large stretches began depopulating in the late 1880s, when a string of bad winters killed many cattle and much wheat. Even larger swaths depopulated during the ecological catastrophe of the 1930s Dust Bowl, probably twentieth-century America's worst environmental disaster.

By the mid-1980s, the region's persisting slow-leak depopulation meant that much of it was reverting to frontier. Huge stretches of the Plains had six or fewer people per square mile, the density standard of the nineteenth-century Censuses and that used by great University of Wisconsin and Harvard historian Frederick Jackson Turner in the Manifest Destiny era to separate the frontier from more settled places.

(Think Manhattan with at most 138 people.) Much of the region's agriculture—cattle, wheat, corn, and in the South cotton—had become nationally and internationally unneeded, propped up only by a baffling array of federal farm subsidies and more obviously Social Security. Rural Plains' towns had often lost their doctors, lawyers, clergy, bankers, and farm suppliers. The young left to seek better opportunities, the middle-aged remained in place, and the elderly formed the largest proportion of any American region.

In 1987, Deborah and I wrote another *Planning* piece that explored the lessons of the region's hard history. We suggested that the Plains' future, particularly in the many places where settlement had visibly retracted, might lie in new, more environmentally sensitive land uses that fell somewhere between traditional agriculture and pure wilderness. We called our approach the Buffalo Commons. Like smart decline, it at first provoked opposition from parties that felt threatened: local landowners, politicians, and business groups. It appeared to them to be a deliberate undoing of settlement, Manifest Destiny running in perverse reverse.

But in the years since farmers, ranchers, Indian tribes, state governments, banks, and non-profit groups like the Virginia-based Nature Conservancy, the country's largest land-preservation group, and the Texas-based Great Plains Restoration Council (disclosure: I chair its board) have taken a range of serious steps to achieve the Buffalo Commons. Ted Turner, the CNN mogul, bought seventeen Plains cattle ranches totaling over 3,100 square miles, larger than Delaware and Rhode Island combined, replaced the cattle with buffalo, antelope, and deer, replanted the original grasses, and culled some of the buffalo to supply his national restaurant chain, Ted's Montana Grill. Animals rarely go extinct if people eat them.

In Kansas, a former Republican governor who denounced the idea in the 1980s while in office supported it by 2004. In 2009, the state's two largest papers editorially supported it (the first such endorsements anywhere) and suggested two small adjacent counties on the state's Colorado border—with a total population of 2,600—as the core of a presumably multi-state Buffalo Commons. (The counties predictably resisted.) In 2010, a Kansas Democrat ran for the U.S. Senate on a platform that went out of its way to incorporate the Buffalo Commons.

Deborah and I expect in our lifetimes to see a large clear Buffalo Commons. When we began our Plains research in 1985, the standard political/environmental wisdom on buffalo was that they had experienced terrible nineteenth and twentieth centuries. Estimates suggest that 30 to 70 million of them roamed the Plains in 1750. With the coming of the Whites and their Indian collaborators, the number dropped under 1,000 by 1900. Now the conversation is different. There are perhaps 500,000 Plains buffalo, the numbers are growing fast, and they figure in many Plains restoration efforts and schemes, including those that expect major temperature rises in the Southern Plains because of global warming.

The rhetoric looks forward rather than backward: it often regards the twenty-first century return of the buffalo as a national mission, a second chance to finally do right by the Plains and its people, particularly its Indians. The success of our Plains work led us to formulate the idea of smart decline 15 years after our first Buffalo Commons piece. It is in truth a generalization of the Buffalo Commons, an extension of it to new, often more urban places.

To review: large American rural agricultural regions have seen population decline, economic shrinkage, and sometimes social recovery since the nineteenth century. Large and mid-sized heavy-industrial Rustbelt cities have followed roughly the same path since 1950, but it is too early to know whether they can recover. Sunbelt Information Age middle-class cities and suburbs have just entered the path. All three types of places—rural, urban, and suburban; Agricultural, Industrial, and Information Age—can keep depopulating together, a trifecta of decline.

Other American places seem likely to continue growing: for example, large cities such as New York, Los Angeles, Chicago, Seattle, or Washington DC, whose populations have enlarged through immigration, adaptation to the Information Age, and attractiveness to young people; rural areas such as Southern New England, the Southern Midwest or the Pacific Northwest coast that are near big cities; or suburbs across the country that never grew as fast or as rashly as Sunbelt ones and so never had to endure their fall.

The analysis fits much of the First World. Many Western European countries face region-scale shrinkage of their once-industrial cities, as in Germany's Ruhr Valley (for starters, Dortmund, Düsseldorf, and Essen) or much of the urban United Kingdom away from London (Glasgow, Liverpool, and Newcastle). Western Europe also has rural regions that are depopulating as their traditional farm/natural-resource bases wither: central Spain (cattle), South Wales (coal) and the Vosges Mountains region of Eastern France along the German border (mixed farming). Most such places are trying, often successfully, to replace their struggling rural enterprises or at least supplement them by finding tourism, recreation, retirement, and cultural amenities: the consumption side of the Information Age.

Russia and its one-time Eastern European satellites have similar rural areas, plus declining deindustrializing large cities, such as nearly all of those in the old East Germany (Chemnitz, Magdeburg, and Rostock) and the monograds, the once-polluting-industry cities of the former Soviet planned economy (Baikalsky, Pikalevo, and Togliatti). Japan and to a lesser extent South Korea have comparable issues, worsened by their especially aged populations, among the oldest in the world.

The analysis offers plenty of gloom. In an American context and an international-finance one, it implies that the ongoing Great Recession will be W-shaped: a second nasty dip looms as the suburban Sunbelt crash intensifies and reverberates with, for instance, the American economy's continuing weakness and the Southern Europe government deficits. Yet this is not the customary quasi-Malthusian environmentalist story of resource shortages or society-wide deprivation.

Many American (and European and East Asian) farm regions suffer, at the same time that food and fiber products are mostly in oversupply. Automobile, steel, and other manufacturing towns bleed, yet good cars and industrial equipment are plentiful. American farmers, ranchers, loggers, miners, and heavy-industrial concerns of all kinds do not have problems of underproduction, lagging demand or outdated technology. They have the opposite problems: overproduction, plenty of demand, and excellent technology. They have been too efficient and successful for their own good. They did their job so well that they harmed their self-interest.

As a result, they have been passed by. The larger society presumably benefits, at least over the long run. But the people and places left behind, typically with no recourse, suffer hugely. Cherished, often characteristically American crafts, skills, and ways of life quietly disappear, with almost no one to notice or mourn them. Every year the culture feels more tediously homogenous—more nationalized, globalized, and unsatisfyingly effective—even as we say we seek and value diversity. As a society we have a backlog of homework piling up for ourselves. So does much of the rest of the First World and nations like Brazil, China, and India that may be rapidly approaching First World status.

Smart decline, planned shrinkage, rethinking growth, the Buffalo Commons— all these ideas of Hollander, my wife Deborah and me need further exploration. It often seems that First World mature capitalism rewards and punishes people, groups, and places unaccountably, for dark comical reasons of its own. Yet Eastern Montana, most of Detroit's neighborhoods, a mounting number of Fresno's, their European and East Asian counterparts, and all the fast-rising competitors demand understanding. This book, which I hope I have made you eager to read, offers a big step in that direction.

Frank J. Popper
Rutgers and Princeton Universities
Highland Park, New Jersey, USA

List of abbreviations

CBO   Community-based organization
CDC   Community Development Corporation
FRB   Federal Reserve Bank
FRS   Federal Reserve System
GIS   Geographic Information Systems
GM   General Motors
HOA   Home Owner Association
HUD   Department of Housing and Urban Development
LISC   Local Initiatives Support Corporation
LOHOA   Laveen Organization of Home Owner Associations
NGO   non-governmental organizations
NIA   Neighborhood Improvement Area
NSP   National Stabilization Program
TNBW   Tomahawk Village Block Watch
USPS   United States Postal Service
VMT   vehicle miles traveled
ZCTA   Zip code tabulation area

CHAPTER 1

Introduction

Detroit, Michigan

Northwest Detroit has always been his home. Leroy and his family would like to stay, but the neighborhood is changing. The wider City of Detroit has lost half of its population since 1950, but this neighborhood of 1920s-era single-family homes on quarter-acre lots always seemed to hold its own. Not anymore. The city's hemorrhaging population is now beginning to bleed into Northwest Detroit. Vacant homes are targeted by arsonists, open lots are left uncared for after derelict structures were razed, the once lively streets are now empty, and the gangs have moved in. Leroy and his family debate leaving the neighborhood themselves, but are determined to stay and make it better.

Petunia Gardens, Florida

Deborah and Hank thought they had finally made it. After toiling away in trailer parks and slumlord rental housing, they could finally afford to buy a home of their own in the converted swamps of the West coast of Florida. The realtor and mortgage officer promised them the American Dream when they signed a contract to buy a new home in Petunia Gardens—a 1,000-unit new housing complex built over wetlands. With no money down and an adjustable-rate mortgage they had no trouble making the monthly payments. Within months of moving in, news began to spread of the national collapse of the subprime mortgage market. Soon, their new neighbors began to flee, some voluntarily and others by the force of foreclosure. Petunia Gardens today sits half built and half empty, with Deborah and Hank joined by only a few dozen other hold-outs. This new housing development is priced too high for the market, a credit crunch limits any new homebuyers, and the dream community is now a ghost of its former self.[1]

The goal of this book is to analyze the widespread phenomenon of population decline and its impacts on Sunbelt urban neighborhoods—to learn from the past experiences faced by Leroy and his family in the Rustbelt city of Detroit and to offer detailed understanding and guidance concerning the conditions faced by Deborah and Hank in the Sunbelt. In the past, public policy and planning would have little constructive to say about depopulation except to try to reverse it. But today, under the broad umbrella of "shrinking cities" there is hope for places that are losing population and unlikely to reverse course. These shrinking cities' activists have focused primarily on perennially declining places such as St. Louis and Detroit, but the concept of shrinkage also has saliency as policymakers and planners attack the problem of depopulation in the formerly booming Sunbelt.

When faced with problems related to depopulation, urban planners globally have turned to growth as a panacea (Portney 2002; Pinderhughes 2004). Under the guise of "development," these planners try to grow their cities and towns to be bigger and better. Defined by Webster's dictionary as "a step or stage in growth, advancement, etc" (Guralnik 1986, p. 386), development means advancing in a conceptually indeterminate manner. For a city to develop, does that mean healthier children? Does it mean more jobs? Does it mean less crime? Does it simply mean more people?

Without a clear answer, planners have pursued development—have manipulated policies and regulations—to advance without public consensus about where they are advancing to. The results have more often than not been dismal.

In trying to "advance" or "grow," the City of Buffalo built a billion dollar light rail to nowhere, while its public schools are woefully underfunded. In its attempts to develop, the City of Youngstown heavily subsidized the construction of several prisons throughout the city, while less money is available for crime fighting. Part of Bridgeport, Connecticut's strategy to grow involved the construction of several sports stadiums using public resources—facilities that remain vacant most of the year while public housing facilities next door need roof repairs.

Critics of development are common, with big thinkers such as David Harvey, Susan Fainstein, and Neil Smith at the front of the intellectual fight against city policies that oppress the poor, enrich real estate interests, and advance the political ambitions of elected officials. Embedded in these critiques of development is an inherent concern over both how growth impacts on quality of life for residents (particularly those most disenfranchised) and concern over the process by which local government decisions are made. If development does not work, it may be because the concept is so fatally flawed that it should be entirely discarded.

Growth, on the other hand, is more conceptually tight, indicating an increase in population, jobs, and perhaps even income levels. But is growing the only way to advance? Do more people mean that a city can move forward in the next stage in providing fair and equitable education to its children? Do more jobs mean that a city can advance in its provision of parks and recreational amenities? In some cases, the answer is yes, but for some cities there may be another way to develop: by shrinking.

There may be a way for planners to develop their cities without growing them, to enhance the quality of life of residents without adding jobs, people, or even increasing income levels. While professional planners might scoff at this idea, there is growing evidence (to which this book contributes) that suggests that development can be achieved through shrinkage.

An emerging group of practitioners and scholars has embraced this kind of thinking into a new way to talk about population and economic decline—they are literally changing the discourse around decline. Proponents of "shrinking cities" reject the growth-based paradigm that feeds much of urban planning in North America. Rather than trying to grow every declining city, the shrinking cities approach argues that not all cities are going to grow back to their former glory.

Instead of chasing industry with hefty incentives and the other standard economic development tools, for some cities it would be prudent to just focus on improving the quality of life for those left behind.

This book presents original research from the storied history of the decline of the Rustbelt to inform a new conceptual framework for city planning. This conceptual framework reinvents development using the language of shrinking cities and provides a path forward for Sunbelt cities that have been devastated by the affects of the foreclosure crisis and the Great Recession, what I call Sunburnt Cities. These Sunburnt Cities can learn from the mistakes of the shrinking Rustbelt and plan for smaller futures. Sunburnt Cities can adopt this conceptual framework of planning to rightsize their physical landscapes to fit declining populations, to reconfigure infrastructure and amenities to serve fewer people. While much of the damage has essentially been done in places such as Camden, New Jersey and Syracuse, New York, there is hope for Sunburnt Cities: St. Petersburg, Florida can manage its shrinkage; Tempe, Arizona can get smaller in a good way.

This all may sound defeatist, giving into the forces around us and succumbing to loss. The conceptual framework presented here does just the opposite, it provides a new way for cities to approach depopulation but it also provides direction when a place begins to grow again. I offer here a way for cities to escape the false dichotomy of growth and decline and instead manage change in their neighborhoods, to address problems directly.

One way to escape the discourse of decline is to rethink measures of success for cities. New ways to gauge effectiveness must change for cities to be able to fundamentally rethink and re-prioritize their investments in neighborhoods, their investments in places. The old metrics told us that success was measured in the number of new jobs, but by that logic a place bleeding jobs cannot feature high quality of life. We know that is not true. Despite its fairly consistent loss of jobs and people over the last 30 years, Pittsburgh is considered one of the most desirable cities in America. Throughout America and across the world, some of the most popular, attractive, and desirable places are, in fact, shrinking. So instead of focusing on bad measures, planners ought to focus on managing change in their communities, whether that change is growth or decline.

Planning for development in growing places is logical. A suite of growth management, community empowerment, and environmental protection policies and planning approaches (often under the banner of smart growth) is well suited to creating (or trying to create) development (see Meck 2002 and others). Central to this ideology is the contention that when a region is growing (even if urban areas are declining), new growth should be concentrated in existing urban areas to reverse their population loss (Lucy and Phillips 2000; Calthorpe and Fulton 2001). Concentration of new growth into existing urban areas has been a central tenet of planning for decades, if not longer (see Real Estate Research Corporation 1974). But what if the growth is not going into the urban areas? What if the region, itself, is not growing?

Some critics have raised this question from other perspectives. Ophuls (1996) takes a political economy perspective and critiques any reliance on development as the road to a just, equitable, and ecologically sound society.

Hempel (1999) and others have advanced a version of development that is built on the foundation of sustainability. The American Planning Association has also stepped away from formally using the term development, but a close reading of their 2000 policy guide shows otherwise. Following is an excerpt from the guide, where planners are invited to take up the challenge of meeting "the demands of a growing human population that has rising aspirations for consumption and quality of life, while maintaining the rich diversity of the natural environment of biosphere" (APA 2000, p. 1). The guide presupposes that population growth is what demands planners' focus, grounding the policy statement on the premise of development, growth, and advancement. The American Planning Association provides little policy guidance to its 35,000-member practicing planners about what the demand of a shrinking human population can have on neighborhoods, cities, and regions. This omission is largely due to the field's close ties to the real estate development process and illustrates the difficulty in responding to decline.

Depopulating cities

Cities that lose population are first challenged by the fiscal impact of lost revenues from taxes and reduced revenues from state and federal aid. With fewer businesses and residents, they will experience reduced revenues from taxes. Because of how states and the federal government structure their aid programs, local governments can also lose aid when their population falls below certain threshold levels.

The economic and population decline of Rustbelt cities has been widely studied since the 1980s (Bluestone and Harrison 1982). Persistent population loss in some of America's largest cities is well known: of the largest cities in the country nearly half lost population, on average, every decade from 1950 to 2000 (27 of 64 cities). Cities such as St. Louis, Detroit, Buffalo, and New Orleans lost as much as half of their populations during those 50 years. With the collapse of manufacturing industries and the shift to a service economy, scores of cities in the Northeast and Midwest have been losing jobs and people for decades. Demographers have written and analyzed this phenomenon well, we know about the kind of population loss that has occurred and we have a high degree of certainty about the further population losses that are coming.

While only now emerging, the Sunbelt is beginning to witness widespread housing abandonment and population loss. Rapidly rising home prices, subprime mortgage lending, and an unrelenting building boom have been credited as the sources of the collapse of the real estate market in 2006, which is widely seen as the impetus for the Great Recession (Immergluck 2009).

The region's meteoric rise in population from 2000–2006 suddenly halted and reversed course. Headlines in *The New York Times* announced on Christmas Eve 2009 that the Sunbelt's unstoppable population growth had finally stopped and that states such as Florida, Nevada, and California had more residents move out than move in. These facts and figures testified to the shocking end of a long-held tradition of people migrating from cold Rustbelt cities to the sun and warmth of the South and West.

This shift in demographics has contributed to and been affected by a foreclosure crisis not seen in the U.S. in decades. The Mortgage Bankers Association has estimated that, nationally, 900,000 borrowers were in foreclosure in September 2007 (Mullins 2008). But "formerly booming Sun Belt cities are the epicenters of this economic downturn" and are bearing the greatest burden in managing the land-use changes due to mortgage foreclosure. In Southwestern Atlanta, some neighborhoods have witnessed 40 percent abandonment rates due to mortgage fraud and delinquency (Leland 2007). In 2008, Phoenix's Maricopa County had 13,000 homes in foreclosure, 600 percent higher than the previous year (Fletcher 2008).

The kind of decline seen in the Sunbelt is unquestionably different than what the Rustbelt has experienced. In fact, the Sunbelt's woes may simply be episodic and the sun-drenched growth machines of the past may begin quickly to rev up. But they also may continue to sputter and with future economic conditions uncertain, the past few years may presage a future of ongoing decline.

If decline in the Sunbelt continues, unchecked, these population and land-use changes will radically alter the American urban, suburban, and rural landscape. While planning and public policy officials are engaged primarily in fighting the core demographic and economic changes at work—a development agenda of bringing jobs and people back, some are beyond the reach of government. A good example is from Orlando, Florida, where at the beginning of the foreclosure crisis, city officials were desperate to grow back their faltering economy. They put together a relocation incentive package for the internationally renowned Burnham Institute for Medical Research to the tune of $367.2 million. The Institute agreed to come to Orlando and bring its projected workforce of 303 jobs, at a recruitment cost of $1.2 million per job. In this case, the City effectively won out over other cities vying to host the Institute, but at $1.2 million per job it shows how difficult it is to change the fundamental economic conditions of a city. At the time, Orlando could afford to use public monies to "buy" jobs, but with an unemployed workforce of roughly 7,500, the ability to address all of the cities' economic challenges is limited.

For those cities experiencing changes that are persistent and long term, for those neighborhoods that are not going to repopulate any time soon, the answer for them may lie in managing those changes in a sound and sustainable manner instead of fighting those trends at over $1 million per job.

Of course population is only one factor in the myriad of variables that contribute to the physical shaping and re-shaping of neighborhoods. Racial, ethnic, and class change in neighborhoods can have a profound effect on stability, harmony, and vitality. With the explosive growth in immigrant population in the U.S. in the last decade, it is hard to believe that population decline is a challenge at all. But much of that new immigrant population has followed the jobs, and places without job growth are seeing few new immigrants. This book is about those places, the places where few are migrating to, and many are leaving. Lucy and Phillips (2000) write about the constantly moving American public: the average renter moves every three years, the average homeowner moves every seven years. As Lucy and Phillips put it, if your neighborhood does not constantly replenish your population with new immigrants (domestic and foreign) then your net population change will be negative over time.

The mongrel cities of the twenty-first century that Leonie Sandercock (2003) writes about have people of all types, languages, size, and shape coming together in communities, changing them physically and socially. Gottlieb (2007) describes the widespread impact of immigrant Latino culture on the environmental movement in Los Angeles. A key player in this movement is the urban planner, James Rojas, an activist in the effort to create more dense urban spaces and a re-fashioning of urban neighborhoods in the image of Latino residents' south of the border homelands (Gottlieb 2007).

These cultural, linguistic, and social factors have a physical effect on neighborhoods and can even contribute to growth and decline in population. Throughout this book, close care will be paid to how such factors impact on neighborhood change in shrinking cities. How communities plan for decline will vary depending on their composition, their history, and the eclectic personalities of those who live there.

Taking a step back, it becomes clear that both the history and the future of human settlement is about unevenness. When we look back at Roman ruins and imagine crumbling skyscrapers ahead, there is always a physical remnant—an artifact left behind when people leave a place. While astronomical growth rates in developing countries and booming suburbs in developed countries lead many analysts to focus on the physical effects of growth on the landscape, the physical effects of decline are equally pronounced. I will argue in this book that decline wreaks even greater havoc on established human settlements than growth (a message oft told).

But I stake new ground in this book through an optimistic note. This physical change that decline brings, it is not universally bad. While my focus is on the physical, the research presented herein transcends the built-up world of urban planning to broader societal concerns about decline. Through this investigation, larger lessons about how to confront loss and decline are being made available to other disciplines as they confront change. For the planner, *change* itself is the challenge to overcome not whether that change is good or bad. The job of the planner is to *manage* that change so that the outcomes are always good (for residents, businesses, and communities).

For other fields, confronting change can be difficult and especially the kinds of changes that include decline or shrinkage. What does it mean for a business to shrink? What does it mean for an educational curriculum to shrink? What does it mean for an organization when its diversity shrinks? In this study, I show what it means for a city to shrink and can begin to translate those results into a broader, more general discourse on decline.

Cities are a good place to begin this new and novel line of inquiry because the very idea of a city is a hotly contested one. From the early utopian planners such as Ebenezer Howard and his *Garden Cities of Tomorrow* to Le Corbusier's *Radiant City*, to today's New Urbanist visionaries and their transit-oriented developments, the solution to the problem of the city has, throughout the past few centuries, been to create non-cities. These non-cities have taken many different forms, but in many policy and planning solutions it has meant starting fresh, starting anew in a field or forest or swamp. Regardless of the rectitude of these past practices of planning, the results have been an anti-city legacy that traces its legacy in America back to Thomas Jefferson and his commitments to an agrarian society over an urban society. Barring any major social, political, or demographic shift, the declining city is likely here to stay and planners ought to focus their energies on managing the changes that come with smaller cities.

Book outline

More than anything else, this book is an investigation into the paradox of planning for growth in shrinking Sunbelt cities. The book's organization follows a simple argument: as Sunbelt cities face a new era of depopulation and disinvestment, there is much to be learned from the experiences of the Rustbelt. The unique political and geographic history and context of the Sunbelt help to explain why depopulation is occurring, but also help to show how it impacts on the physical landscape in both different and similar ways as the Rustbelt (Chapter 2).

Over the last 30 years, Rustbelt cities have physically changed as they lost people. This change is documented in two chapters, the first being a macro-level view of how dozens of Rustbelt cities have changed demographically and physically (Chapter 3), the second is a micro-level view of the ways in which this change occurred in three neighborhoods in Flint, Michigan (Chapter 4).

Understanding this change then lays the foundation for a conceptual framework for urban planning that can then be applied back to the Sunbelt (Chapter 5). The framework introduced builds directly on the empirical evidence presented in Chapters 3 and 4, but also builds on the rich and diverse literature presented in Chapter 2.

Turning back to the Sunbelt, and using the new framework as a guide, a documentation and analysis of the demographic and physical change underway in the region is presented at the macro-level (Chapter 6) and then at the micro-level in three case studies of shrinking Sunbelt cities where the role of local officials and community leaders in responding to decline is examined (Chapters 7, 8, and 9).

The book concludes by tying the findings to the original goals of the book, while offering policy recommendations (Chapter 10).

CHAPTER 2

Ways to think about decline

Introduction

Urban planners have, for decades, been caught up in a false dichotomy: when a community grows in population it prospers, when it declines in population it suffers. E.F. Schumacher challenged that false dichotomy with his legendary volume *Small is Beautiful* in 1975. Finkler *et al.* followed with *Urban Nongrowth* in 1976. But the on-the-ground world of practice never really responded to those critiques and the growth/decline link prevailed. That is, until just recently.

Some planners are beginning to ask whether their communities can thrive and improve while staying small or even declining in population. In many ways, it is out of desperation with the profound failure of growth-oriented economic development strategies over the last several decades to arrest decline in scores of cities throughout the U.S. and beyond. The infusion of public monies into new stadiums, job training centers, infrastructure, and new housing in cities, big and small has had an effect on some but not all. Called the "forgotten cities" by Lynn Fisher and her colleagues at the Massachusetts Institute of Technology, the power and success of economic turn-around has simply not worked everywhere. In fact, there is mounting evidence that economic development fails more often than it works in reversing structural economic conditions contributing to population and employment decline (Boyer 1983; Schumpeter 1983; Logan and Molotch 1987).

Urban decline has a bad reputation. Beauregard's 2003 book *Voices of Decline* documented in fastidious detail the ways that the discourses of decline were developed and positioned in American culture. Beauregard concludes that modern society's drive for bigger, faster, more of everything required that population and employment loss in mid-twentieth century cities be viewed in antipode to the growth and vitality of the suburbs. Thus, instead of the depopulation of cities such as Newark, St. Louis, and Detroit being described as a neutral demographic fact, those changes were positioned as something very bad in contrast to the good of the suburb.

But population loss does not have to be a bad thing for a community. Fewer people can mean less congestion; it can mean more open space and recreational opportunities. Fewer people in a city can mean lower student-to-teacher ratios in the classroom and faster response times from the police and fire departments. A smaller population has a smaller environmental footprint, helping a city to reduce its impacts on global climate change. Fewer jobs mean fewer cars on the roads and improved air quality. Fewer factories mean less pollution and better water quality. While population and employment declines are never the aim of public policy and planning, the affect (if managed properly) can be quite beneficial to residents and workers left behind.

But, unfortunately, cities know very little about what it takes to manage decline. More often, the loss in population is either caused by or contributes to a wide range of social, economic, and fiscal challenges. So, in a knee-jerk fashion local governments simply work to reverse the process of depopulation—a skill that only a handful have mastered.

In this chapter, I bring some order to the chaos of the urban decline phenomenon. First, I synthesize the relevant and important ideas about how neighborhoods physically change when they lose population—introducing a basic economic model of housing stability. Next, I review the choices that planners and policymakers face when their city or town loses population, presenting smart decline as an idea emerging from the shrinking cities ideology.

The notion of smart decline is a compelling one and very quickly it went from backwater to national think-tank status, as policy wonks all over have sought to find solutions to the problems of the Rustbelt. I review the brief history of the ascendancy of the language of shrinking cities in order to provide context for the focus here: the Sunbelt. Despite all of the attention to the idea of shrinking cities, there has been, to date, no serious examination of what it might mean for these Sunburnt Cities. Some historical and political context is offered to help understand how these cities have faired in the past and why they are an appealing place to look at to rethink city planning practice.

How neighborhoods physically change when they lose population

When speaking of population decline, there is no single rationale or explanation as to why a place depopulates. Depopulation has been explained by everything from natural disasters (Vale and Campanella 2005), to deindustrialization (Bluestone and Harrison 1982; McDonald 2008), suburbanization (Jackson 1985; Clark 1989), globalization (Sassen 1991; Hall 1997) and of course the natural economic cycle of boom and bust (Rust 1975). Beauregard's (2009) analysis of shrinking U.S. cities from 1820 to 2000 identified three key dimensions of shrinkage (prevalence, severity, and persistence) and concluded that the causes of population decline vary from one historical period to another.

Understanding the theoretical and conceptual explanations for decline is important, but this is not a book about why places lose population. Instead, I am focused on understanding the results of the loss and what it is that local planners and policymakers can do to manage that change.

When employment falls in a territory, people are expected to act rationally and to leave that territory and relocate to a place where new employment exists. There are several problems with this expectation, the first being that when people leave a neighborhood, the physical form of the city does not naturally shrink. Glaeser and Gyourko (2005) studied the durability of housing in their time series sample of 321 U.S. cities and towns with at least 30,000 residents in 1970, showing how housing prices declined at a faster rate in depopulating cities than prices grew in growing cities. Their research suggests that the durability of housing poses a long-term threat to neighborhood stability. Others come to the same conclusion, that is, if housing does not disappear as quickly as people do, then those abandoned structures will drag down neighborhoods by serving as a haven for criminal activity (Wallace 1989).

Another problem of population decline is that only those urban residents with means can relocate, leaving behind the poorest and most destitute residents. With fewer middle and upper-income residents in a neighborhood, there are fewer role models available to youth and prospects for upward mobility are dimmer (Wilson 1987; Sugrue 1996).

Widespread past and present discrimination in hiring and in the housing market have systematically limited relocation options for African Americans and Latinos (Massey and Denton 1993; Sugrue 1996). As such, when a neighborhood loses jobs, African Americans and Latinos have fewer choices for places to move to, which causes a further racial concentration in ghettos.

In depopulating residential neighborhoods, housing moves first from high rent (and affluent residents), to lower rent (and less affluent residents) as demand declines. In a process described as filtering, poorer economic conditions results in lower demand for housing and a filtering through economic classes of owners or renters (Hoyt 1933; Temkin and Rohe 1996). Ultimately, when demand sinks to a certain threshold level owners tend to abandon their structures (Keenan *et al.* 1999). In time, many abandoned structures become derelict and may be subject to arson. Thus, in a depopulating neighborhood, occupied housing units are replaced by both unoccupied housing units, derelict structures, and vacant lots where fire consumed the unit(s). This is a process that suggests the appropriateness of analyzing physical change through the lens of occupied housing unit density.

Rust's (1975) comprehensive study of population and employment decline in 30 U.S. metropolitan areas from the 1800s to 1970s revealed much about both why and how places decline. He found that these shrinking places experienced dramatic population loss and then "a long period of profound resistance to demographic or economic change which continues until the people, artifacts, and institutions which were assembled in the truncated growth era gradually erode away" (p. 169). The very physical fabric of neighborhoods—these artifacts are expected to "erode away" in a period of decline.

Rust's study also found that for many cases he studied, once the decline began, the effects are "expected to be felt most strongly a generation after the cessation of growth and to persist for up to 50 years" (p. 187). For the booming Sunbelt, these results present a clarion call for a new way to do planning—a new model is needed to think about neighborhood change in the face of ongoing population loss.

Conventional responses to shrinkage

Local officials effectively face three choices when presented with population decline: public redevelopment, smart decline, or no action. With public redevelopment, these agencies are essentially fighting population loss by attempting to manipulate both endogenous and exogenous factors to encourage private investment to create new jobs and generate new demand for real estate. Smart decline (the antonym of smart growth) is a way to accommodate population loss in a way that does not require a manipulation of exogenous factors and with a focus on quality of life improvements in a neighborhood. Lastly, communities may simply do nothing (this is the most popular choice).

For local government policymakers and planners, there is very little they can do about changing their population and employment levels.[1] After completing his study of 30 metropolitan areas in the U.S. over 200 years of boom and bust, Rust (1975) concluded, "national forces often overshadow local efforts to direct growth and change" (p. 169). Dewar's (1998) close examination of the effectiveness of economic development policies in Minnesota reached the same conclusion. Bradbury et al. (1981) ran a series of rigorous mathematical models to study how public redevelopment policies might impact on the continuing depopulation and economic decline of Cleveland. They also found little to no effect of such policies on the broader trends of economic decline, housing abandonment, and population loss.

Despite these challenges of trying to combat decline, politics make it a popular choice. On its own or through a redevelopment agency, a local government may choose to fight decline through publicly financed redevelopment, streetscape improvements, grants or loans to encourage new private investment, or other economic development strategies. An example of public redevelopment is when the local government funded Community Development Corporations (CDCs) to develop affordable housing in Pawtucket, Rhode Island (Doyle 2001). Another example is when local governments in Tennessee encouraged people to move to cities with financial incentives in an urban homesteading program (Accordino and Johnson 2000). The dearth of public monies available for the redevelopment of vacant and abandoned property makes partnerships with non-profit and private companies an appealing avenue for many local governments.

A movement has arisen over the last decade to redevelop brownfields. Brownfields are, statutorily, real property where redevelopment "may be complicated by the presence or potential presence of a hazardous substance, pollutant, or contaminant" (Section 101, 42 USC 9601). Addressing environmental problems head-on can be an effective way to redevelop sites left abandoned or vacant. The brownfields movement has galvanized state and federal funding in support of brownfields projects as well as a change to the federal Comprehensive Environmental Response, Compensation, and Liability Act, removing some of the most intractable legal hurdles for redevelopment. Following on the success of brownfields programs, another land-use classification has emerged: greyfields. They are essentially the same as brownfields, without the real or perceived contamination. In other words, greyfields are abandoned or underutilized property (Sobel et al. 2002; New Jersey Department of Community Affairs 2003). The State of New Jersey established a

Greyfields Task Force and is leading the way in focusing public policies to addressing decline by way of new nomenclature. The focus of much greyfields work has been the redevelopment of abandoned suburban malls (Sobel *et al.* 2002).

In a study of six large U.S. cities that tried to intervene, that attempted to shift the underlying forces shaping economic and population forces, Perloff (1980) found that none considered the possibility of failure. In devising long-term plans to address urban problems, none of these cities confronted the possibility that their efforts to shape exogenous forces might not work. Perloff calls on planners to draw on decision theory in approaching possible futures. Decision theory suggests that the dangers and risks of certain outcomes are higher than others, therefore the risk that decline could occur (with all its potential dangers) ought to be part of community planning efforts.

Perloff goes on to conclude his study of planning-in-action, stating that:

> Growth is commonly regarded as an aid to reducing unemployment and raising levels of living within a city, but a review of the statistics suggest that the connections are often tenuous. Population growth in some cases attracts many unemployed persons and many poor families so that the problems remain or are exacerbated.
>
> (Perloff 1980, p. 201)

Where fighting decline may be effective in some places, the urban studies and planning literature suggest a real opening exists for an alternative policy response that does not require growth.

Free market advocates on the one hand, argue that no local government response is needed to address decline. Clark (1989) devoted much scholarship to this perspective, proposing that governments "facilitate, even to encourage, the run-down of cities and to use such resources as may be released to promote the growth of new urban forms in the locations most suited to the needs of modern industry" (p. 129). But more often, cities do nothing because they are not able to acknowledge population decline (for political reasons or simply out of embarrassment). As just one example, Indiana County in Southwest Pennsylvania has been consistently losing population every decade since 1980, yet its planning is all focused on growth—officials seem to be ignoring the demographic trends and projections that point to further decline. In fact, there is only one master plan ever produced in the U.S. that has ever come to terms with population decline (Youngstown, Ohio in 2004); the other scores of plans produced every year in shrinking cities simply ignore population decline.

Critics of the do nothing policy approach point to research that demonstrates a contagion effect with population decline—if you do nothing, the extent and level of the population loss can increase. Wilson and Margulis (1994) showed that some neighborhoods that were economically and socially vital in the 1980s experienced severe decline in the 1990s, largely due to the spread of abandonment and crime from proximate declining neighborhoods. By doing nothing, by either ignoring or taking a philosophical stance away from public action, communities may be exacerbating their problems.

A new approach to address shrinkage

Popper and Popper (2002) define smart decline as "planning for less—fewer people, fewer buildings, fewer land uses" (p. 23). The clearest practical example of smart decline is their proposal to establish a Buffalo Commons in severely shrinking parts of the Great Plains (Matthews 2002). The Poppers' research (1987) found that the preservation of a large portion of the Great Plains as "somewhere between traditional agriculture and pure wilderness" offered "ecologically and economically restorative possibilities" (Popper and Popper 2004, p. 4). Vergara (1999) proposes an American Acropolis in downtown Detroit to preserve the scores of abandoned skyscrapers. He sees cultural benefit in establishing a park at the site to attract visitors to walk the crumbling streets.

Also, Clark (1989) encourages preservation of declining areas as vacant, arguing that these areas can be greened for "parkland and recreational spaces" (p. 143)—a suggestion echoed recently by Schilling and Logan (2008). Armborst *et al.* (2005) introduced the idea of widespread sideyard acquisitions of vacant lots as a means of reducing housing density, a process they described as blotting. They found that the urban fabric of Detroit was changing on a daily basis not by city plan or regulation, but by the actions of individual landowners in expanding their lots to more closely mirror density patterns seen in suburbia.

Community leaders in Youngstown, Ohio (which has lost half of its population since 1950) adopted this smart decline approach with a new Master Plan to address its remaining population of 74,000 (U.S. Census 2008). In the Plan, the city came to terms with its ongoing population loss and called for a "better, smaller Youngstown" focusing on improving the quality of life for existing residents rather than attempting to grow the city (City of Youngstown 2005; Hollander 2009).

Central to smart decline is a recognition of the "fallibility of the myth of endless growth" (Popper and Popper 2002, p. 23). Policy advocates in Philadelphia are also well aware that they should not place all their bets on growth. The non-profit Public/Private Ventures office issued a report calling for "the consolidation of abandoned areas and, in some cases, the relocation of those households that remain in blocks that too often look like Dresden after the Second World War" (Hughes and Cook-Mack 1999, p. 15).

To help further explain smart decline, below I offer short descriptions of two smart decline tools I have studied: Relaxed Zoning and The Reverse Land Use Allocation Model.

Relaxed Zoning addresses the fundamental economic problem in shrinking cities: excess supply of structures (housing, stores, schools) relative to demand (the number of people). Rybczynski (1995) painted a compelling picture of how this problem affects mall owners: when shopping decreases and tenants leave, the owner can decrease rents or refurbish the mall. If those strategies do not work, the mall owner can absorb the losses, but only for so long. Eventually the mall owner needs to either raise rents or go bankrupt. Rybczynski argues that city governments face the same dilemma when dealing with shrinking populations. But continuing with the mall metaphor, he offers hope through smart decline:

> The mall owner who has tried everything and finds that there is simply no demand for space has a final option: make the mall smaller. Consolidate the successful stores, close up an empty wing, pull down some of the vacant space, and run a smaller but still lucrative operation.
>
> (Rybczynski 1995, p. 37)

The process of neighborhood change described earlier in the chapter showed how depopulation causes problems. Here, I add a wrinkle: depopulation does not have to cause problems. As Rybczynski notes, a mall can be smaller but still "lucrative."

In a neighborhood, falling demand (often due to worsening economic conditions and falling employment levels) for housing will result in falling rents and house values (Hoyt 1933; Temkin and Rohe 1996). As prices fall, the ability of owners to sell is impaired (especially if their mortgage exceeds the value of their property).[2] As prices fall, the ability of landlords to recoup in rents the costs of protecting and maintaining their properties is likewise compromised (Keenan et al. 1999). A spiral of declining values, disinvestment, and deteriorating housing stock typically destroys stable neighborhoods and spreads dereliction (Bradbury et al. 1982).

More than anything else, this process highlights how fewer people means a decreased demand for housing. The conventional responses to decline highlighted above argue for public subsidy to reverse the population decline, but what about reducing the supply of housing instead? A proactive strategy that reduces housing supply concomitantly with dropping population levels means that rents and housing prices should remain stable. But how do you reduce the supply of housing in a neighborhood or an entire city?

The origins of zoning—still the primary local land-use regulation—at the beginning of the twentieth century was aimed to manage the ill effects of growth and now new kinds of zoning can provide a remedy for decline. Today, zoning legally restricts the use of most houses, duplexes, and apartment buildings to residential use. For a shrinking city with falling population levels, the need for residential uses will fall, as well. A new Relaxed Zoning is the answer for either adaptively reusing or demolishing surplus housing.

The mechanism here is a zoning regulation that lays dormant in municipal code books, but is only triggered by a specificied level of housing vacancy. For example, the trigger might be that once more than 20 percent of the homes in a neighborhood are vacant for more than 90 days, the regulation is activated. The new Relaxed Zoning code would no longer restrict the use of houses, duplexes, and apartment buildings to residential use but would provide for a wide range of new uses. Alternative uses for homes and apartments would come from community-based planning processes, where residents have a say about what vacant homes and lots can be used for. New uses can include farms and gardens (now permitted in Cleveland), parks and open space (as Detroit is proposing), and a wide range of office, storage, and artistic uses.

The code would also be temporary, allowing for alternative uses for a specified number of years, perhaps from three to ten. At which point a trigger would cause the original zoning to revert back in place, requiring the relaxed uses to turn back into housing within a reasonable timetable. This Relaxed Zoning tool allows for proactive, vigilant response by local government to shifting conditions of growth and decline on a sub-community level. As of the time of this writing, no communities have yet adopted Relaxed Zoning, but in theory it offers strong potential for effectively shrinking cities—and unshrinking them when economic and demographic conditions change.

Another smart decline tool I have studied in depth is the Reverse Land Use Allocation Model (Hollander and Popper 2007). This tool is an adaption of a mainstay urban planning tool: the Land Use Allocation Model. In growth planning, a Land Use Allocation Model uses stochastic regression to predict land use change. By reversing the model operators, the model can predict land-use changes in a declining area. This Reverse Land Use Allocation Model can be used to determine the boundaries of the most severely declining areas—that is, decline nodes.

When a metropolitan region is growing, urban planners will employ land-use allocation models to predict where the future growth will occur (Krueckeberg and Silvers 1974; Landis 2001). With that knowledge, planners can delineate growth zones and implement appropriate zoning, open space protection, transportation and utilities infrastructure, and other measures, in anticipation of change to the area (Burchell et al. 1998).

A model that can predict which areas will decline the greatest can be quite useful in guiding specific neighborhood-oriented, community-based planning. For example, if the model predicts that the blocks between Seventh Street and Tenth Street along Vine Avenue will lose 50 percent of their housing units in the next ten years, then local residents could utilize that information to envision appropriate successor land uses to empty lots and/or abandoned housing units.

Of course, nobody wants to live in an area predicted to become a decline node, especially because the model will be able to predict that no one will be living there at a certain point in the future. The imposition of such a pejorative label seems antithetical to sound deliberative planning (Forester 1999). Perhaps the label can be discarded, but the boundaries and idea are powerful. Frank and Deborah Popper experienced this in the way their Buffalo Commons metaphor provoked death threats, hate mail, and derision (Matthews 2002). Knowing that your neighborhood is going to physically change is a wake-up call to local residents.

Designating decline nodes offers an important innovation for inner-city, community-based planning. Community-based organizations (CBOs) have been at the forefront of addressing urban decline efforts in inner cities and engage in innovative physical and social planning (Thomas 1997; Thomas and Grigsby 2000). Decline nodes can present CBOs with an objective, rational view of what their neighborhood will look like in the future and then turn the discussion to alternative views. What are other possible successor land uses to the housing units that will be left behind, besides abandoned buildings and vacant lots? What else can become of the homes left behind? What can the existing vacant lots become? If we can expect residents to abandon housing units in the blocks from Seventh to Tenth Street along Vine Avenue, what would early neighborhood intervention accomplish? Can we convert those entire blocks into community gardens, into an urban forestry project, into a baseball field, into a human-made lake? The options are as unlimited as the imaginations of local residents—and planners can help realize them.

With these two tools, Relaxed Zoning and Decline Nodes—and with others tools—planners can begin to use smart decline in the field. They can think about what possible futures are available to shrinking cities and then make changes to local regulations and formal plans to manage those changes. This nascent field of smart decline still has much to do in refining techniques and strategies, but some published research has shown that smart declining is happening in the U.S. and around the world—the proliferation of tools and techniques will come, as well (Armborst *et al.* 2005; Schilling and Logan 2008; Hollander et al. 2009).

The genesis and maturity of the shrinkage idea

In the last few decades, mass migration from the former East Germany to West Germany following the fall of the Berlin Wall has left cities and towns emptied. The German Federal Cultural Council responded in 2004 by funding an arts-grounded Shrinking Cities Project (Oswalt 2006). The Project included an international ideas competition that generated scores of ideas on how to make smart decline happen— in the process defining the scope of the problem and outlining the boundaries of policy and planning responses—initiating a sketch of what smart decline looks like.

The Shrinking Cities Project then spawned a travelling exhibit showcasing these novel ideas in dozens of cities throughout the world. The interest created by the Project resulted in a conference on the topic sponsored by Kent State University in 2005 and another in 2006 convened by a newly formed group at the University of California, Berkeley, Shrinking Cities in a Global Perspective (Pallagst *et al.* 2009).

While academics and artists were singing the praises of shrinkage, the popular media was slow to catch on. In fact, for some years after the German event, the media was still using the same old language of decline as death. *Forbes* magazine, which loves to rank the best and worst of everything, the richest CEOs, the best place to vacation, the worst places to work, may have hit a new low by profiling the Fastest Dying Cities in its August 2008 issue (Zumbrun 2008). The issue took specific aim at Buffalo, NY; Canton, OH; Charleston, WV; Cleveland, OH; Dayton, OH; Detroit, MI; Flint, MI; Scranton, PA; Springfield, MA and Youngstown, OH.

So, hurt and inspired by such a label, activists in Dayton, OH decided to fight back. Co-opting the term "dying," they organized local officials and activists for a *Forbes* 10 Fastest Dying Cities Symposium and Art Exhibition held in August 2009. Over 200 people from eight of the ten cities attended, celebrating what is good and alive about their cities, such as spirit and passion, dimensions not so easily calculated in *Forbes* statistical analysis. Dayton's city planner argued for a shrinking cities approach to city planning, "the future in front of us is different from what we knew in the past. We won't recreate the Dayton of the '50s and '60s."

The Brookings Institution tried a few years before the Dying Cities raucous to rebrand declining cities as Weak Market Cities. Their effort garnered some attention and helped somewhat to reframe the discussion around depopulation (Katz 2006). More recently, Brookings issued two reports on what the federal government should do about shrinkage (Mallach 2010) and a policy guide directed specifically at Ohio local and state governments (Mallach and Brachman 2010).

The federal report calls for a rethinking of the concept of affordable housing in shrinking cities, questioning what is gained by providing government-subsidized affordable housing (through the low-income tax credit program) in places where market-rate housing is already quite affordable. The result, the report author argues, is the proliferation of new, federally subsidized affordable housing in areas desperately in need of reducing the number of housing units to meet a smaller population.

Mallach (2010) also criticizes U.S. Department of Housing and Urban Development (HUD) policies that requires an annual Consolidated Plan without any meaningful consideration of future demographic change. Mallach (2010) calls for new HUD language that requires communities to design "targeted strategies for reconfiguration of land uses and economic activity around the reality of population loss" (p. 27). The Ohio report echoes some of the same themes as the federal report, adding the need for state and local policies to promote urban agriculture and land banking.

The Federal Reserve System (FRS) has also been toying around with the benefits of shrinkage. The Federal Reserve Bank (FRB) of Cleveland produced a report in 2008 that held the Youngstown planning example up as a good practice and called for demolishing homes that are vacant. The recommendations are intended to fix a broken housing cycle that occurs in a period of economic malaise. The FRB of Cleveland is on record for arguing that demolition of vacant housing is an effective way to break this cycle of crisis and to help stabilize neighborhoods. It is a radical policy recommendation to call for destroying sound structures that could help meet society's housing needs. But at the very core of the shrinking cities idea is that the needs of neighborhoods to maintain some kind of equilibrium in their housing market trumps policies that purport to increase the stock of affordable housing. If we cannot stabilize the physical changes occurring in shrinking cities by managing them (through demolition, reconfiguration, or reuse) the FRB of Cleveland and the Brookings Institution argue the overall quality of life in these places will fall so low that these new affordable housing units will be in quite undesirable neighborhoods.

In 2004, I travelled through the Brightmoor neighborhood in Northwest Detroit, physically ravaged by the affects of decades of depopulation. My guide was a community development professional and as we drove the streets he kept pointing out the new housing built through low-income tax credits or by Habitat for Humanity. Not all, but the vast majority of these affordable housing units were either damaged by arson or partially abandoned.

Brightmoor was not able to reach an equilibrium between the supply of housing and the demand for housing. Instead of an active demolition program, the city government was working closely with affordable housing developers to build more housing, further straining the housing market and leading to more and more abandoned buildings, derelict structures, and poorly maintained public spaces and infrastructure.

A focus on the Sunbelt

As the Sunbelt faced the growing economic problems of the Great Recession beginning in 2006, neighborhood after neighborhood started to suffer from the same disequilibrium that so worries groups such as the FRB and Brookings. While the precipitous drop in demand for housing was first met with falling house prices, widespread foreclosures in the region has also meant high levels of abandonment and vacancy—problems more commonly associated with Detroit than Tucson.

Foreclosure itself does not cause abandonment or vacancy, but research has shown that the eviction of owners (and sometimes tenants) through a foreclosure process often results in vacant homes for years (Immergluck 2009). The reluctance of banks to move quickly to re-sell foreclosed homes can lead to vandalism, derelict conditions, and sometimes even arson.

For Sunbelt cities, the problems of depopulation are not well understood and how smart decline might help such places has not yet been explored at all. The Sunbelt has been the subject of in-depth, comprehensive study for decades as a place of growth and prosperity. The movement of people and jobs from the Rustbelt to the Sunbelt has been described as "one of the greatest population shifts in American history" (Bernard and Bradley 1983, p. 1). For a region defined by growth, the contemporary period of decline presents a vexing problem for local, state, and federal officials. This study sheds light on the way that decline is impacting this region and how smart decline might be a promising path forward for some affected urban neighborhoods.

The very idea of the Sunbelt is a relatively new one, first coined by Phillips (1969) in a book about the growing Republican majorities in the South and West. Since then, scholars and practitioners have debated the boundaries of the Sunbelt with great ferocity.[3] Most, though, settle on the boundary of the 37th parallel, suggesting that cities and states below it are part of the Sunbelt. I offer a minor refinement on this boundary in Chapter 6, excluding a couple of deep South states that have not seen the kind of wild growth that the other Sunbelt states have seen.

To understand the broad changes afoot over the previous four decades, it is useful to review the results of a study conducted by McDonald (2008) of Census data in both Sunbelt and Rustbelt cities. He closely examined 12 large Sunbelt metropolitan areas and contrasted the results against 12 large Rustbelt metropolitan areas. In a series of multivariate regressions of this Census data, McDonald found that central city population growth was due primarily to two factors: the first is through an increase in central city land area (also known as annexation). For cities that expand their borders, the population increases. This is so obvious, but for Rustbelt cities it simply does not happen. Rusk (1995) studied this topic and concluded that a city's elasticity was key to its ability to grow. He found that Sunbelt cities, generally, maintained strong annexation powers, which Rustbelt cities did not. Through the regular absorption of new, growing areas outside city borders, the central city is able to capture new sources of tax revenues. A 1955 editorial in the *Arizona Republic* (Phoenix's major newspaper) explained the predicament well:

> Phoenix faces a problem common to all growing metropolitan areas. It must keep pushing its limits out into the country as new housing and industrial

development are built up. Otherwise, the new area will become incorporated and Phoenix will find itself hemmed in by a group of independent satellites.

(*Arizona Republic* editorial, 1955, p. 317)

The second factor that McDonald found contributed to center city population growth was employment growth in the metropolitan area. Likewise, this is an expected finding. Cities that are part of booming metropolitan areas with ample jobs will be attractive as places to live and do business. But McDonald also finds that "causation runs both ways" between population and employment growth. As an area becomes popular for residents and second-home owners, businesses tend to follow (certainly the case in much of the Sunbelt).

In actual performance, the 12 Sunbelt metropolitan areas studied by McDonald grew by 21.7 percent, while the central cities for each metropolitan area grew by 9.2 percent. Constrast that against population change in the 12 Rustbelt cities McDonald examined where the metropolitan areas grew by 5.7 percent and the central cities grew by 2.8 percent, on average.

Within the Sunbelt, there is great diversity and variety of experience. But, on the whole the region is quite different from its antipode. During the Great Recession, Rustbelt cities experienced much distress and depopulation, but those patterns of decline and responses to it have been well documented. What we do not know is how decline impacts on Sunbelt urban neighborhoods, how they respond, and most importantly how this new shrinking cities mentality could aid local officials in shrinking to greatness.[4]

Concluding thoughts

The term "decline" is not a favorite of planners. In fact, the planning profession has a "bias towards growth" (Popper and Popper 2002, p. 20). The basic facts of decline are clear: due to forces largely outside the control of local governments, cities, suburbs, and rural areas will continue to experience population decline and combating it can only help in some cases, some of the time. In considering the three choices that communities have when faced with population loss, the smart decline option offers great promise for managing the physical changes that happen in a depopulation place.

Unfortunately, little is known about how neighborhoods change when they lose population so today's planners are limited in their ability to manage that change. The remainder of this book probes this very question in the hope that a clearer understanding of the relationship between population loss and land use will open up possibilities for smart decline. I opened this chapter with an attack on growth-oriented economic development strategies for shrinking cities. For some places, economic development can and will work. For others, it is time to consider smart decline and the following chapters will provide the theoretical and empirical foundation for doing so.

CHAPTER 3

The shrinking Rustbelt

A pattern of decline

There are a number of different views on why cities lose population and what should be done about it, but there has been little debate about what fewer people means for a neighborhood; it is generally understood to be a bad thing. But now, with the emergence of the shrinking cities ideology, a possibility begins to appear that losing population might not have to be a bad thing for a neighborhood.

It is best to begin here by looking at causal connections: do decreased jobs and/or dispersal of populations to the suburbs and exurban fringe cause social and functional malaise in neighborhoods, or do they simply cause decreased demand for housing in such neighborhoods leading to depressed housing values and rental prices?

The economics literature offers a wealth of evidence that both things occur. Exogenous factors (such as fewer employment opportunities and higher amenity housing choices in suburban areas) drive down demand for some urban neighborhoods, which in turn result in fewer residents (and often poorer residents because rents and housing values are more affordable). Among these fewer, poorer residents, there can be higher crime levels and worse public health conditions. But part of the reason why these fewer, poorer residents are exposed to greater crime and worse public health is tied directly to the lack of access to employment and educational opportunities. As this discussion illustrates, the fate of a given neighborhood located in an area experiencing economic decline or metropolitan dispersal is complex and hard to predict. Understanding the isolated impact that fewer people contribute to a neighborhood's quality of life is the objective of this chapter. In the subsequent chapters of this book, I will examine the ways that exogenous forces bear directly on neighborhood quality of life.

Planners are prone to dwelling on these very exogenous conditions in lamenting the difficulties faced by depopulating neighborhoods. "If only we could have economic development," I hear planners and other local officials remark with regularity. There is ample published statistical evidence that points to a strong correlation between population decline and a range of indicators of social and health ills (Berg 1982; Bradbury et al. 1982; Lucy and Phillips 2000). But what about neighborhoods that have lost population and have not seen an appreciable decrease in quality of life? Are there ways that neighborhoods depopulate that involve a "management" of the ill effects of depopulation? Unfortunately, to date, nobody knows. Nobody has done a systematic study to answer such a question, until now. This chapter reports on a study I conducted with the help of several research assistants looking at hundreds of depopulating neighborhoods. While the geographic focus of this book is the Sunbelt, it is a region that has only recently faced widespread depopulation. The Rustbelt—the broad swath of post-industrial, former manufacturing cities and towns spread throughout the Northeast and Midwest has, on the other hand, faced falling population for decades (White *et al.* 1964; Bluestone and Harrison 1982; Hollander 2009).

This chapter takes aim at this other region in the hopes of building a conceptual framework to be applied to the Sunbelt. The legacy of the Rustbelt is a complex one, while some cities and towns have faced major depopulation, others have thrived. The future of the Sunbelt is expected to be equally complex and diverse; the aim of this chapter is to provide further foundation to understanding how cities with persistent population loss physically change and what can be done to manage that change.

If we know how neighborhoods physically change when they lose population, can we plan for such changes? Can we devise physical plans that will limit the presence of abandoned buildings and vacant lots by "right-sizing" neighborhoods to physically match their smaller populations? If we can, then the hope is that such physical changes will inhibit the detrimental effect to quality of life that depopulation causes.

Over the last two generations, the Midwest and Northeast have seen some of the highest levels of population and employment decline in the country. The decay of these regions' industrial prowess in the middle of the last century has led to a twenty-first century legacy of widespread abandonment in its cities. I examined the ten Midwestern and Northeastern cities that have seen the greatest loss of population since 1950 and then focused on neighborhoods that have lost more than 30 percent of their population since 1970.

This research begins with the idea that a given urban neighborhood has a certain stable population, a relatively high housing density, and high quality of life. The exogenous forces of job loss and metropolitan migration will cause a decline in population and with conventional planning (either public redevelopment or no public response) the result is often lower housing density and lower quality of life (due to increased crime, increased risk of arson, and other negative community impacts outlined earlier in Chapter 2). With the intervention of smart decline the now less dense neighborhood can retain a high quality of life (just with fewer people). This chapter demonstrates how this process works by documenting changing physical neighborhood conditions in depopulating areas. Chapter 5 then takes this raw evidence in combination with the direct field research presented in Chapter 4 to build a model for how smart decline can operate within these depopulating landscapes.

Assembling the data and devising the methods

In contrast to the study of land-use change in growing areas with aerial photography, Geographic Information Systems (GIS), or by enumerating building permits, the study of land-use change in declining areas is largely an uncharted arena. It is quite easy to measure new growth in terms of new structures and developed land, while it is more difficult to measure the abandonment associated with decline. Ryznar and Wagner (2001) attempted to study urban decline using GIS and Remote Sensing techniques, but could only measure net change in forested and agricultural land, extrapolating their findings to housing and commercial land-use changes.

Brownfields researchers have developed some tools to measure the abandonment of commercial and industrial properties, but most examine just a single case study location or set of locations (for example, see a recent study done by Leigh and Coffin 2005). On the other hand, housing researchers have developed more rigorous approaches to measuring residential abandonment (Wilson and Margulis 1994; Hillier et al. 2003). The approach used here attempted to build on both the work of brownfields researchers and housing scholars to better understand the unique land-use changes that occur in depopulating urban neighborhoods.

Because the impacts of depopulation can strike residential neighborhoods the hardest, this study is limited to exclusively examining residential land uses. Housing researchers have looked at changing patterns of housing density in urban neighborhoods as a proxy for land-use changes from single-family to multi-family housing. For example, a neighborhood with 50 occupied housing units per acre in 1990 has a very different physical form than that same neighborhood ten years later with only 40 occupied housing units per acre.[1]

Table 3.1 Top 25 most declining cities in the Northeast and Midwest, 1950–2000

City	1950	2000	Difference	Region	% change	Change rank
St. Louis	856,796	348,189	−508,607	MW	−59%	1
Youngstown	168,330	82,026	−86,304	MW	−51%	2
Pittsburgh	676,806	334,563	−342,243	NE	−51%	3
Buffalo	580,132	292,648	−287,484	NE	−50%	4
Detroit	1,849,586	951,270	−898,316	MW	−49%	5
Cleveland	914,808	478,403	−436,405	MW	−48%	6
Scranton	125,536	76,415	−49,121	NE	−39%	7
Newark	438,776	273,456	−165,320	NE	−38%	8
Camden	124,555	79,904	−44,651	NE	−36%	9
Cincinnati	503,998	331,285	−172,713	MW	−34%	10
Rochester	332,488	219,773	−112,715	NE	−34%	11
Trenton	128,009	85,403	−42,606	NE	−33%	12
Syracuse	220,583	147,306	−73,277	NE	−33%	13
Dayton	243,872	166,179	−77,693	MW	−32%	14
Hartford	177,397	121,578	−55,819	NE	−31%	15
Canton	116,921	80,806	−36,115	MW	−31%	16
Providence	248,674	173,618	−75,056	NE	−30%	17
Albany	134,995	95,658	−39,337	NE	−29%	18
Philadelphia	2,071,605	1,517,550	−554,055	NE	−27%	19
Minneapolis	521,718	382,618	−139,100	MW	−27%	20
Boston	801,444	589,141	−212,303	NE	−26%	21
Reading	109,320	81,207	−28,113	NE	−26%	22
New Haven	164,443	123,626	−40,817	NE	−25%	23
Flint	163,143	124,943	−38,200	MW	−23%	24
Gary	133,911	102,746	−31,165	MW	−23%	25

Census data was downloaded for the 25 Midwestern and Northeastern cities that experienced the greatest loss of population since 1950 (see Table 3.1). From that list, I used Geolytics software to download population data for all of the census tracts for those ten cities.[2] The census tract was used as a unit of analysis because the Geolytics software has a special feature whereby the data is normalized to 2000 boundaries across all four time periods, supporting time series analysis. I focused my analysis on those tracts that lost more than 30 percent of their population from 1970 to 2000 (n=914).[3] The 30 percent threshold was devised based on the assumption that population loss of less than 30 percent over 30 years may not result in enough significant physical change to neighborhoods to effectively study the relativity between depopulation and land use. As a counterbalance to my review of tracts with declining population, I also examined a reference group of tracts in the selected cities that grew by at least 10 percent of their population from 1970 to 2000 (n=224).

For both the declining tracts and the growing tracts, I first conducted a correlation analysis between population loss and a variable to serve as a surrogate for residential land-use change. I used "change in occupied housing unit density per decade" to help understand the changing physical form of residential structures in a given neighborhood.

For the first regression, the dependent variable used was "change in occupied housing unit density 1970–1980." In trying to explain that change in housing density, I included several independent variables that the literature suggests may influence housing vacancy, key among them population change from 1970 to 1980 (Cholden and Hanson (1981) used a similar set of explanatory variables in their study predicting neighborhood change in depopulating sub-community zones). Other independent variables include income levels, age of residents, racial characteristics, and poverty levels (for this first regression, I used 1980 data for each). By using these control variables, I am able to isolate the independent effects of population change on increased housing vacancy. Because depopulation will be different from city to city (Boston's neighborhoods are very different in form and character from Columbus') I also included variables to control for those differences. By using these control variables, I am able to isolate the independent effects of population loss on increased housing vacancy. The regressions were then run again for each of the other two time periods (1980–1990 and 1990–2000) and then again using robust regressions, in order to limit the influence of outliers on the results.[4]

Results of data analysis

The descriptive statistics for both the shrinking census tracts are presented in Table 3.2. The first step in the research was a correlation analysis I did between my key variable of interest, percent change in occupied housing unit density, and population change. As seen in Table 3.3, the two variables are highly correlated for the shrinking tracts. In all three time periods examined, population change and change in occupied housing unit density are highly correlated for the declining tracts. I also ran a similar correlation analysis for the growing tracts and the variables were highly correlated during the first (1970–1980) and second (1980–1990) periods, with a somewhat weaker correlation in the third period (1990–2000).[5] In fact, there is a steady decline over time in the strength of the correlations for growing tracts between change in population and change in housing density.

A potential explanation for this is the well-documented trend, particularly in growing neighborhoods, toward smaller household sizes since the 1970s (Kobrin 1976; Bradbury *et al.* 1982). This phenomenon would mean that as a neighborhood grew in population, the addition of new housing per new resident grew at a faster rate in the 1990s relative to the 1970s and 1980s.

Table 3.2 Descriptive statistics of shrinking census tracts included in the study

	1970		1980		1990		2000	
	Mean	**Standard dev.**	**Mean**	**Standard dev.**	**Mean**	**Standard dev.**	**Mean**	**Standard dev.**
Population	4,874	2,502	3,457	1,858	2,889	1,623	2,443	1,418
Total housing units	1,685	919	1,417	759	1,255	701	1,134	666
Number of occupied housing units	1,667	906	1,331	702	1,168	650	1,035	610
Occupied housing units per acre (density)	9.09	7.05	7.27	6.04	6.29	5.36	5.54	4.92
Number of Black population	2,526	2,731	2,046	2,024	1,755	1,666	1,538	1,388
Percentage Black population	47%	0.39	68%	3.21	58%	0.39	61%	0.37
Number of persons 65 years and older	507	315	418	276	393	279	326	243
Percentage persons 65 years and older	11%	0.05	15%	0.51	14%	0.07	13%	0.08
Number of persons foreign born	220	240	133	163	94	137	105	163
Percentage persons foreign born	5%	0.05	5%	0.13	3%	0.05	4%	0.07
Number of persons 16 years and older who are unemployed	132	91	190	133	190	133	138	108
Percentage persons 16 years and older who are unemployed	7%	0.03	19%	0.61	18%	0.11	15%	0.1
Number of households receiving public assistance income	160	148	271	200	271	200	215	164
Percentage households receiving public assistance income	14%	0.11	28%	0.85	26%	0.15	24%	0.14

N = 858
Note: Mean Land Area (Acres) = 310.7, St Dev. = 480.8

Table 3.3 Correlations between occupied housing density and population change for shrinking tracts

		% change in occupied housing unit density 1970–1980	% change in occupied housing unit density 1980–1990	% change in occupied housing unit density 1990–2000
% change in population 1970–1980	Pearson correlation	0.65	0.00	−0.05
	Sig. (2–tailed)	0.00	1.00	0.14
	N	854.00	855.00	851.00
% change in population 1980–1990	Pearson correlation	−0.02	0.08	−0.01
	Sig. (2–tailed)	0.63	0.02	0.89
	N	852.00	855.00	850.00
% change in population 1990–2000	Pearson correlation	−0.04	0.00	0.43
	Sig. (2–tailed)	0.23	1.00	0.00
	N	851.00	853.00	850.00

Because other confounding variables may be contributing to the effect of population change on occupied housing unit density I ran an Ordinary Least Squares regression (see Table 3.4). Separate regressions were run for each time period, 1970–1980, 1980–1990, and 1990–2000. First, I will discuss the results for the primary dataset of interest, those census tracts that experienced declines in population during the study period.

The ability of each model to accurately account for changes in occupied housing unit density is assessed through a model fitness statistic. Here, I employed R-squared as a measure of model fitness—its values range from 0 to 1, with 1 indicating a model that perfectly explains the dependant variable. The 1970–1980 model had a very high R-squared, 0.831, whereby model fitness declined in the two subsequent decades to 0.726 (still quite good) for 1980–1990, and 0.641 (passable) for 1990–2000. While higher is better, these R-squared statistics are satisfactory enough to draw conclusions from the results.

The regression results for the declining tracts show that for each decade, population change (in this case, it was population loss) during the same decade was a statistically significant indicator of change in occupied housing density, controlling for other relevant variables. The same results held true when the three time periods were run using a Robust regression tool Weighted Least Squares Regressions. These results verify that when holding all other variables constant, there is a statistically significant relationship during these three time periods between population loss and occupied housing unit density.[6]

Across both regressions for all three time periods, the direction of the influence of population loss on housing unit density was always positive. That is, a decline in population meant a decline in housing unit density, as expected. The degree of that influence ranged across the time periods.

Table 3.4 Regression results for shrinking and growing census tracts

	Shrinking tracts			Growing tracts		
	Ordinary least squares			Ordinary least squares		
	R-squared 0.837			R-squared 0.792		
	b	st. error	sig.	b	st. error	sig.
Intercept	80.571	80.032		35.509	113.725	
Absolute change 1970–1980						
Population	0.174	0.011	***	0.36	0.029	***
Receiving public assistance	−0.243	0.075	***	0.06	0.208	
Older than 65 years	0.749	0.05	***	0.435	0.074	***
High school graduates	0.396	0.057	***	−0.007	0.098	
Foreign born	0.215	0.055	***	−0.175	0.072	
Unemployed	0.361	0.104	***	0.63	0.279	**
African American	0.052	0.075	***	−0.091	0.032	***
Living in poverty	0.138	0.025	***	0.069	0.079	

Dependent variable = change in occupied housing units from 1970–1980

	Shrinking tracts			Growing tracts		
	Ordinary least squares			Ordinary least squares		
	R-squared 0.735			R-squared 0.583		
	b	st. error	sig.	b	st. error	sig.
Intercept	50.138	55.9		48.8	122.145	
Absolute change 1980–1990						
Population	0.088	0.12	***	0.318	0.039	***
Receiving public assistance	0.32	0.072	***	0.085	0.259	
Older than 65 years	0.623	0.039	***	0.362	0.093	***
High school graduates	0.164	0.04	***	−0.108	0.1	
Foreign born	0.308	0.051	***	−0.111	0.059	*
Unemployed	0.159	0.073	**	0.011	0.297	
African American	0.117	0.012	***	−0.111	0.04	***
Living in poverty	−0.009	0.021		0.162	0.073	**

Dependent variable = change in occupied housing units from 1980–1990

	Shrinking tracts			Growing tracts		
	Ordinary least squares			Ordinary least squares		
	R-squared 0.642			R-squared 0.405		
	b	st. error	sig.	b	st. error	sig.
Intercept	32.011	43.658		−33.503	113.558	
Absolute change 1990–2000						
Population	0.165	0.013	***	0.118	0.028	***
Receiving public assistance	0.338	0.055	***	0.211	0.14	
Older than 65 years	0.364	0.039	***	0.225	0.088	**
High school graduates	0.076	0.036	**	0.176	0.086	
Foreign born	0.051	0.044		−0.097	0.039	
Unemployed	−0.048	0.045		−0.202	0.066	***
African American	−0.005	0.012		0.012	0.029	
Living in poverty	0.073	0.017	***	0.134	0.055	

Dependent variable = change in occupied housing units from 1990–2000

Notes: Not presented here are the regression results for the city dummy variables, which with a few exceptions were not statistically significant. The exceptions are 1970–1980: Boston, 1980–1990: Trenton, Detroit, and Providence, and 1990–2000: St. Louis and Gary, all significant at the 90% confidence level.

* = 0.05 signficance
** = 0.05 signficance
*** = 0.01 signficance

For the 1970–1980 regression, occupied housing units decreased by an average of 0.174 units for each fewer person in a given census tract, holding all other variables constant. Put differently, in a neighborhood with 100 occupied housing units, a decrease in population of 100 persons would reduce the number of occupied housing units by 17.4, leaving only 82 units remaining. The 1980–1990 regression showed a lower value, where occupied housing units decreased by an average of only 0.088 units for each fewer person. The 1990–2000 regression was much closer to the 1970–1980 results, where the decrease was 0.165 units.

These results can be translated back to the language of land use by being restated in terms of occupied housing units per acre. In a neighborhood with ten occupied housing units per acre (for example, 200 units on 20 acres), that same drop of 17.4 units (based on the 1970–1980 regression) can be reinterpreted as a fall in density to 9.13 units per acre. For a neighborhood to change from 10 units per acre to 9.3 units per acre means a fall in density of 9 percent. As Table 3.5 indicates, the degree of predicted fall in density will depend on original density levels. A low density neighborhood of only two units per acre, would be expected to lose the same 17.4 units when 100 people departed as a high density neighborhood. The difference though is how each neighborhood's density would shift—the impact of 100 people leaving a high-density, 20 unit per acre neighborhood would be a drop of 4 percent in density. This would be a less noticeable change than the emptying of 17.4 units in a neighborhood of only two units per acre (where the decline in density would be 44 percent). For planning purposes, for smart decline strategies, this difference is essential to understand and use as the basis for planning.

Table 3.5 Predicted values for change in occupied housing units in Buffalo, NY

Buffalo

Units	Acreage	Density (units/acre)	Change in population	Change in occupied units	New number of units	New density	% change in density
300	100	3.0	−100	−26	274	2.74	−8.52%
250	100	2.5	−100	−26	224	2.24	−10.22%
200	100	2.0	−100	−26	174	1.74	−12.77%
150	100	1.5	−100	−26	124	1.24	−17.03%
100	100	1.0	−100	−26	74	0.74	−25.55%

Note: These predicted values are based on keeping all variables at their mean but setting population change to −100.

A specific understanding of the expected changes in occupied housing unit density is critical to the kind of planning needed to transform neighborhoods from one "ecozone" to another—from 12 units per acre to 10 units per acre, for example (as will be explained further in Chapter 5). These regression results, combined with the density change tables (Table 3.5 and Appendix A), provide a roadmap for devising smart decline strategies.

When I ran the same regressions for the growing tracts I arrived at similar results. For each time period, the relationship between population change (in this case, growth) and occupied housing unit density was a positive one and statistically significant. For the 1970–1980 regression, occupied housing units increased by an average of 0.36 units for each one additional person in a given census tract, holding all other variables constant. The 1980–1990 regression was similar (0.32 units) but the 1990–2000 regression showed a lower figure (0.12 units). Changing political and economic conditions in the 1990s may account for the lower rate of new housing being added during the decade, relative to the number of new people who migrate into a census tract. This confirmed and validated the findings from analyzing the depopulating tracts, where the relationship was also positive.

What do these results mean?

An example is useful for making meaning of these results. A fictional 1,000 person neighborhood is comprised of 250 two-family homes covering 50 acres (at a density of ten dwelling units per acre) in year 2000. Demographers project that the area will lose 15 percent of its population in the coming decade. This research suggests that planners employing a smart decline orientation could expect that a fall in 150 persons could be expected to result in the loss of between 12 and 17 occupied housing units and an overall drop in density of 3 to 9.6 units per acre. With this information in hand, planners could then work closely with property owners, city building inspectors, and community groups to proactively convert some of those 12–17 housing units to non-residential uses in order to adjust to the lower neighborhood population and diminished demand. The findings from this research can potentially inform smart decline practice in a range of different types of neighborhoods with different building types and density levels.

In Appendix A, I list all the Rustbelt cities examined and show how a loss of 100 persons over the course of a ten-year period (1970–1980, 1980–1990, and 1990–2000) in neighborhoods in that city resulted in a concomitant decrease in occupied housing units for neighborhoods in that city, holding all other variables constant at their mean. For example, in Buffalo (NY) from 1970 to 1980, a loss of 100 persons for a neighborhood with average change in poverty levels, educational attainment, foreign-born population, unemployment, racial composition, public assistance recipients, and population older than 65 years, would be expected to have lost 26 housing units during that same time period. When placed in the context of occupied housing unit density, Appendix A illustrates how that loss of units will have varying impact depending on the original density of the neighborhood. For a low density neighborhood like the last row in the Buffalo example in Table 3.5, that loss of 26 units is a big deal because at one unit per acre, a 100-person drop in population means a drop to only 0.74 occupied housing units per acre in 1980, 25 percent less than in 1970. But that same drop for a higher density neighborhood, take the top row, for example, would also mean a loss of 26 units, but would result in a more modest fall of only 8.5 percent in occupied housing unit density. As Appendix A shows, there is some degree of variation among the cities in how many units lost would result from a reduction of 100 persons, thus reflecting broader differences that exist in how occupied housing unit density changes in the face of depopulation from one city to another.

There are a number of important limitations to this analysis. First, by only looking at neighborhoods that experienced either heavy population decline or growth the results can only be generalized to other such neighborhoods. Second, by relying on Census data little is known about what other land uses replaced the decreased number of occupied housing units. The assumption was that much of what replaced occupied housing units were unoccupied housing units or vacant lots, an assumption that is verified in the next chapter on Flint, Michigan.

Planning practice has traditionally been geared toward issues of growth and new real estate development. Planning for decline is only beginning to emerge as an alternative strategy. As such, communities lack the skills and resources to respond to decline in an effective and positive way. Physical plans and design strategies for shrinkage need to be built upon sound empirical evidence about the ways cities decline. This chapter quantifies the phenomenon of urban decline and begins to lay the foundation for the development of planning and urban design tools that respond to the unique needs and characteristics of shrinking cities. Before doing so, it is important to return to the central causal challenge of studying depopulating urban neighborhoods: an understanding of the effects of how exogenous forces interact with endogenous (neighborhood-based) physical conditions. To do so, the following chapter describes an in-depth case study of three depopulating neighborhoods in Flint, Michigan to attempt to untangle these causal connections and to clarify the findings from the research presented in this chapter.

CHAPTER 4

Lessons from a declining city

Flint, Michigan after 40 years of
population loss

Few places in America are so reviled as Flint, Michigan. For a city that was the
birthplace of the modern automobile and only three decades ago the home of the
largest car maker in the world, Flint has fallen mightily. But the news is not all bad.
In fact, just as Flint's employment fell, so did its population, and so did its housing
stock. The shrinkage of Flint, Michigan can offer valuable lessons to Sunbelt cities
today facing the early stages of prolonged depopulation.

First settled in 1818, Flint, Michigan is located 60 miles northwest of Detroit
along the Flint River. The city was largely dependent on the timber industry until
General Motors (GM) was founded there in 1908, turning the city into the world
capital of the automobile industry in just three decades (May 1965; Edsforth
1982; Matthews 1997). As GM and the American automobile industry shrunk its
workforce in the 1970s, so went Flint's fortunes. Unemployment and reduced taxes
translated to a reduction in city services—firefighters and police officers were laid
off (Matthews 1997). City officials responded with hundreds of millions of dollars in
tax abatements and redevelopment financing in the 1980s and 1990s to encourage
new industrial development and bolster the city's central business district and to
market the city as a tourist center (Matthews 1997). At the same time, the U.S.
government and the State of Michigan invested tens of millions in grants and loans
while local philanthropists pushed vast sums of money into rebuilding downtown
(Gilman 1997). In his review of 14 redevelopment projects executed in Flint from
1970 to 1992 costing $568.5 million, Gilman (1997) found that all but one of these
initiatives were explicitly intended to foster greater economic growth.

While some benefits accrued to the city and its residents through these
projects, the overwhelming evidence available shows that these efforts largely
failed to reverse the city's continuing economic decline (Matthews 1997; Gilman
1997). Flint's total employment went down from 69,995 in 1970 to 40,213 in
2006 (U.S. Census 2008). Flint's population fell by almost a third in the last half-
century, going from 163,143 in 1950 to 112,524 (U.S. Census 2008). The city's
changing racial composition is harder to pin down due to the differing ways in
which the Census characterized race and ethnicity between 1960 and 1980. While
the definitions were being consistently used from 1980 to 2006, there was a rise
in the percentage of non-Hispanic African Americans in Flint, from 41.1 percent
to 56.3 percent. See Table 4.1 for a summary of how the city changed from 1970
to 2000.

Table 4.1 City-wide demographic and housing data, Flint, 1970–2000

	1970	1980	1990	2000
Total population	193,854	160,114	141,089	124,954
% White	71.7%	56.2%	49.8%	42.7%
% African American	28.0%	41.3%	47.7%	54.7%
% Latino	1.7%	2.4%	2.7%	3.0%
Total population foreign born	3.7%	2.7%	1.6%	1.5%
% < age 18	37.4%	31.7%	30.6%	30.6%
% > age 64	8.8%	10.0%	10.6%	10.5%
Total households	61,082	57,883	54,118	48,823
Total housing units	64,362	61,094	58,912	55,468
Total occupied housing units	61,082	57,794	54,089	48,748
% occupied housing units	94.9%	94.6%	91.8%	87.9%
Average household income prior year	$10,283	$19,310	$26,043	$40,343

Source: U.S. Census Bureau, Census 1970–2000 Summary File 1; Geolytics, Neighborhood Change Database

My approach to studying Flint

As with the previous chapter, I use the metric "occupied housing units per acre" to understand and measure the way that Flint's physical form has changed during its period of population and employment decline over the last three decades. Census data was downloaded using the Geolytics software program for census tracts in Flint for 1970, 1980, 1990, and 2000. The census tract was used as a unit of analysis because the Geolytics software has a special feature whereby the data is normalized to 2000 boundaries across all four time periods, supporting time series analysis.

The key variables examined from the census were population loss and occupied housing unit density, which served as a proxy for residential land use. I chose to use "occupied housing unit density" to help understand the changing physical form of residential structures in a given neighborhood, in part, to follow up on the results from the previous chapter.

Based on a review of the Census data and on prior fieldwork in Flint, I selected three neighborhoods to focus this research on. Working with a research assistant, we conducted background research on each neighborhood through electronic database searches in Thomson Gale Expanded Academic ASAP and Academic OneFile; LexisNexis; ISI Web of Knowledge; ProQuest; Social Sciences Citation Index; Journal of Planning Literature; and, CSA Illumina. We also conducted Google searches to identify relevant planning reports or news items for each neighborhood. Articles were limited to those printed from 1980 to the present. Next, we consulted with local experts to begin generating a list of potential interviewees.

From April through August of 2008, we conducted at least two semi-structured in-person or telephone interviews with individuals in each of the following two categories for all three neighborhoods: 1) long-time residents and 2) professionals who work in the development, redevelopment, or planning fields in each neighborhood. In addition, we also conducted three interviews with individuals who are professionally involved in neighborhood development, redevelopment, or planning city-wide but not necessarily in one of the study area neighborhoods. Lastly, I conducted on-site visits to each of the three neighborhoods in June of 2008 and directly observed and recorded my observations of current land use and signs of historic land use in each.

Results of Flint's decline

Flint has changed dramatically as its population has fallen. In some places of the city, the rapid departure of people has resulted in a new pastoral landscape where houses were once packed tightly together. In others, the derelict structures that once housed people now serve as a deterrent to investment and a haven for criminals. In each neighborhood, a certain percentage (often large) of the population has no place else to go. Together, the desperately poor huddle together and are stuck in an economic ghetto. In some parts of Flint, the ghetto is not just economic but also racial. The discrimination in employment and housing that laid the foundation for the urban crises of the 1980s and 1990s continues today to haunt vast stretches of Flint.

Socio-economic and racial considerations aside, the Flint landscape has changed dramatically. The following is a summary sketch of the ways that residential land use changed in three of Flint's neighborhoods as each faced significant population loss over the last three decades.

Grand Traverse: open spaces and group homes

Grand Traverse experienced a dramatic decline in occupied housing unit density and population levels from 1970 to 2000. Since then, according to U.S. Census and county estimates, population levels have continued to drop, as with occupied housing unit density (Genesee County 2007; U.S. Census 2008). In 1970, the census tract containing both Grand Traverse and Carriage Town had 5,100 persons and 2,446 occupied housing units in its 614 acres, for a density of 3.6 occupied housing units per acre (see Table 4.2). In 2000, the occupied housing unit density fell sharply to only 1.4 units per acre with a population of 2,562.

Table 4.2 Demographic and housing data, Carriage Town and Grand Traverse neighborhoods, Flint, 1970–2000

Variable	1970	1980	1990	2000	% Δ '70–'80	% Δ '80–'90	% Δ '90–'00
Population	5,100	3,536	3,203	2,562	−30.7	−9.4	−20.0
Total number of households	2,200	1,601	1,197	889	−27.2	−25.2	−25.7
% African American	11.4	18.4	41.5	49.0	61.4	125.3	18.2
% over 65 years old	17.1	16.7	8.6	3.4	−2.4	−48.7	−60.8
% living in poverty	22.4	31.8	48.8	45.0	42.0	53.5	−7.8
Total housing units	2,446	1,770	1,536	1,264	−27.6	−13.2	−17.7
Total occupied housing units	2,199	1,550	1,235	849	−29.5	−20.3	−31.3
Occupied housing units per acre	3.6	2.5	2.0	1.4	−29.5	−20.3	−31.3

Source: U.S. Census Bureau

In Grand Traverse, I validated the land-use changes discovered through the Census data analysis through interviews and direct observation of current housing conditions. Hundreds of housing units throughout the neighborhood underwent a process described in the housing literature as filtering, but with a unique twist. As White flight and employment cuts has reduced demand for housing in Grand Traverse since the 1960s, single-family homes (which accounted for a vast majority of the neighborhood's housing stock historically) were divided into multi-family homes and rented. This phenomenon would be expected to, in fact, increase the occupied housing unit density of the neighborhood, but the period of multi-family use was often quite limited. According to interviews with long-time residents, many of these multi-family homes were not cared for by their owners, leading to accidental and often intentional fires (see Figure 4.1). Over time, the neighborhood association, working closely with foundation and city resources arranged for the demolition of many (if not all) of these fire-damaged structures, leading to a further decline in occupied housing unit density and the emergence of a more open, pastoral landscape in the city (see Figure 4.2). One long-time resident active in the neighborhood association celebrated the new feel of his neighborhood: "So it's expanded the size of their properties and they have a nice big green space on the side…They use it for gardens and bigger yards."

Figure 4.1 Partially damaged home due to accidental fire in Grand Traverse neighborhood.

Figure 4.2 Pastoral landscape in the Grand Traverse neighborhood.

Armborst *et al.* (2005) labeled this phenomenon blotting in their work in Detroit. They found that the urban fabric of Detroit was changing on a daily basis not by city plan or regulation, but by the actions of individual landowners in expanding their lots to more closely mirror density patterns seen in suburbia. In Grand Traverse, some parcels are over two acres and the neighborhood feels more rural than suburban. Perhaps more important, the active control and management of vacant land and abandoned buildings has contributed to a sense in the neighborhood that it is safe from crime. According to one long-time resident:

> The main social change is, I think, that crime is way, way down. It used to be scary to go out at night and it just isn't anymore. There are a lot more people active and aware; a lot more eyes on the streets. I think that has been a real improvement and I attribute that to the removal of the worst of the housing. There are just very few places for criminals to hang out anymore.

Two other factors influenced land-use change in Grand Traverse during this time period: conversion of homes to offices and conversion of homes to group living quarters. Grand Traverse is strategically located in close walking distance to city, county, and federal courthouses and during the 1960s and 1970s several dozen homes in close proximity to the courts were converted into office use for local attorneys. At the same time, local and regional social service agencies orchestrated the conversion of dozens of owner-occupied and rental housing units into group living quarters for mentally disabled adults throughout the Grand Traverse neighborhood. While these new uses can have a range of impacts on the neighborhood, ultimately, they bear little overall effect on the broader shift toward lower occupied housing unit density in Grand Traverse. In sum, the quantitative results in Table 4.2 accurately reflect the widespread change in the physical form of Grand Traverse, with dramatically fewer homes and new vast stretches of open space.

Carriage Town: the historic preservation conundrum

The Carriage Town neighborhood is located within a city designated historic district. The benefits that accrue to the neighborhood owing to that designation are also accompanied by restrictions placed on the demolition of derelict structures. As a result, Carriage Town has an inordinate number of derelict, historic structures, in contrast to Grand Traverse. Direct observation of neighborhood conditions, as well as interviews validated the quantitative evidence presented in Table 4.2 that Carriage Town has experienced a dramatic fall in occupied housing density over the previous several decades. While that change was accompanied with demolition and the creation of wide open spaces in Grand Traverse, restrictions on demolishing historic structures in Carriage Town has meant that far fewer derelict (or even partially burned-down) structures have been razed.

Like Grand Traverse, single-family homes have historically accounted for the majority of the neighborhood housing stock, and like in Carriage Town, scores of these homes have gone through a process whereby they are converted into multi-family rentals, then, owing to owner neglect, are (partially) consumed by fire. Also like Grand Traverse, the Carriage Town neighborhood has seen a major influx of group homes. In spite of the restrictions on demolishing historic homes, there has still been massive population and housing unit decline over the study period in Carriage Town. "There are now half the homes in our neighborhood as there were 30 years ago," said one long-time resident. Both new and long-time residents agreed that Grand Traverse has halved its supply of housing over the last three or four decades as the demand for living there dropped precipitously.

While the rural feel of Grand Traverse is absent in Carriage Town, the remaining residents left behind are comfortably spread out on large lots with ample green space: somewhat of a suburban quality to the neighborhood form (see Figure 4.3). Just as was seen in Grand Traverse, homeowners buy abutting parcels after the homes are demolished to add additional yard space or room for more parking, "blotting" the physical form of their neighborhood. By reclaiming these abandoned spaces, they leave no spaces untamed, no place to hide, and few structures to turn into criminal havens. Residents I interviewed in Grand Traverse don't perceive crime to be a serious issue in their neighborhood. One resident recounted what happens when he invites friends from the suburbs over for dinner:

They can't believe how beautiful my home is. "We don't feel like we're in Flint," they always say. Which on the one hand feels good, but on the other it's like "what do you mean it doesn't feel like Flint?" "Why is Flint a bad thing?"

These friends from the suburbs are accustomed to the idea that Flint is a dangerous place, but, in fact, neighborhoods such as Grand Traverse have depopulated, lost huge numbers of housing units, yet are quite attractive places to live.

Max Brandon Park: lack of community, lack of commitment

The final neighborhood studied was different in many ways than Grand Traverse and Carriage Town. First, its location outside of walking distance to downtown, second its racial composition (see Table 4.3), and third the lack of a vital neighborhood association or even large numbers of homeowners. In the three census tracts that comprise Max Brandon Park, the occupied housing unit density fell by 27 percent from 1970 to 2000, while the population dropped 40 percent.

While Grand Traverse and Carriage Town are diverse racially and in terms of tenure, Max Brandon is primarily African American and primarily rental. Houses throughout the neighborhood have been demolished, but many derelict structures remain. While unimproved lots are adopted by neighbors or utilized for park space in Grand Traverse and Carriage Town, they are mostly left fallow in Max Brandon Park (see Figure 4.4). There, the large tracts of vacant land are untamed and uncared for. These wild vacant lots provide habitat for vermin, hiding spots for criminals, and dumping grounds for others.

Figure 4.3 The Carriage Town neighborhood has a distinctive suburban quality.

Table 4.3 Demographic and housing data, Max Brandon neighborhood, Flint, 1970–2000

Variable	1970	1980	1990	2000	% Δ '70–'80	% Δ '80–'90	% Δ '90–'00
Population	16,189	14,426	11,432	9,831	−10.9	−20.8	−14.0
Total number of households	4,745	4,372	4,119	3,459	−7.9	−5.8	−16.0
% African American		60.2	87.1	93.5	95.9	44.6	7.4	2.6
% over 65 years old		8.2	6.0	8.8	9.8	−26.6	45.9	11.6
% living in poverty		16.6	20.5	41.4	38.8	23.5	102.0	−6.3
Total housing units	4,981	4,657	4,473	4,106	−6.5	−4.0	−8.2
Total occupied housing units	4,744	4,378	4,055	3,463	−7.7	−7.4	−14.6
Occupied housing units per acre		5.0	4.6	4.3	3.6	−7.7	−7.4	−14.6

Source: U.S. Census Bureau

In Max Brandon Park, when owners of single-family homes departed, the homes were most often reused for single-family rentals, thus keeping the occupied housing density constant. Owing to the same kind of lack of care and responsibility as seen in other parts of Flint, many of these rentals were also victims of arson. When I asked a long-time resident about other uses in the neighborhood, beside residential, she said, "the only other uses is a drug house." The quantitative results show how occupied housing unit density has fallen in Max Brandon Park over the prior several decades, but the qualitative investigation has highlighted the successor land uses of the housing units—drug houses and vacant lots—and validated the overall finding that the physical form of the neighborhood has shifted with its depopulation.

Figure 4.4 Most empty lots in the Max Brandon Park neighborhood are overgrown with weeds and unattended.

The meaning of population decline in Flint

The inability of the city or the neighborhood association to effectively reuse or demolish abandoned buildings makes Carriage Town susceptible to higher levels of criminal activities than Grand Traverse. Where one neighborhood leader told me she could count on a single hand how many drug houses there were in Grand Traverse, the squatters occupying the vast supply of abandoned and semi-abandoned structures in Carriage Town has a more universal quality. Interviews with long-time residents revealed that Carriage Town was much beloved by its homeowner population due to its historic charm, but the neighborhood's ability to demolish or rehabilitate derelict structures is limited.

Both in Grand Traverse and Carriage Town, local residents and community development professionals have successfully used the blotting process to change their urban-ness, to move from high density to low density neighborhoods. From the Max Brandon Park case, we learn that the lack of strong community organizing and low levels of homeownership resulted in a different outcome. There, there are few examples of blotting and what typically succeeds a demolished home is, qualitatively, perhaps worse than a derelict structure. Where both Grand Traverse and Carriage Town have recoded their neighborhood physical form to be more rural and suburban, respectively, after decades of declining occupied housing density, Max Brandon Park remains a high-crime, high-rental, unstable community. Both Grand Traverse and Carriage Town have achieved a rural/suburban density level (1.4 units per acre), signaling perhaps a slow-down in their continued depopulation. But Max Brandon Park was still a somewhat urban 3.6 units per acre in 2000 and likely has more shrinkage to go.

While each neighborhood witnessed change, the change was most painful in the Max Brandon neighborhood. This suggests that depopulation, physical neighborhood deterioration, and decline in quality of life are not all perfectly correlated, but rather are subject to variation. As a neighborhood's occupied housing unit density declines, quality of life does not necessarily fall concomitantly. By focusing on the value of the single occupied housing unit density measurement it is possible to capture all the social, physical, environmental, and economic forces at work in a neighborhood that are shaping its physical form, while allowing for varying outcomes in quality of life. Some places will shrink well, others will not—community development and planning interventions can potentially make the difference.

This research offers some empirical weight behind the possibility of a smart decline ideology. A smart decline planning intervention can maintain a high quality of life, despite a lower population and a lower housing density. While the research presented in this chapter contributes to our understanding of the ways that housing density (and by proxy land use) changes in depopulating neighborhoods, it also suggests that a smart decline approach can go far in maintaining high quality of life when that density decreases, a hypothesis that will be further tested through the following chapters. In the next chapter, a new model for thinking about and implementing smart decline is presented that incorporates the findings from this chapter and the previous one on Rustbelt-wide shrinkage.

CHAPTER 5

A new model for neighborhood change in shrinking cities

Before I turn to the empirical evidence about the Sunbelt, this chapter offers an opportunity to consider what lessons the Rustbelt offers for theorizing decline. Building on the evidence collected in the last two chapters, a conceptual framework is presented here to introduce a new way to plan for Sunburnt Cities.

During the recent real estate and economic boom of the 2000s, it was Sunbelt cities that were most affected. From San Jose to Fort Lauderdale, the boom brought great wealth to the warmer climates south of the 37th parallel. It also brought sprawl. It brought overtaxed public utilities, crowded schools, and environmental degradation at an unprecedented scale. While the growth machine apparatus and local elites of these places benefited greatly from growth, dissent was strong and grassroots opposition to the bulldozer simmered in many places. As we will see in the coming chapters, each case study city was struggling with growth when the foreclosure crisis hit. Each was crafting strong growth management strategies designed to restrict the unfettered development that was seen as threatening quality of life.

For the cities profiled here as well as dozens across the U.S. the answer to growth was widely recognized to be one form or another of a new breed of sustainable development called smart growth or New Urbanism. I have personal experience engaging with the practice of planning holding the banner of smart growth. It was 1999 in Central Massachusetts. The real estate industry was in a frenzy to meet the space needs and growing populations of the Internet and technology revolution. Central Massachusetts was far enough from the Greater Boston area that it was not only a bedroom location for many commuters, it also generated its own jobs in its own cities such as Fitchburg and Worcester. But when demand creeped up, the region was overwhelmed with new growth and real estate development; 30 and 40 mile commutes were no longer unusual as Boston area commuters piled into the Central Massachusetts region.

I was hired for my first professional planning job and was eager to get into the fray, ready to apply the language of New Urbanism and smart growth to my new home. With a grant from the State of Massachusetts, my agency, the Montachusett Regional Planning Commission, embarked on a regional plan and I was put in charge. Swooping across the region, from town halls to public libraries, I was filled with the ideas of smart growth and tested the discourse on half-empty, unenthusiastic crowds. The script basically read like this:

Demographic projections suggest that your town will grow by 10 percent over the next ten years. We predict that will mean 1,000 new homes and 750 new school children. The forces at work creating this growth are outside of our control and frankly outside of the reach of state and federal government: growth is inevitable. The question for us to decide is how are we going to manage growth? Do we conduct business-as-usual and continue to build low-density, sprawling new housing projects or do we focus on building and rebuilding mixed-use, compact communities with a strong sense of place?

These speeches were often met with blank stares, but some regular citizens were able to connect with the choices being presented. Others left the meeting befuddled. Other planners I met in the course of promoting this new vision for growth and real estate development were often sympathetic but concerned about how they would modify zoning, building, and subdivision regulations to adequately manage this new growth. Most people simply did not want the new growth, they did not want any change.

But in this work, I learned unequivocally that change happens. In the towns I worked in, from Lunenberg to Shirley, change was happening every day as bulldozers cleared forests and "for sale" signs dotted farm roads. Growth was coming and the people of this region were not prepared for managing it in order to preserve any semblance of the kind of quality of life that they had become accustomed to.

Years later, I reflect on that and other similar experiences and can not help compare those speeches I made with speeches I make today in talking about the inevitability of decline. On some levels, the argument I made back then resonates today—simply replace "growth" with "decline." The diatribe cited above about how ordinary citizens ought not to resist the exogenous forces of growth else they will perish can be easily restated in terms of decline. Ordinary citizens can make a difference in their declining communities by focusing on *managing* that decline, by paying attention to the ways that their built environment is changing and stepping in to *shape* that change.

This odd relationship between smart growth and smart decline deserves further exploration, which I do throughout this book. In the remainder of this chapter, I focus on a new way to think about smart growth that provides a foundation for smart decline practice. This new thinking will serve to orient the reader in exploring the possibilities for cities to successfully shrink.

Some definitions

Where sprawl means spread out real estate development with large residential lots in suburbia, smart growth focuses on city centers and encourages high density development (Burchell *et al*. 1998). Smart growth promises more efficient use of land, decreased dependency on automobile use, and protection of environmental resources. Smart growth advocates highlight wasteful development patterns and promote alternative patterns based on land recycling and conservation. Smart growth has been implemented in a number of unique ways, including green development, people-based development, and brownfields reuse (Taylor and Hollander 2003).

People-based development focuses resources and amenities at the pedestrian scale, to the detriment of automobile users. The typical automobile-based development results in great distances between residential and commercial land uses, requiring heavy automobile use (and the accompanying air pollution and energy waste). People-based development is central to the urban planning movement, New Urbanism (Calthorpe 1993). The New Urbanists call for a new urban development pattern that pays attention to traditional architecture and both pedestrian and transit orientation.

Smart growth is conceptually ambiguous and New Urbanism even more so. Smart growth advocates have introduced a series of key policy innovations that, taken together, offer the clearest definition of the concept (see Table 5.1). Each tool is designed to support compact, mixed-use, pedestrian, and transit-oriented development in a growing region. Herein lies the problem: what happens when economics and demographics shift and a place is no longer growing? The answer is that smart growth tools are designed to address growth and their efficacy in either population stagnation or decline is unknown.

Table 5.1 Smart growth policies

Policy tool	Cities where adopted
Regional vision documents or plans	Portland, Salt Lake, Seattle, NYC, Chicago
Scenario process and concept plans	Portland, Salt Lake
Community design options (photo-selection preferences)	Salt Lake
Urban growth boundaries	Minneapolis/St. Paul, Seattle, Portland
Rural legacy program	State of Maryland
Transportation/infrastructure required concurrently with new development	State of Washington, State of Florida
Regional appeals boards	State of Washington
Urban centers strategy	Seattle
Priority funding areas	State of Maryland
Transit-oriented development	Portland
Pedestrian environment factor	Portland
Regional tax sharing	Minneapolis/St. Paul
Fair share housing requirements	Minneapolis/St. Paul, State of New Jersey

New Urbanism was conceived by architects and is a national movement dominated by architects. They are in the business of designing buildings, neighborhoods, even entire towns and the New Urbanism movement reflects that. The movement's most remarkable contribution is the Transect System. Developed by architects Andres Duany and Elisabeth Plater-Zyberk, the New Urbanist transect was an adaption of the ecological transect that suggests that natural systems function well when appropriate elements are co-located: a pine tree does not belong in a desert; a coral reef does not belong in a river valley. The transect idea was developed and refined further in 2002 for an academic audience in an article co-authored by Duany and urban planning professor Emily Talen in the *Journal of the American Planning Association*.

In this now well-accepted presentation, the transect serves as a model for sustainable urban growth and development (see Figure 5.1). Each ecozone of the transect cuts across different segments of the landscape, beginning out in the remote rural zones with T1 (Rural preserve) through T2 (Rural reserve), T3 (Sub-urban), T4 (General urban), T5 (Urban center), and culminating in the heart of a metro area, T6 (Urban core).

Associated with each ecozone of the transect are maximum density levels and associated urban design and landscape elements. T2 has homes on large lots with narrow winding roads and scenic vistas, while T3 allows for limited multi-family housing, woodlands, and arterial roads. T4 and T5 allow for increasing levels of housing density and higher capacity roadways, along with mixes of uses (particularly retail and office uses). As presented in the Duany and Talen (2002) article, T2 has a low housing density (to be determined by local boards), while T3 has a maximum housing density of six units per acre, T4 allows for up to 12 units per acre, and T5 allows for up to 24. The New Urbanist's greatest innovation with the transect is their insistence that each ecozone is special—no one better than the others. The key, they argue, is to preserve and protect their cohesiveness as distinct ecozones.

This argument was accepted broadly during the recent period of economic growth and prosperity. Cities across the U.S. and abroad have explored incorporating the transect model and its associated zoning apparatus into their own regulatory systems.[1] Miami, Florida, has advanced this agenda quickly and as of this writing appears close to being the first major U.S. city to formally adopt form-based zoning.

The transect model teaches us that growth does not have to be a bad thing for communities and neighborhoods if it is planned for and managed such that each ecozone is preserved. For this book, the central hypothesis is that decline does not have to be a bad thing for communities and neighborhoods if it is planned for and managed. The transect model offers a useful starting point for examining that very question in the context of the Sunbelt. To begin, I ask: can the transect model work in reverse?

As currently constructed: no. However, a Reverse Transect Model provides a possible path forward to address some of the inconsistencies and contradictions of smart growth and sustainable development introduced earlier in this chapter. It allows for a conception of development that advances a neighborhood both forward and backward along a path of change, without placing greater value on growth or decline. Figure 5.2 depicts a reformulated Transect Model. Reading Figure 5.1, the logical path of development reads left to right, from rural, undisturbed landscapes, to suburbs, to central city. To read the Reverse Transect requires a different set of assumptions whereby a neighborhood can either develop (or advance itself) by either growing or declining in housing density.

Here we assume that a neighborhood begins at T5 with 15 housing units per acre. In the diagram presented in Figure 5.2, I worked with two research assistants to sketch out an actual urban neighborhood in Somerville, Massachusetts with 15 units per acre.[2] If the neighborhood loses 20 percent of its housing units due to depopulation, it will have just 12 units per acre and will appear now in the T4 ecozone. Normally, such a loss would be viewed as tragic but the transect concept teaches us that neighborhood change does not have to be a bad thing. From the New Urbanists, we learn that T4 is no better or worse than T5, simply different. From the New Urbanists, we learn that a variety of urban design and landscape architecture techniques can be useful to retrofit a neighborhood to install or redesign elements within the ecozone to protect and preserve its integrity.[3]

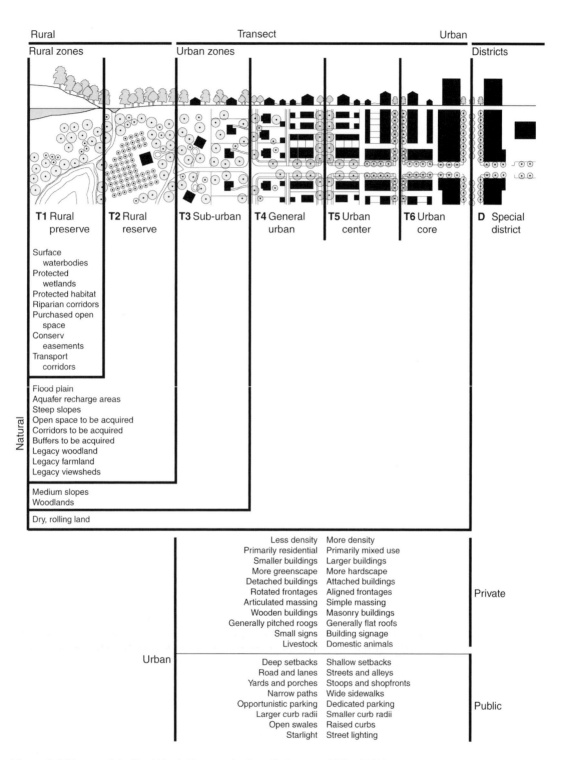

Rural · Transect · Urban

Rural zones · Urban zones · Districts

T1 Rural preserve | **T2** Rural reserve | **T3** Sub-urban | **T4** General urban | **T5** Urban center | **T6** Urban core | **D** Special district

Surface
 waterbodies
Protected
 wetlands
Protected habitat
Riparian corridors
Purchased open
 space
Conserv
 easements
Transport
 corridors

Flood plain
Aquafer recharge areas
Steep slopes
Open space to be acquired
Corridors to be acquired
Buffers to be acquired
Legacy woodland
Legacy farmland
Legacy viewsheds

Medium slopes
Woodlands

Dry, rolling land

Natural

Less density	More density
Primarily residential	Primarily mixed use
Smaller buildings	Larger buildings
More greenscape	More hardscape
Detached buildings	Attached buildings
Rotated frontages	Aligned frontages
Articulated massing	Simple massing
Wooden buildings	Masonry buildings
Generally pitched roogs	Generally flat roofs
Small signs	Building signage
Livestock	Domestic animals

Private

Urban

Deep setbacks	Shallow setbacks
Road and lanes	Streets and alleys
Yards and porches	Stoops and shopfronts
Narrow paths	Wide sidewalks
Opportunistic parking	Dedicated parking
Larger curb radii	Smaller curb radii
Open swales	Raised curbs
Starlight	Street lighting

Public

Figure 5.1 Diagram of the New Urbanist Transect, developed by Duany and Talen (2002).

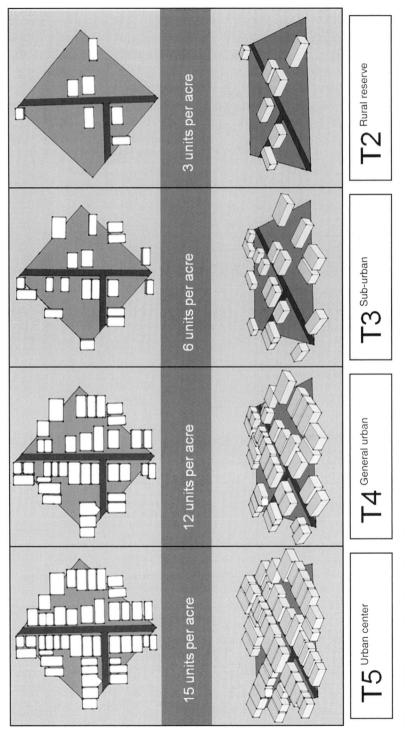

Figure 5.2 Diagram of the Reverse Transect.

While smart growth and New Urbanism appear prima facie to offer little guidance to planners and policymakers confronting depopulation, both ideologies provide important supports for the Reverse Transect Model introduced here. This revised version of the transect provides a new way of thinking about managing decline in a way that focuses on preserving architectural, urban design, and landscape features that maintain the integrity of an ecozone. The Reverse Transect Model provides a way to think about how a neighborhood might go from being 15 units per acre (T5) to only 12 units per acre (T4).

CHAPTER 6

Unfamiliar patterns in the sun

What postal workers already know

It is a virtual truism in the field of urban studies that hot, sunny places always grow, or do they? The deep and rich literature on the American Sunbelt tells the story of the attractive powers of these warm environs—where the introduction of air conditioning made them ideal for jobs, workers, and retirees. A 1926 cover story in *Liberty* magazine suggested that there were no brakes on the Florida growth engine (Cave 2009). Cheap land and abundant amenities made Arizona, Texas, New Mexico, South Carolina, and other states desirable in the second half of the twentieth century beyond any booster's wildest dreams. The new alignment of power, money, and people away from the Rustbelt to the Sunbelt has been viewed by many scholars since the 1970s as largely permanent (see Perry and Watkins 1977; Weinstein and Firestine 1978; Bernard and Bradley 1983; Sawers and Tabb 1984; Schulman 1994; Pack 2005).

Except for the occasional boom–bust cycles, the Sunbelt has been viewed as a place of perpetual prosperity and limitless growth. In this chapter, I introduce empirical evidence to refute that idea and to begin to fill in the conceptual framework introduced in Chapter 5. Sunbelt cities are presently in a state of economic and population decline: they are shrinking. More importantly than demographic change, many of these declining Sunbelt cities are physically shrinking, presenting an unprecedented opportunity to reshape and retrofit urban neighborhoods in a positive way.

This late twentieth-century thinking about the Sunbelt has been shaped primarily by interpretations of past data. Bowman and Pagano's (2004) *Terra Incognita: Vacant land and urban strategies* report on a survey and Census data analysis that was influential at the time and serves as a useful introduction to my own findings. The study involved a survey mailed to city officials in U.S. cities with populations of 50,000 or more from 1997 to 1998 (531 were sent, 186 responded) and a second survey mailed to 81 with follow-up questions. The survey results showed a massive amount of vacant land in Southern (n=23) and Western (n=30) cities, 20,011 acres and 10,349 acres, respectively. With Midwestern and Northeastern cities reporting 5,903 and 5,004 acres, on average.

The survey also asked local officials to report the number of abandoned buildings in their cities (only 20 Southern and 23 Western cities reported data for these questions). Among those who reported data, the Southern cities had an average of 1,632 abandoned buildings and the Western cities had only 93. These numbers are important when contrasted against Northeastern and Midwestern cities that reported on average 4,025 abandoned buildings.[1] While there was certainly an abandoned building problem in some Southern cities in 1998, Western cities had no problem at that time, on average. This disparity is part of a larger well-documented split among Sunbelt cities into poorer, formerly industrial cities such as Mobile, Alabama (2,009 abandoned buildings) and Richmond, Virginia (3,000 abandoned buildings) and the growing, new economy cities such as Pembroke Pines, Florida (one abandoned building) and Santa Clara, California (five abandoned buildings). In this new millennium, with the advent of the foreclosure crisis and the Great Recession, it is worth studying the whole of the Sunbelt to understand the impacts and responses for both sides of the coin. But recognizing the historical differences among Sunbelt cities and between Sunbelt cities and other U.S. cities is critical to conducting this analysis. Bowman and Pagano demonstrate this variation with respect to abandonment and through their surveys of vacant land they raise important questions about how undeveloped land fits into local planning strategies (we will return to this point in the case study chapters).

In approaching the current shift afoot in the Sunbelt, I relied on two primary data sources that provide demographic and land-use data at the neighborhood level. The first is the well-known and popular U.S. Census, which enumerates population, employment, and housing levels at the city and, in some cases, zip code level. Census data collected on a decennial basis is also available at an even finer geographical level called the census tract (usually smaller than a zip code geography and comprising, on average, a few thousand households). I compiled this data for every Sunbelt city with over 100,000 in population in 2005. In defining the Sunbelt, I adapted boundaries employed by several demographers and geographers to include cities in those states that are located below the 37th Parallel.[2] The cities are in the following states:

- AL
- AR
- AZ
- CA
- FL
- GA
- LA
- MS
- NC
- NM
- NV
- SC
- TX

Due to data errors, seven cities were removed from the analysis, leaving a total of 140 cities in the above 13 Sunbelt states.[3] Most (86 percent) of the 140 Sunbelt cities studied were growing rapidly just a few years prior to the housing crash. In total, these cities gained 2,372,033 persons between 2000 and 2005 (474,406 per year, on average). As the housing crash approached in 2006, many of these cities began to change course. But the Sunbelt, as a whole, did continue to grow (albeit at a slower pace). In total, these cities increased in population by 1,138,245 persons between 2006 and 2008. But a closer look reveals a crack in the sustained growth patterns. As housing prices began to sink in 2006, populations also began to dwindle in a select group of cities. Twenty-six Sunbelt cities lost population from 2006 to 2008, including cities in Florida, California, Louisiana, Georgia, Alabama, and Mississippi (see Table 6.1, Figure 6.1). In this group of losing cities, the mean loss was 1,660 people (with a standard deviation of 1,603), while the highest decline was 6,680 persons in Baton Rouge, Louisiana.[4]

Table 6.1 Cities with greatest population loss (Jul 2006–Jul 2008)

City	State	Jul '08	Jul '06	Change '06–'08
Baton Rouge city	Louisiana	223,689	230,369	–6,680
Columbus city	Georgia	186,984	191,578	–4,594
Jackson city	Mississippi	173,861	177,999	–4,138
Hialeah city	Florida	210,542	213,854	–3,312
Long Beach city	California	463,789	466,751	–2,962
Pembroke Pines city	Florida	145,661	148,069	–2,408
Coral Springs city	Florida	125,783	128,023	–2,240
St. Petersburg city	Florida	245,314	247,515	–2,201
Hollywood city	Florida	141,740	143,853	–2,113
Birmingham city	Alabama	228,798	230,733	–1,935

Source: U.S. Census Bureau (2009)

While population changes are surprising, a closer look at land-use change within Sunbelt cities reveals more chilling statistics. Six days a week, every week of the year, a postal worker walks up and down nearly every street in America. And they track what they see. I am not interested in how much mail people receive (but those numbers appear to be in decline, as well). I am interested in how many housing units are empty and no longer receiving mail. After 90 days of unoccupancy, the Postal Service removes an address from its active inventory.

Figure 6.1 Change in occupied housing units in Sunbelt cities with greater than 100,000 persons, 2006–2009.

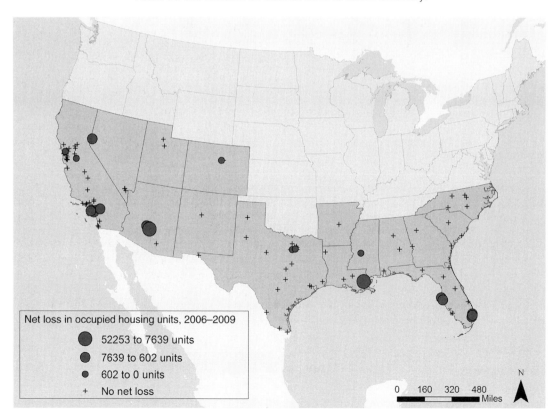

Net loss in occupied housing units, 2006–2009

● 52253 to 7639 units
● 7639 to 602 units
● 602 to 0 units
+ No net loss

0   160   320   480
Miles

N

For example, take my own street with four single-family homes and two multi-family homes (each with three units). When I moved here, all ten housing units were occupied and receiving mail. If the house across the street goes into foreclosure, and is left vacant for more than 90 days, then the Postal Service will begin tracking my street as having only nine housing units. This 10 percent decline can be both meaningful and misleading. By just looking at a 10 percent decline, an observer might not know if this meant fewer residents, if it meant an abandoned building, if the 10 percent decline occurred because one of the multi-family homes was converted from three units to two. An observer of the data would not know any of this, but the planner would know something: there is now a decrease in occupied housing unit density.

Occupied housing unit density was introduced in Chapter 3 as an essential concept in smart decline practice, as it is already an essential concept in smart growth planning practice. The Postal Service data provides a window into changing occupied housing unit density, but only a window. Just as the chapter on Flint, Michigan validated the usefulness of using census tract generated occupied housing unit density data, I will present the findings from three in-depth case studies on Sunbelt cities to check the accuracy of the findings here.

The bounds of this study necessitate a narrow time window to study neighborhood change in Sunbelt cities. My own review of housing sales data from Zillow.com and a general consensus in the popular media suggest that the housing boom peaked on or about the beginning of 2006 in most parts of the Sunbelt (Goodman 2007; Leland 2007; Cauchon 2008). I obtained complete raw data from the Postal Service from February 2006 through February 2009.[5] The data was difficult to work with, but I was successful in matching zip codes in the Postal Service database with the U.S. Census Bureau's Zip Code Tabulation Area (ZCTA) files. Then, I filtered out only those zip codes located within each of the 140 Sunbelt cities in the study. I did this by conducting searches on USPS.gov to obtain a list of each zip code in each city—for a total of 2,241 zip codes. Lastly, I needed to attend to the fact that the Postal Service regularly changes zip code boundaries. Working with a research assistant, I read through all issues of the *Postal Bulletin* (an online Postal Service newsletter) for announcements of changes or eliminations of zip codes. As a result, I removed 607 zip codes from the study, leaving 1,634 remaining.

Such a loss of information might be seen as potentially damaging to the results. But that would only be true if those zip codes with changing boundaries are systematically different from the typical zip code. In fact, they probably are different in that they are generally the growing neighborhoods, with new homes and businesses demanding expansion of zip code boundaries into unincorporated areas. Zip codes also change in growing areas when a zip code splits into two. While I might expect those zip codes that were removed to be more of the high growth zip codes, this is a study about decline. All conclusions and generalizations drawn from this analysis will be limited by this bias in the data.

Land-use change in Sunbelt cities

At the city level, most Sunbelt cities faired well during the foreclosure crisis. Among 140 Sunbelt cities with populations over 100,000 in 2005, 29 experienced a net loss in housing units between 2006 and 2009 (see Table 6.2 and Appendix B). For those 29 shrinking cities, the mean loss in housing units was 2 percent, with New Orleans accounting for more than half of that loss. Beyond hurricane-ravaged New Orleans, this loss was spread out throughout the region. The average shrinking city had six zip codes that lost housing units, with many having ten or more zip codes losing units.

But this is a study about neighborhoods more than anything else and a close look at sub-city scale reveals a more striking picture. For those 140 cities, there are a total of 1,647 total zip codes where data was available from USPS for both 2006 and 2009[6]—601 (more than one-third) of these zip codes lost housing units, 1,044 of these zips grew in size. More than one-third of all zip codes included in the analysis lost occupied housing units from 2006 to 2009—the finding is an astounding one. In addition, 79 percent of all the Sunbelt cities (n=112) had at least one zip code that lost housing units during the time period.

The prevalence of this physical shrinkage is impressive, but what about the severity? Using the variable occupied housing unit density, it is clear that there was real change afoot in Sunbelt cities from 2006 to 2009. Among the 601 shrinking zip codes in the region, the mean decline in occupied housing unit density was 4 percent, with a standard deviation of 9.7 percent. To translate these results, take the example of a neighborhood of 20 two-family homes on five acres. In 2006, suppose these units are all occupied (that is, they have received mail within the last 90 days). The neighborhood has 40 units divided by five acres, for a total of eight occupied housing units per acre (in planning practice this is a typical medium/high density urban neighborhood). For this neighborhood, a reduction in 10 percent of occupied housing unit density means a decline from eight units per acre to 7.2 units per acre, or only 36 housing units (7.2 × 5 acres). What happened to the missing four housing units? Some are still there, but vacant. Some have suffered from neglect and vandalism and may be in derelict condition. Some may have even been demolished. And some may even have been combined with adjacent units (in the case of a duplex, this would mean a conversion to a single-family home).

Summing up the stats

The big question is what have all these changes meant for the people who live in these neighborhoods and for the planners who are responsible for managing land-use change? The following three chapters test these findings further through ground-truthing of actual neighborhoods, as well as through interviews with residents and local officials. As demonstrated above, there are scores of Sunbelt cities where the challenges of abandonment and the opportunities for smart decline might be examined. Above all other Sunbelt states, four have been recognized both in the results in this chapter and in other studies as the epicenters of the vacancy crisis: California, Florida, Arizona, and Nevada. A 2009 report by the private firm RealtyTrac showed that the greatest number of foreclosures are concentrated in cities in those four states (Associated Press 2009).

Table 6.2 Cities with greatest housing unit loss (Feb 2006–Feb 2009)

City	State	Combined acreage of all ZCTAs within city boundaries	Feb '06 occupied housing units (OHU)	Feb '09 occupied housing units (OHU)	Difference in OHU '06–'09		OHU density Feb '06	OHU density Feb '09	Number of zip codes that lost OHUs
					No.	%			
New Orleans city	Louisiana	105,163	217,451	165,198	−52,253	−24%	2.1	1.6	16
Chandler city	Arizona	81,478	96,992	87,241	−9,751	−10%	1.2	1.1	5
Scottsdale city	Arizona	536,280	150,482	144,325	−6,157	−4%	0.3	0.3	9
Gilbert town	Arizona	25,309	44,307	42,539	−1,768	−4%	1.8	1.7	2
Glendale city	Arizona	52,078	106,098	101,951	−4,147	−4%	2.0	2.0	7
Reno city	Nevada	1,036,474	80,775	78,745	−2,030	−3%	0.1	0.1	2
Clearwater city	Florida	36,098	91,022	89,264	−1,758	−2%	2.5	2.5	9
St. Petersburg city	Florida	55,359	176,961	173,839	−3,122	−2%	3.2	3.1	13
Pompano Beach city	Florida	58,839	182,880	179,833	−3,047	−2%	3.1	3.1	10
Fort Lauderdale city	Florida	125,086	334,285	328,744	−5,541	−2%	2.7	2.6	21
Pembroke Pines city	Florida	14,007	43,999	43,353	−646	−1%	3.1	3.1	3
San Bernardino city	California	106,139	69,207	68,331	−876	−1%	0.7	0.6	5
Mesa city	Arizona	173,988	182,805	180,895	−1,910	−1%	1.1	1.0	9
Hollywood city	Florida	11,620	50,581	50,137	−444	−1%	4.4	4.3	2
Downey city	California	8,008	34,662	34,372	−290	−1%	4.3	4.3	3
Norwalk city	California	6,268	27,436	27,226	−210	−1%	4.4	4.3	1
Santa Ana city	California	27,450	102,039	101,296	−743	−1%	3.7	3.7	5
Long Beach city	California	44,603	196,119	195,045	−1,074	−1%	4.4	4.4	11
Modesto city	California	136,310	87,614	87,192	−422	0%	0.6	0.6	5
Richmond city	California	24,191	58,551	58,297	−254	0%	2.4	2.4	3

Source: U.S. Postal Service, Active Residential Deliveries (March 2006 and March 2009)

In selecting case study cities, I sought to include a range in population size, geography, and policy responses to abandonment. The first two variables were easy to collect; to identify policy responses to abandonment, I conducted informal phone interviews with city officials in more than a dozen cities that experienced major occupied housing unit loss in at least three zip codes. In those interviews, I sought to understand, generally speaking, what the city government was doing. While some of those preliminary findings were later contradicted in the field, it ensured that the three cities I examined would provide a range of outcomes in order to help in painting an intricate picture of the dimensional range of the concepts being studied. I also had to limit the selection of cities to those where I was granted access to both local officials and community leaders. For all these reasons, I selected Fresno, California, Phoenix, Arizona, and Orlando, Florida for the case studies.

Fresno (2008 population = 475,050) is the capital of a century-old agricultural region that started growing houses as a new crop in the beginning of the 21st century. The city's aggressive response to a sudden turn of fate in the real estate business has meant new opportunities for converting homes into skate parks, among other innovations. It was in Phoenix (2008 population = 1,567,924) that President Barack Obama chose to announce his plan to spend $50 billion to address foreclosures and housing abandonment—a city whose growth appeared unstoppable until quite suddenly in 2006 when the entire economy began to fall apart like a house of cards. And lastly, there is Orlando, home to Mickey Mouse and year-round sun, the smallest city of the three (2008 population = 230,519). Orlando faces hard times trying to reconfigure its long-held New Urbanist policies to meet the demands of a shrinking city.

While not a random sample, the three cities are varied enough in terms of population, geography, and policy responses to abandonment for the following chapters to provide a rich and enlightening story about both a problem and the potential of a smart decline solution. Lessons from the next three chapters can, in fact, be generalized to other similar cities in similar regions operating under similar policy frameworks. The methodology employed in each case study follows closely the approach used in studying Flint, Michigan in Chapter 4. While Census data was at the heart of the quantitative analysis of Flint's changing housing and demographic conditions, new data sources are examined in the Sunbelt city cases. After the following three chapters, I will return to the key lessons of the book by comparing across the cases and connecting back to the larger questions of how to confront decline.

CHAPTER 7

Facing change in the Central Valley

A declining Fresno

Nathan Gans loves Fresno. He got married and raised two children here in the heart of California's Central Valley. Mid-way between the Bay Area and the Los Angeles Basin, Nathan was able to find good work as a welder and could afford to buy a three-bedroom detached home in the booming West of 99 neighborhood of Fresno.

While he bought low, housing values started to grow rapidly during the early 2000s and by the middle of the decade he had built up quite a lot of equity on his home. Like many of his friends and neighbors, Nathan tapped into that equity through a home equity loan. He used the money to buy a modest boat that he could take out on the wild rivers in nearby Yosemite National Park.

Then, a couple of years later Nathan took out another home equity loan to buy a bigger boat, and the following year he did it a final time and bought an even larger boat. A few months later, Nathan lost his job and the spiral of financial ruin quickly followed. He defaulted on his loans, the house went into foreclosure and still with no income he moved in with his father out in Minnesota. Left behind was a home that the Gans family took great pride in but was now rotting away in the hot Fresno sun. The grass and the trees on the property began to die and local teenagers tried to get inside to party. For more than a year and a half, the deteriorating building sat empty and was a scar on the neighborhood until eventually the bank rented out the home.

People come to Fresno for all kinds of reasons—the sun, the affordability, the jobs. But today, people are leaving because they are losing their jobs and losing their homes. Instead of offering financial security and stability, homes in Fresno and beyond were used as banks to buy boats (and bigger boats) leaving the owners exposed when property values plummeted. Official State of California estimates tell us that Fresno's population has stayed relatively steady—even growing slightly, but traveling around the city's neighborhoods tells a different story. The overbuilding of 2005, 2006, and 2007 has left thousands of empty houses scattered throughout the city. Data collected from the Postal Service shows that some Fresno neighborhoods have lost between 2 and 3 percent of their occupied housing units.

This chapter is the first of three where I examine the complex story of how each city has been impacted by economic malaise and how people have responded: both professional urban planners and local politicians as well as ordinary residents and leaders of community organizations. Before delving into the present, we begin this story with the past: the history of Fresno and the Central Valley is critical to understanding the phenomenon we are studying today.

A brief history of planning and real estate development in Fresno

Any history of Fresno is, more than anything else, a history of water. Its use, its abuse, and its limits. Worster's (1985) definitive treatment on the topic of water and the American West is a useful point for beginning to understand what has occurred in the Central Valley and what its future portends. Worster argues that water "more than any other single element, has been the shaping force in the region's history" (p. 5).

The wholesale reconstruction of the Central Valley to provide for massive scaled irrigation has both wreaked havoc on the region's natural systems as well as brought great wealth. Worster's study explores how the 1933 Central Valley Project brought great water works to a fertile, yet dry basin, allowing for an unprecedented transformation of a sleepy train station town into the agricultural center of the world. Estimates are that the valley produces 25 percent of all U.S. table food; it's been called by one environmental scientist the "richest agricultural region in the history of the world" (Johnson *et al.* 1993). This inconceivable change has been the subject of much attention in planning and real estate development literatures. In her study of the modern history of the Central Valley, Nash (2000) writes, "Perhaps no other landscape has been so discussed, studied, and planned over the last century" (p. 3)—thus making Fresno a uniquely interesting place to understand contemporary urban change.

Settled first in 1878 by Minnie Austin and three other San Francisco-based school teachers, Fresno was eyed even earlier by railroad magnate Leland Stanford as the main midway station stop along his Central Pacific route. A small town grew up around the train station and farming in the desert community took off.

But the desert climate meant little water was available for irrigation and the small town remained small. Once the Central Valley Project got the water flowing, the City of Fresno and surrounding communities transformed their landscape into a hard-working agricultural center.

The very seasonal nature of agriculture has meant much work during the growing season and much unemployment the remainder of the year. Fresno's agricultural economy demands a "malleable and eternal lower class" as Johnson *et al.* (1993) put it—this "shadow society" of as many as 86,000 live throughout the valley with few benefits, no security, and low wages (p. 14).

In the 1960s, city officials, armed with millions in federal dollars, cut wide swaths through Fresno's neighborhoods either literally by building highways, or figuratively by labeling the swaths as high density districts. The high density classification was made with no regard for what structures or uses were actually there; according to one planner, "non-conforming uses were created within structures!"

Today's planners conjecture that the mid-twentieth century planners' aims were to generate new construction and reinvestment within the city boundaries so as to rejuvenate the city and its neighborhoods. By upzoning land, they would provide an incentive to property owners to build, thus enhancing economic activity. But the building was often very low quality apartments and "not anything that will stabilize neighborhoods." In exchange for a temporary infusion of construction jobs and incomes, the city effectively destroyed owner-occupied stable neighborhoods. The densification of housing in a shrinking city did effectively attract capital and reinvestment but at the same time transformed quiet, owner-occupied places such as Lowell-Jefferson into primarily tenant-occupied congested places. A planner in Fresno told me, "we never really respected ourselves, we just wanted new real estate development." And with all the physical improvements, not much progress was made in enhancing the physical aesthetics of the city. As Setencich (1993) put it, "Fresno will never win any beauty contests" (p. 11).

For decades, the city recoiled from the urban renewal disasters and by the mid-2000s the economy began to boom with increased overall wealth and growth for Fresno. Population rose, number of jobs grew, and number of houses also climbed (see Table 7.1). To accommodate these new residents, thousands of acres of agricultural land every year were being converted into housing developments (Johnson et al. 1993, p. 199). The region's very economic base—agriculture—was losing out to its newly favorite industry: home building. This sprawling, placeless new growth was recognized by planners and others as a serious threat to the sustainability of the region. Some demographers went as far as to predict a doubling of population between 2007 and 2050 for the region. A key policy report behind much of the planning warned, "In order to prepare for this growth, today's leaders and residents will need to make intelligent choices regarding the shape and future of the valley's communities and land" (Great Valley Center 2007, p. 1).

Beginning in early 2006 a broad coalition of local politicians, planners, and non-profit community leaders in the Fresno region[1] came together to shape a BluePrint, to respond to the warning of four million more people, to guide future growth. The goal of this BluePrint project is to reduce vehicle miles traveled, enhance housing affordability, and decrease long-distance commuting by bringing more jobs into the immediate region. One regional planner remarked that they want to "get more jobs here so people don't have to commute so far."

Table 7.1 City-wide demographic and housing data, Fresno, 1970–2000

	1970	1980	1990	2000
Total population	289,225	358,813	477,389	570,163
% White	91.1%	76.9%	64.7%	58.3%
% African American	6.4%	6.8%	6.6%	7.5%
% Latino	19.2%	22.0%	26.5%	36.4%
Total population foreign born	5.6%	7.7%	14.9%	18.0%
% < age 18	34.8%	28.0%	30.7%	31.8%
% > age 64	9.3%	10.2%	10.4%	10.1%
Total households	92,091	131,772	165,962	190,127
Total housing units	96,134	141,298	174,767	200,543
Total occupied housing units	92,091	131,725	165,719	189,723
% occupied housing units	95.8%	93.2%	94.8%	94.6%
Average household income prior year	$9,264	$19,837	$37,663	$48,447

Source: U.S. Census Bureau, Census 1970–2000 Summary File 1; Geolytics, Neighborhood Change Database

The approach is recognizable along the lines of other contemporary regional planning efforts modeled on the New Urbanist and smart growth approaches of the later 1990s in Portland, Oregon and Salt Lake City, Utah (see Calthorpe and Fulton 2001 for other examples). Emphasizing concentrated growth in existing urban areas, transit-oriented development, protected open space, and controlled fringe development, this BluePrint responded well rhetorically to the kinds of growth pressures Fresno was facing up until the tide turned in 2006.

While farmland was being gobbled up in the mid-2000s by new housing developments, center city Fresno was struggling to keep its stores and residents and to fight off crime. The regionalist idea of restoring center cities and curbing suburban sprawl was an appealing one to Fresno. From 2002 to 2005, 7,424 single-family building permits were issued by the city (see Table 7.2). That represented an increase of 135 percent from 2002 to 2005. During this period, the population was estimated to have grown by 14,547 persons (U.S. Census 2009). The building boom was not limited to single-family housing, with the number of multi-family permits issued quadrupling during this period. Oddly, student populations were falling during this period as birth rates declined and young families left the city (Fresno Unified School District 2009). Kindergarten through 12th grade populations dropped 5 percent from 2002 to 2006, according to the Fresno Unified School District.

To make matters worse, broader environmental challenges have hit the region and the city with a double whammy. A couple of thousand acres of agricultural land on the city's West Side was put out of production in early 2009 owing to lack of water for irrigation. Declining agricultural production has meant lost jobs on those acres as well as further job losses in warehousing and processing, the ripple effect has further compounded broader economic challenges facing the city and the region. Troubles relating to water are long term and hinder any efforts by city and regional leaders to expand agricultural employment. For the remainder of the chapter, I will put these concerns on the backburner for now but I will return to them at the end when discussing opportunities for smart decline.

Table 7.2 Building permits issued, Fresno, 2002–2009

	2002	2003	2004	2005	2006	2007	2008	2009*	ch 2002– 2005	ch 2006– 2008
Residential single-family	1,134	1,514	2,109	2,667	1,959	2,039	1,529	1,231.5	135%	−37%
Residential multi-family	26	161	220	152	49	163	58	9	485%	−82%
Total permits	3,162	3,678	4,333	4,824	4,014	4,209	3,595	4,254	53%	6%

* 2009 data was estimated based on a an annual linear extrapolation of data from 1/1/09 to 8/31/09, 1FAM=821, M-FAM=6, TotalPERM=2836
Source: City of Fresno Building Department

Using 2006 as the beginning of the economic and housing problems of the Sunbelt, we see a different Fresno emerging in 2006. While city-wide population continued to grow,[2] according to the State of California and the U.S. Census, an examination of USPS data shows that individual neighborhoods began to see widespread housing loss (see Figure 7.1). Building activity plummeted during this bust period, where the number of single-family building permits fell 35 percent and the number of multi-family building permits fell 82 percent from 2006 to 2009. The impacts of this decline have been severe.

Reduced tax collection has crippled city services, with the planning department cut in half and lower budgets for critical city services such as code enforcement and police. In 2008, the city reduced spending by $27 million from the previous year and at the close of 2009, the city was facing a further budget gap of $27.8 million (Clemings 2009). Fresno's mayor has promised layoffs to address the continuing shortfalls, but some observers fear that the current situation is only going to get worse as a second wave of foreclosures hits the city (Clemings 2009).

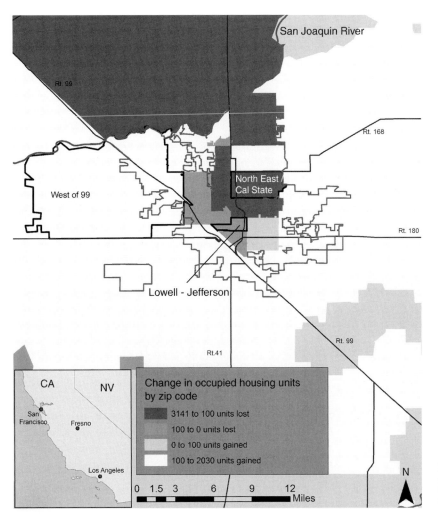

Figure 7.1 Fresno area: change in occupied housing units, 2006–2009 (by zip code).

Table 7.3 Housing occupancy patterns for Fresno zip codes, 2006–2009

| Study neighborhood | Zip | LISC foreclosure score (Intrastate Foreclosure Component Score) ** | Neighborhood name | 2000 Census | | |
				Total population	Total housing units	Land area (acres)
	93703	10		31,168	10,241	2,996
✓	93726	8.7	Northeast/Cal State	39,135	15,038	4,071
	93704	3.1		26,565	11,667	3,623
✓	93701	4.7	Lowell-Jefferson area	13,844	3,943	977
	93705	10.7		35,443	13,084	3,007
	93728	4.8		16,339	6,283	1,956
	93721	0.9		6,836	1,860	1,303
	93650	0.9		3,257	849	314
	93702	22		47,997	12,737	3,362
	93710	3.3		29,327	11,557	4,214
	93711	1.7		36,269	15,589	7,163
	93706	8.5		35,781	10,323	101,812
	93725	4.6		20,998	5,970	41,501
	93727	13.1		54,681	18,344	20,819
	93720	3.9		–	–	–
✓	93722	26.2	West of 99 *	–	–	–

* Zip codes where boundaries changed were removed from the analysis in Chapter 6, but 98722 was one such zip code which had a boundary change but was examined further due to its extraordinary foreclosure rate.
** Local Initiative Support Corporation with Foreclosure Response project, Table 1: November 2008, http://www.housingpolicy.org/assets/foreclosure-response.

Because zip code boundaries change often, longitudinal analysis is challenging. It is difficult to be able to calculate exactly how many housing units Fresno has lost since 2006. In Chapter 6, I provided a broad brush accounting of the major changes afoot throughout the Sunbelt. In this detailed case study of Fresno, it is useful to highlight the neighborhoods that saw major losses as indicated by Table 7.3. As with the chapter on Flint (Chapter 4), I approached this case study analysis with both statistics on neighborhood change and an open mind. After interviewing several city officials and community leaders, I narrowed my focus to three neighborhoods that all experienced major housing loss from 2006 to 2009. One of these neighborhoods was actually eliminated from the analysis earlier due to a change in its zip code boundaries during the study period. But, the neighborhood West of 99 (93722) offers unique insights and is included in the analysis. The other two study area neighborhoods show huge housing unit losses: Lowell-Jefferson (93701) lost nearly 100 homes from 2006 to 2009 and Northeast/Cal State (93726) lost almost 150 homes—together these three neighborhoods contribute to an understanding of the larger Fresno story.

USPS active residential delivery statistics

Occupied housing units – Feb '06	Occupied housing units – Feb '09	Change in occ. housing units Feb '06–Feb '09	Occupied housing units per acre – Feb '06	Occupied housing units per acre – Feb '09	% change Feb '06–Feb '09
10,194	9,918	–276	3.40	3.31	–3%
15,196	15,049	–147	3.73	3.70	–1%
11,618	11,500	–118	3.21	3.17	–1%
3,729	3,632	–97	3.82	3.72	–3%
12,948	12,871	–77	4.31	4.28	–1%
6,201	6,128	–73	3.17	3.13	–1%
1,753	1,722	–31	1.35	1.32	–2%
1,483	1,454	–29	4.72	4.62	–2%
12,484	12,539	55	3.71	3.73	0%
11,414	11,562	148	2.71	2.74	1%
15,751	15,918	167	2.20	2.22	1%
10,260	10,654	394	0.10	0.10	4%
5,971	6,395	424	0.14	0.15	7%
19,691	21,641	1,950	0.95	1.04	9%
21,029	18,318	–2,711	–	–	–
–	–	–	–	–	–

Table 7.4 Neighborhood-level demographic and housing data, Fresno, 2000

Neighborhood	Total population	% White	% African American	% Latino	% < age 18	% > age 64	Total housing units	Total occupied housing units	% occupied housing units
93701 – Lowell-Jefferson	13,844	27.8%	6.9%	64.6%	43.4%	4.3%	3,943	3,451	87.5%
93722 – West of 99	60,879	57.0%	8.0%	35.2%	23.4%	6.9%	20,695	19,744	95.4%
93726 – Northeast/Cal State	39,135	53.4%	7.6%	35.7%	29.5%	11.8%	15,038	14,122	93.9%

Source: U.S. Census Bureau, Census 2000 Summary File 1

Northeast/Cal State (93726)

Primarily built up in the 1950s and 1960s, the Northeast/Cal State neighborhood is known today for hosting Cal State Fresno, a comprehensive university of 22,000 students. But when it was first built it was emblematic of a new breed of Sunbelt real estate development that consisted of modest structures layed out primarily in cul-de-sacs, with plenty of pools, close to downtown. One city official described the areas as consisting of "a lot of lower quality homes." The first wave of suburbanization occurred within Fresno's boundaries and was first inhabited by middle-class working families who were predominantly White. According to the most recent available demographic data, Whites maintain a plurality of the population (53 percent), but 36 percent of the neighborhood is Latino, 8 percent African American, and 11 percent Asian (U.S. Census 2009) (see Table 7.4).

As the real estate boom headed toward Fresno, prices began to climb in this modest neighborhood of bungalow homes. Many long-time residents got caught up in the same problems profiled at the beginning of the chapter of using their home as an ATM machine. As Northeast/Cal State homeowners began to face foreclosure, a new group of investors moved in. While I observed and my interviewees confirmed that the neighborhood could have 10 percent vacancy, those foreclosed homes are attracting the interest of investors who come primarily from out of the area and rent the properties out to tenants. Some in the neighborhood have detected a clear pattern of change since 2006, where the people living in the area are increasingly Hispanic and increasingly renters.

State budget cuts have meant a drop in 40,000 students in the coming academic year for the entire Cal State system. That means 400 fewer freshmen each year for the coming years will be attending Cal State Fresno and a concomitant drop in demand for housing in the Northeast/Cal State neighborhood (Miller 2009).

As indicated in Table 7.3, the Northeast/Cal State zip code (93726) is one of the larger zip codes in Fresno with 39,135 people and 15,038 housing units in 2000 (according to the U.S. Census). The USPS data indicates 15,196 occupied housing units in February 2006, a modest growth over the 2000 data. Given that the neighborhood has been built out for decades, a small increase over six boom years can be expected. But as things soured in the Fresno economy around 2006, the USPS data shows a drop in occupied housing units by February 2009. The 147 unit drop can be translated into a measure of decreased residential land-use density when the number is divided by the total land area of the zip code (in this case, 4,071 acres). By dividing the number of housing units by the zip code area, the results are normalized and can be compared across time and space.

Table 7.3 shows that Northeast/Cal State went from a neighborhood of 3.73 occupied housing units per acre in February 2006 to 3.70 housing units per acre just three years later, roughly a 1 percent drop. At that rate, the neighborhood would be expected to fall 3.33 units per acre in 30 years—a total loss of 1,470 units. There is no evidence to suggest that either external or internal economic or market forces would result in continuation along such a trend, but from a planning perspective it is useful to understand whether they did.

So far, the forces bearing down on Northeast/Cal State have resulted in major changes to the physical form of the neighborhood, consistent with the USPS findings (see Figure 7.2). According to one community leader who lives in Northeast/ Cal State, "we see what it [foreclosure] is doing to neighborhoods. People do tend to break into the houses. [My neighborhood] it's turning into a rental area" as investors buy up properties and rent them out. One community development professional commented about the changes afoot in Northeast/Cal State, "there is a tipping point, as more and more rentals are concentrated in an area, you may lose a sense of community."

Crime is on the rise, break-ins by "kids and gang members" are frequent for abandoned homes—the tell-tale sign for intruders is the dead lawn (see Figure 7.3). Homeowners in the community have set up a crime watch, "there's about six or seven of us that sit out, until 11pm at night, we've noticed a change in the neighborhood." People from outside the neighborhood walk through, that's something that never use to happen in Northeast/Cal State. A long-time resident who monitors crime statistics drew a link between the foreclosures and abandoned buildings and higher crime: "I think there's a direct connection with what's happening…there's a creeping crud [spreading through the neighborhood]."

Figure 7.2 Typical single-story vacant home in Northeast/CSU at 9th Street, dead lawn is evident as well as the "for sale" sign squirreled away under portico.

Figure 7.3 Dead lawn and damaged garage identify this as a vacant home on Buckingham Way in Northeast/CSU.

Lowell-Jefferson (93701)

Demographically speaking, Lowell-Jefferson looks more like an urban neighborhood in a Rustbelt city than in a Sunbelt city. Its housing stock is, on average, 50 years old. It is largely built out with few large open spaces, except where foreclosures today dot the landscape. The population living there today is largely non-White, Hispanic, with high numbers of younger people—relative to the city as a whole (U.S. Census 2000) (see Table 7.4). But Lowell-Jefferson has changed over the last century. It evolved from an agricultural village on the outskirts of Downtown Fresno, first settled in the early 1900s, into a bustling in-town desirable residential community in the 1940s, and then into a neighborhood of last resort for some of the region's poorest residents. The story of the neighborhood's transformation, in many ways, mirrors the larger city's own rise and fall (see Figure 7.4 for a photograph of a formerly grand mansion in Lowell-Jefferson).

From the time of the neighborhood's first settlement, some of the region's wealthiest residents chose Lowell-Jefferson as their home, building grand mansions on the neighborhoods' tree-lined boulevards. As the city's wealth diminished and suburbanization emptied the city of population, Fresno implemented an urban renewal plan that 1) bisected the neighborhood with a limited access above ground highway, and 2) allowed for greater housing density in low density neighborhoods such as Lowell-Jefferson. In my interviews with Lowell-Jefferson residents and with city officials, there is near uniform agreement that the two initiatives successfully accomplished the opposite of what they intended to. By building a major highway, the city acquired hundreds of existing homes and obliterated the sense of place in these neighborhoods by replacing idyllic streets and gardens with a roaring overhead highway. When the dust had settled, by the turn of the millennium Lowell-Jefferson had a reputation as being the poorest neighborhood in Fresno and a breeding ground for crime.

Figure 7.4 This derelict mansion on L Street in Lowell-Jefferson is an icon of the neighborhood's past wealth.

Figure 7.5 This Park
Street house in Lowell-
Jefferson shows multiple
signs of abandonment,
including the poor
condition of the resident
palm tree.

As real estate prices began to climb in the mid-2000s, investors descended on what many hoped would be Fresno's next "hot" neighborhood. But these gentrification pressures did not last long; as the market turned in 2006, these outsiders fled en masse and this poor neighborhood began to see extraordinary levels of foreclosure and then housing abandonment.

In February 2006, Lowell-Jefferson had 3,729 occupied housing units (according to USPS data) at a housing density of 3.82 units per acre, the third highest density among zip codes in Fresno.[3] Three years later, the zip code had lost 97 units and was down to 3,632 units, with a 3 percent drop in housing density to only 3.72 units per acre (see Table 7.3). Direct observation of neighborhood conditions and interviews with local residents and community leaders confirmed these findings. There has been a dramatic up-tick in foreclosure and abandonment in the neighborhood. Scores of units have been left to rot away, blighting the surrounding blocks (see Figure 7.5). Some streets feel like veritable ghost towns, where a single house or two sit surrounded by empty ones (some for sale, some for rent, others seemingly forgotten about by their custodial banks).

The depopulation of Lowell-Jefferson has meant boarded up homes, increased crime, and a further transformation of the neighborhood into a renter's community. "A few [home] invasions, a lot more vandalism," reports one community leader as she observes the proliferation of boarded-up houses. "Now it's really bad. Pool goes bad, then mosquitoes." She goes on to say, "lawns are dead, landscape dying" (see Figures 7.5 and 7.6).

For those housing units that are selling, it is investors that are buying. A lifelong resident explained the change: "2006 saw a lot of infill and low-rent apartments come in. Things really started going bad two to three years ago, after the boom. Since then, a lot of owner-occupied homes have since become rentals."

Figure 7.6 This vacant lot on MacKenzie Avenue abuts an empty rental complex—the broken chain link fence and denuded "for sale" sign show a lack of care and attention to the property.

"A lot of these foreclosures are being scooped up by slumlords," said a resident. The foreclosure crisis is giving greater fuel to the broader transformation of Lowell-Jefferson into a primarily renter-occupied neighborhood. "This used to be a single-family neighborhood," lamented one long-time resident. And because of the tightening of the credit market, owner-occupiers are having difficulty getting mortgages, according to one city official.

West of 99 (93722)

A neighborhood called West of 99 did not even exist 30 years ago. Interstate 99 had, for decades been a western barrier of the City of Fresno, but beginning in the 1980s builders introduced new subdivisions just west of I-99, seemingly overnight to accommodate a boom in demand for new housing. The neighborhood remained small until the recent real estate boom of the mid-2000s transformed the country outpost into a sprawling urban complex for middle-income residents.

Some of the new housing that went up in 2004, 2005, and 2006 remained unoccupied when I visited in 2009 (see Figure 7.7). Subdivision projects are unfinished, roads half built, and construction debris strewn about. With housing values plummeting in this remote location, "far away from services and amenities," as described by one city official, owners are walking away from their homes when facing foreclosure.

Six-lane arterial roadways lead cars to and from West of 99 along the long established grid road network that cuts north–south and east–west at regular intervals. Huge automobile volume never came to this neighborhood designed to accommodate tens of thousands of new residents. "Over planning" may have led to this neighborhood's problems. A slow and steady growth pattern could have meant a different outcome today for a big neighborhood ready for big growth that never came.

Figure 7.7 Housing in the Vassar Street subdivision was brand new and never occupied at the time of this photograph (June 2009). The open land across the street was intended for more housing, but for now it remains vacant.

Instead of growth, 2006 marked the beginning of a period of steady depopulation and abandonment that lasted up until the time of this writing in late 2009. Most of the zip codes included in the study did not experience changes in their boundaries, but some of the very high growth areas did—including West of 99.[4] Therefore, Table 7.3 does not include any housing data for West of 99 and I needed to rely exclusively on my field research and interviews.

In that research, I found a similar pattern to what appeared in the two other Fresno neighborhoods, abandoned homes, break-ins, and increased crime. Residents I interviewed said that 10 percent of homes in their neighborhoods are empty; my own observations confirmed that. With all that abandoned housing, crime is on the rise; one resident I spoke with said, "this is a scary neighborhood at night," though he does walk the neighborhood alone during the day. He went on to give more details:

> A slightly rowdier group of teenagers, more graffiti, more gatherings at night that make some people uncomfortable. We had a murder at a nearby park... [West of 99] has changed [since 2006], any neighborhood that gets more renters and transients, that is always going to happen.

Neighbors feel that for the empty homes, break-ins are one of the biggest problems. "The druggies come in, they party...there were people who were setting fires, there was no heat so they lit fires."

West of 99 is unique in that it is so new and has such a large inventory of new, never occupied homes. During my field research, I drove ploddingly along the neighborhood's main drag (West Clinton Avenue), passing one new subdivision of homes after another. I pulled my car into the entrance to one such complex and before me opened up a vast wasteland of construction debris, brand new roads, and a smattering of fully-built and half-built homes. The homes all appeared to be empty. I parked my car, cautiously, and walked over to inspect more closely. The homes did all appear empty, but signs of life were apparent in the graffiti strewn across dividing walls (see Figure 7.8).

Figure 7.8 Eight-foot walls separate subdivisions from one another and are quickly tagged by competing gang members. Here, in the Westpointe project, three plus acre tracts remain empty, half-built homes rot away without any protection or maintenance.

Figure 7.9 The tattered flags for the Westpointe housing development whip wildly in the wind above a vacant (brand new) home to the right and a dividing wall to the left (at the end of Harvard Avenue in the West of 99 neighborhood).

All alone, I jumped at a sudden whipping noise that filled my ears and echoed throughout the subdivision. Searching around, I saw the sounds emanated from the real estate developer's tattered flags as they whipped violently in the wind (see Figure 7.9). The brand new structures were once celebrated by gleaming new flags, but years of failed sales bankrupted this developer and the disintegrating flags dance a final dance.

Planning/policy response

As Fresno's neighborhoods crumble under the weight of the foreclosure crisis, what is it that the city, non-governmental organizations (NGOs), and ordinary residents are doing to respond? In considering some of the larger research questions of this book, it is critical to understand the planning and public policy responses to depopulation in Sunbelt cities so as to test whether a smart decline approach might be an appropriate alternate response.

City governments are complex, unwieldy beasts and the City of Fresno is no different. As is common in city management, some parts of the city government are controlled directly by elected officials (particularly the mayor), where other parts of the city are managed primarily by civil servants—career city employees not connected or affiliated with elected officials. As can be imagined, each division of the city government has its own power structure, values, and goals—all ostensibly under the auspices of the mayor. In analyzing the planning and policy responses of the city and others to the foreclosure crisis, much of this division is laid open for inspection. When I arrived in Fresno to conduct my field research, a new mayor, Ashley Swearengin, had just months before taken office. Running for office on a reformist platform, she swooped in and quickly reorganized the city's Economic Development Department into a Downtown and Community Revitalization Department. This was accomplished at the same time that federal National Stabilization Program (NSP) funds began to pour into the city through a different department: the Planning and Development Department (which includes a community development function). In its response to the foreclosure problem, the city's approach had four dimensions: 1) leverage most resources on a single neighborhood, 2) quality of life strategy, 3) overcome the NSP straightjacket, and 4) a limited view of land use as active only.

As the foreclosures and abandoned homes piled up, the new Mayor refocused city and federal resources around a major investment into a single neighborhood in Fresno: Lowell (a smaller subset of Lowell-Jefferson). This means close coordination among police and code enforcement, as well as other key agencies. Through most of 2009 that meant monthly meetings among the departments. The goal is to make some progress in Lowell and then fan the coordination out to other priority neighborhoods in the city.

"We are working to coordinate city departments to figure out how to revitalize a neighborhood," explained one city official. What is particularly unusual about this project is the focus on quality of life instead of growth and economic development. City leaders told me, "we want Lowell to be a healthy, thriving, attractive, mixed-income neighborhood"—of course, defining "healthy" and "thriving" could employ measures of growth, but not necessarily.

Also unusual about the initiative is the pilot nature of it. City leaders are saying explicitly that they do not know what it takes to "revitalize" a neighborhood, but suspect that if they can focus all of their resources in one place, they will figure it out. It appears to be quite a wasteful strategy, given the decades worth of empirical evidence available about what policy and planning interventions have been effective in poor, depopulating urban neighborhoods.[5] City officials might better utilize their resources by studying that extant literature before conducting an experiment of their own.

A major component of the Lowell initiative is in direct contradiction to the goals of the regional planning effort described earlier in the chapter: the Regional BluePrint. City efforts during the foreclosure crisis are directed at stabilization and quality of life, rather than planning for growth and concentrated new real estate development. There is interest within city offices to implement densification along key city corridors and nodes, and to also de-densify large swaths of residential neighborhoods throughout the city as was accomplished in the Tower District. There, form-based codes and design guidelines were employed to de-densify the neighborhood, and by all accounts it worked well and Tower District is one of the most stable of Fresno's neighborhoods.

One city official explained that they "need to guide things towards good development, good design"—in this case good development is high density along the cores and nodes, low density elsewhere—good design is based on New Urbanist principles tying the effort directly to the Transect Model.

While still in an embroyonic stage, this thinking represents a major departure from the conventional planning for growth strategies Fresno has adopted for decades and offers a way for the city to be a part of the regional BluePrint effort while ignoring its assumptions of growth. A senior city official said:

> I don't think we have to accept growth, when we plan for growth we get growth…We have two times the number of road miles as San Jose, but half as many people. Per capita we are maintaining more roadways than San Jose!

While not tied directly to the Lowell-Jefferson initiative, the focus on quality of life is strong in the city's introduction of a foreclosure registration ordinance and its update to its vacant property ordinance both in 2009. The foreclosure registration ordinance was copied from a nearby California city that had used the policy tool to keep track of banks who were holding abandoned buildings. The measure is viewed within City Hall as a positive measure, but more than anything else it requires contact information for the entity responsible for the protection and maintenance of foreclosed structures—someone to call if the windows get broken. The update to the vacant property ordinance updates penalties for absentee custodians of abandoned buildings.

The city subscribes to monthly reports on foreclosures, notices of default, and trustees' sales, and their code enforcement team visits all properties on the report within 72 hours in order to be proactive. While there is a serious abandoned property problem in the city, given the staggering levels of foreclosure, this proactive approach appears effective in containing the problem. City officials estimate that there are well over 4,000 empty homes in the city but aggressive code enforcement has meant only a few hundred have on-going code violations.

Despite the city's stated focus on code enforcement, there is a distinct sense in the neighborhoods studied that the city is not doing enough. "When a house goes into foreclosure, nothing is done about it…Lawns are dead, the interiors are trashed," complained one community leader. A long-time resident in Northeast/Cal State agreed: "I don't think the city does enough to make the banks keep up the property, because that has a big effect on the neighborhood."

The major infusion of federal aid through the NSP would ordinarily be a boom to city officials' ability to tackle a problem, but in Fresno the NSP functions so narrowly it will likely have little impact on the city's success in addressing abandoned properties. When interviewed, a city official explained that their aims are to get properties "into the strongest hands possible"—code for owner–occupiers with good credit. But NSP gives priority to low-income households, regardless of credit, hamstringing the entire endeavor.

One local official attacked the design of the program, saying that it showed no understanding about the challenges on the ground: "It's a local problem, but the solution came from the top…in the meantime the communities continue to suffer."

The city has allocated acquisition monies and roughly $75,000 in renovation monies per unit, with the hopes of fixing up a couple of dozen units. The active investor community made it a challenge for the city and county to even acquire properties, owing to the city's own internal procedures and the accompanying delays. Investors are actively buying foreclosed homes and some are rehabbing them and renting them out, whereas some are just sitting on them.

Where use of land could logistically extend across a broad range, city policies constrain that band so narrowly such that the only legal uses on virtually all private property in the three study neighborhoods are residential or institutional structures. One local official described an episode where her office acquired two abandoned properties as part of a larger redevelopment project and "couldn't get anyone to build on them." There is clear evidence that Fresno officials have a myopic view that prevents them from being able to recognize the value of latent uses. Without that understanding, the only legally possible reuse of abandoned buildings is with another residential unit, a questionable investment in a shrinking city.

A fundamental assumption of smart decline is that successor uses of abandoned buildings and vacant lots be alternative non-active uses such as cemeteries, parks, community gardens, or even parking. Fresno's, as well as most other city's, zoning and land development regulations essentially prohibit creative reimagination of successor land uses and, in effect, prohibit reductions in density. This is of course ironic considering the city's own strong interests in reducing housing density in residential neighborhoods. But the problem is that they want to reduce density by changing zoning requirements for maximum density—move certain districts into lower housing unit per acre categories. These very tools are growth-based tools and do little to effectively reorient a city around planning for depopulation. By changing the maximum housing density of a neighborhood, the city is restricting the development of new housing. They are not addressing the existing crisis of existing housing and using the opportunity of housing abandonment to rethink successor land uses to achieve lower density residential neighborhoods—as is already happening organically according to the USPS data analysis shown above and in Chapter 6.

The City of Fresno is not the only entity active in responding to foreclosures and housing abandonment in Fresno; there is the county and a small but active NGO sector and a large and active skateboarder community that are changing the face of "abandoned" Fresno.

Fresno County includes unincorporated areas throughout the region, including islands of unincorporated lands within the boundaries of the City of Fresno. These few residents receive few public services and pay little in taxes. But predatory lending practices were high in these county islands and county officials report high foreclosure and abandonment statistics in these areas.

Most of the time, county residents want nothing to do with their local government, but with the huge foreclosure and abandoned housing problem there has been a reversal of interest and Fresno County is unprepared to meet the demand for services. One county official said, "most of the time they are like 'leave us alone'" but now they want help desperately. Just as city neighborhoods have witnessed changing housing tenure patterns, so have county islands—where the biggest concern reported is who is moving into these foreclosed homes and what it means for neighborhood stability.

Skateboarding and urban planning are rarely discussed in the same sentence, except that is in Fresno.[6] The city has one of the largest collections of official city-owned skate parks in California and is considered a major capital of the sport (McKinley and Wollan 2008). In late 2009, Los Angeles-based filmmaker Steve Payne premiered his documentary *Fresno* about how skateboarders are descending on Fresno's abandoned homes, draining their pools, and skateboarding for weeks on end. The skateboarders' exploits were also covered by local and national news sources, making them a key player in the Fresno scene (McKinley and Wollan 2008; ABC News 2009). City officials I interviewed denied the relevance of skateboarders and there appeared to be no evidence that the skateboarders had spent much time in any of the three neighborhoods I studied. But, their import comes through in the Fresno documentary—their relevance as temporary heroes for struggling neighborhoods, draining and cleaning pools, preventing mosquito infestation, preventing accidental drownings, and most importantly, bringing people to enliven and monitor what are often otherwise desolate neighborhoods—emptied out of residents.

Armed with iPhones and Google map applications, the skateboarders scout out aerial photos of homes with pools and then overlay foreclosure data from RealtyTrac.com. This high-tech trespassing allows them to quickly and easily find the best locales for skateboarding. Despite their illegal activities, there is a notable public service performed by the skateboarders that involves respect for the vacant properties and a wholly organic role in creating an effective temporary successor land use to abandoned buildings that is otherwise prohibited by law. These skateboarders are giving use to land and structures that otherwise have no immediate use and in so doing help to keep some neighborhoods thriving—in decline but not dying.

A second notable NGO response is the quite extraordinary efforts of the residents of Lowell-Jefferson. In late 2008, frustrated by the city's apparent apathy toward their spiraling abandoned building problem, residents of Lowell-Jefferson, under the auspices of the Lowell Residents Association/Union de Familia, assembled a report documenting the blighting conditions of their neighborhood. The 26 page report documents in fastidious detail the 47 street addresses where abandoned or otherwise dangerous conditions exist, along with both descriptive text and photographs of each property. The grass-roots initiative is impressive in many ways, but its direct attachment to 216 signatories (local residents) and a group photo of the activists is most astounding (see Figure 7.10).

Mayor Swearengin was equally impressed and quickly integrated the results of the report into her Lowell-Jefferson neighborhood initiative, demanding that city agencies rally around to try to make a difference in this troubled neighborhood.

A third important way that the non-governmental sector responded to the foreclosure crisis was in specific acts of neighborliness that were practices by Fresno residents. While not widespread, the willingness of ordinary citizens to water their neighbors' lawn, to clean-up trash on sidewalks, and to cut down errant weeds are all part of an important informal response. The most neighborly residents that I met acted primarily out of self-interest, fearing what might happen to their own property values if their immediate block was to begin to fall apart. One local official felt that sharing in the care of neighbors' abandoned property builds community, though fatigue does tend to set in after a year or so.

When the sewer overflowed into the street in front of an abandoned home in Northeast/Cal State, "the whole neighborhood came, everyone brought a green can and we filled up eight to nine cans of trash, we started watering the lawn, in some neighborhoods the neighbors will come together."

Perhaps worse than sewerage was when a Northeast/Cal State home was foreclosed and the owners left their home and dog behind. "People in the neighborhood are feeding the dog," reported a resident.

Figure 7.10 Group photo of members of the Lowell Residents Association/Union de Familia, included as page 7 in their report to Mayor Searingen demanding action on abandoned properties in their neighborhood.

In general, city officials expressed strong support for these neighborly acts, but internal city disputes over water use made continued volunteer watering illegal—one man in Fresno was actually given a ticket for watering a neighbor's lawn. In the few homeowners' and neighborhood associations I came across in Fresno, this neighborliness is codified in rules and regulations that require residents to cover protection and maintenance expenses of missing owners. I will return to a more complete discussion of these associations in the following chapters on Orlando and Phoenix.

Opportunities for smart decline

There is an old expression: "You can't plan for the future, all you can do is manage the present." Fresno has tried to plan for its future through a sophisticated State of California guided growth management process that has ensured an excess capacity of services, roads, and housing well beyond the city's current needs. Now, stuck with a city physically bigger than its population an opportunity exists for Fresno to explore smart decline.

On some levels, the city is already doing smart decline in its focus on quality of life improvements in the Lowell neighborhood and its efforts to de-densify residential neighborhoods. The region's water crisis provides a third significant avenue for the city to reconsider its physical footprint.

Current planning efforts in the Lowell neighborhood draw on some of the key discourses of smart decline. The official change of the Economic Development Department into the Downtown and Community Revitalization Department is a powerful statement about what local government can and should do. Rather than attempting to create new jobs and attract new residents, the Department's goals are largely about increasing the quality of life for residents left behind by depopulation. What is missing from this effort is an explicit link between the high rates of foreclosure, the sizeable numbers of abandoned buildings, and a new vision for a lower density neighborhood.

In the above analysis, I demonstrated that the larger Lowell-Jefferson neighborhood is one of the densest in the city and that it's density fell by 3 percent from 2006 to 2009. Continued downward trends will mean an opportunity for the neighborhood to reach even lower density levels, more on a par with other city neighborhoods. Successor land uses of the abandoned buildings and vacant lots in today's Lowell-Jefferson could be greater amenities such as parks, community gardens, and recreation sites, as well as conversions of multi-family housing into single-family. Through a concerted physical planning effort, city resources could bring the neighborhood into a condition of lower density (movement along the Reverse Transect Model), while avoiding the blight and dereliction often associated with such a transition.

The city's success in the Tower District has emboldened its planners to apply a similar policy formula throughout the city. The strategy described earlier in the chapter is that of densifying major commercial corridors and nodes while de-densifying residential areas. If executed well, this approach could serve to decrease housing density in areas hit hardest by foreclosures and abandonment.

Specific policies that could benefit this strategy are land acquisition of abandoned buildings by the city, demolition of abandoned housing, and conversion of vacant land into new non-active uses (as described above in the Lowell neighborhood). Taken together, these policies could effectively move city neighborhoods downward along the Reverse Transect Model—preserving the integrity of ecozones through urban design and landscape modifications.

The city's water crisis may be a third avenue for the local officials to consider smart decline. Earlier in the chapter, I wrote about how water shortages have meant hundreds of thousands of acres of farmland have been put out of production in the midst of this broader economic crisis. The drop-off in employment that such an impact will have will likely also translate into a fall in population and eventually housing units. City officials blame climate change for the increased aridity that has diminished water supplies. One said: "There's a coming crisis around water. The desert is slowly reasserting itself."

Rather than looking at this impending environmental disaster as a crisis, a smart decline perspective allows the reassertion of the desert to be an opportunity to make Fresno smaller. A bold sign stretches across a Southern exit to the city and reads: "Your Are Now Leaving The Best Little City in the USA." As agricultural opportunities fade as a result of environmental change, Fresno may want to tweak its slogan to read: "You Are Now Leaving The Best *Even Littler* City in America."

With projected lower employment related to agriculture, Fresno can plan now for fewer jobs, a smaller population, and fewer housing units: a smaller city. The conventional policy response to the water crisis is typically either fight the water problem or reinvent the city's economic base and move away from agriculture. Both conventional responses are fraught with problems that are well documented in the policy literature (Scott 1998; Mitchell 2002). Increasing water in a dry region is exorbitantly expensive and can result in even greater environmental damage (Worster 1985). Converting a city's entire economic base from agriculture to practically anything else is equally costly in terms of requiring vast sums of investment capital and is highly risky. Fresno's unique locational and human resource advantages position it well to have relied heavily on agriculture to support its economy for over one hundred years—what else Fresno is uniquely prepared to offer the world economy is entirely unknown. The economic history of America is littered with scores of cities facing similar crises with just a handful ever truly reinventing themselves (Rust 1975).

Concluding thoughts

As Fresno was heading toward the mid-2000s the abundance of jobs, people, and housing was seen by many elites as the cause célèbre of the day. Combine that growth juggernaut with the environmental disaster of increased aridity and lack of water supply, and a regional BluePrint for managing growth makes a lot of sense as a response. Fundamentally, the flaw in the response, the flaw in a regionalist-based planning effort is that growth is, in fact, not inevitable. Promising a room full of people that exogenous factors like growth are going to happen and we have to plan for them is only true during the upswing of an economic cycle. In the late 2000s, in the midst of the Great Recession, the fight against sprawl in Fresno is like Don Quixote's tilting at windmills—there is no growth, there is no sprawl. Instead, the region and the city of Fresno face an unprecedented emptying out of neighborhoods and the great planning minds of the region are still stuck on stopping sprawl.

The explicit goals of the BluePrint are to reduce VMT (vehicle miles traveled), improve air quality, and increase housing affordability. With one fell swoop, the Great Recession did all that and solved the problems of the Central Valley. Poor economic conditions mean people drive less, which in turn improves air quality. A bad economy has driven housing values to their lowest levels in a decade, opening the real market up to a much broader range of income levels.

In the skateboarder documentary *Fresno* a salon worker was interviewed about the economic crisis and the emptying out of the city: "A lot of my friends from high school went off to college then got jobs in the big cities like LA and SF, but someone who cares needs to stay behind so I'm here." Not all people have attachments to place, but many do. In a long and probing documentary about Youngstown, Ohio's steady economic decline a lifelong resident said the same thing:

> And then [the companies] decide to leave, it's just "tough luck, follow us... we're taking the jobs to the Sunbelt and if you want to work follow us." It doesn't matter that you have roots so deep in the [Mahoning] Valley and friends and homes and loved ones in graveyards that you might like to put flowers on graves on Memorial Day. That kind of stuff doesn't make—the bottom line is money, profits...Wherever the profits are it doesn't matter what they leave behind.
>
> (June Lucas, as quoted in *Shout Youngstown*
> (Greenwald and Krauss 1984))

For those with attachment to Fresno, they should stay and help build their communities, invest in their neighborhoods, and reshape the city for a smaller population. For those who have no such attachment and are happy to leave for the mega-cities with their vast career opportunities so be it. Lucy and Phillip's (2000) research on suburban decline teaches us the simple demographic fact that most Americans are very mobile and the job for any city is to remain attractive to outsiders in order to constantly replenish population from those that are bound to leave every year. For a city to be attractive, the answer lies in more than employment growth—it lies in creating places where the number of people match well with the number of housing units and other physical dimensions of a neighborhood—smart decline could help Fresno do just that.

CHAPTER 8

Endless growth in the desert?

The fall of Phoenix

John and Becky Tollman moved to Phoenix in 1985, to start afresh. Most people do. Since the late 1800s, the Desert Valley has attracted those who were looking to begin a new life far from their family, friends, and colleagues. The thrill of starting anew, combined with the desert climate and ample job opportunities has fueled the growth of the Phoenix region like few places on the globe. Every year for the last 100 years, the Phoenix metropolitan area has grown by 8 percent—that is two times the average growth rate for U.S. regions with more than one million people (Arizona State University 2003). Employment growth in the region rocketed from 1.6 million jobs to 1.9 million in the boom period between 2001 and 2006 (Arizona Department of Commerce 2010).

The Tollmans packed into the growing metropolis by buying a three-bedroom ranch home for barely $200,000, raised two children, and then one day in 2006 a woman rang their door bell and offered them $1,000,000 for their home. They sold it and within weeks relocated to California to be near their grandchildren—this time renting an apartment for a couple of thousand dollars a month. They got out just in time. As 2006 stretched on, the foreclosure crisis grew and Phoenix was one of a handful of epicenters. Defaults led to abandoned homes, led to falling values, which led to more homeowners "underwater"—a condition that precipitates widespread abandonment.

Living next door to the Tollmans for more than a decade were Jack and Rebecca Cantor. The Cantors had also been approached by investors waving zeroes in front of their faces, but they decided to stay—feeling connected to their family and friends in the region. Like the steelworker families in Youngstown, the Cantors wanted to be close to the graves of their loved ones and were not interested in relocating. With their long-term neighbors around them leaving, their newest neighbors were less grounded and committed to Phoenix—many were simply investors looking to flip properties, others were young couples who were over their heads and facing foreclosure. What had been a stable, middle-class neighborhood had in just three years deteriorated in unimaginable ways.

At the two unoccupied houses on the Cantors' street, grass is growing high, paint is peeling, trash is piling up, rodents are suspected to be around, and the crime has never been like this. Scavengers are breaking into homes, stealing copper pipes, ripping out fixtures and appliances. Local teenagers are throwing parties in empty homes and trashing them. The problems generated at these homes are not localized—there is a contagion effect at work that has been likened to a certain tree disease: blight. Down the road, across the arterial street, and into gated communities the story is the same: the empty homes impair neighborhood quality. While the Tollmans got out just in time, the Cantors and thousands just like them are left with depressed property values and lower neighborhood quality—the very physical fabric of their communities is in shambles.

When Phoenix was booming, city planners would sketch out new areas of expansion. But what about today? What are city planners doing to address the deterioration of much of Phoenix? The answers to these questions must be preceded by a clear understanding of how exactly Phoenix is changing. In this chapter, I outline the various physical and demographic evidence of the changing face of Phoenix from the height of the boom, 2006 to 2009. My research has found that Phoenix lost population during that time period and will likely continue to experience depopulation. In the remainder of the chapter, I examine how both city officials and community activists addressed this change and what it might mean for a new conceptualization of smart decline.

The history of planning and real estate development in Phoenix

For generations, the Hohokam people inhabited the land that we recognize today as Phoenix. Their prehistoric society constructed over 1,000 miles of irrigation canals and then, quite inexplicably disappeared around 1450 (Gober and Trapido-Lurie 2006). When Europeans began to explore the region 300 years later, an entrepreneur by the name of Jack Swilling rediscovered the canal network and proclaimed that this settlement would rise like a phoenix from the ashes of the Hohokam city (Gober and Trapido-Lurie 2006, p. 17).[1]

As is the case in Fresno, the challenge of irrigation was key to Phoenix's agriculture expansion and the ancient network of canals were an essential ingredient in addressing that challenge. A massive federal water reclamation of the Salt River added 200,000 acres of irrigable agricultural land to the city in 1912 (Logan 2006). Agriculture was how Phoenix got going, but tourism soon put the city on the map. The dry heat of the desert was widely recognized in the early 1900s as a cure for tuberculosis and the infirm flocked to Phoenix in droves (Gober and Trapido-Lurie 2006). "The desert's clean clear air, brilliant sunshine, and pleasant winter temperatures were an easy sell, as long as visitors avoided the brutally hot summers" (Logan 2006, p. 81).

The 1940s and 1950s brought the military-industrial complex into the region with several new bases and scores of military contractors (Logan 2006). The defense industry came to Phoenix because of "the climate and open space…[and] the federal policy to disperse industry inland away from possible air attacks on the West Coast" (Logan 2006, p. 141).

During this period city leaders were very proactive in shaping new firm recruitment and location decisions. They aimed to avoid the traditional smokestack manufacturing that many were so eager to flee from in the Rustbelt. As Logan (2006) explains:

> the prospect of increasing air pollution might kill the goose that laid the golden tourism egg. Cognizant of this threat to their communities' self-image as healthful and natural locales, civic leaders made it a priority to attract clean

industries, primarily electronic and other high-tech manufacturers, who would bring smokeless factories to the desert (p. 146).

And they were successful at doing so, wooing major high-tech firms while avoiding heavy manufacturing with all its associated contamination. By the end of the 1950s, Phoenix "became the capital of the desert Southwest" (Luckingham 1983, p. 312). In fact, 1959 saw more construction jobs in Phoenix than all the years 1914–1946—a total of 5,060 housing units were added (Luckingham 1983, p. 315).

With new jobs and rapidly expanding tourism, the city's population boomed with no real planning or growth management. In the late twentieth century, "Rather than following a formulated plan, the remarkable growth in Phoenix conformed to the dictates of entrepreneurial imperatives: developers chose building sites that would maximize their profits" (p. 163). The result was a sprawling, low-density ultra-suburban city that was hardly recognizable as urban. Further inciting this pattern is an educational financing system whereby state lands are auctioned and that trust fund is used to pay operating expenses for schools. Local and state governments have a strong interest in the sale of these lands, which in turn generates new development on the fringe.

This sprawling urban morphology was even further reified through a city annexation program that officially stretched from the 1950s through the 1980s, but unofficially continued up until the start of the foreclosure crisis. The city consisted of 9.6 square miles in 1940, 17 square miles in 1950, 190 square miles in 1960, and 330 square miles in 1980 (Luckingham 1983, p. 316; Logan 2006, p. 163; Gober and Trapido-Lurie 2006, p. 35) (see Table 8.1 for demographic and housing characteristics from 1970 to 2000).

Table 8.1 City-wide demographic and housing data, Phoenix, 1970–2000

	1970	1980	1990	2000
Total population	595,989	815,424	1,006,209	1,352,629
% White	93.6%	85.4%	81.8%	73.5%
% African American	4.7%	4.7%	5.1%	5.5%
% Latino	14.1%	14.7%	19.7%	33.8%
Total population foreign born	3.7%	5.6%	8.6%	19.3%
% < age 18	35.8%	28.9%	27.1%	28.7%
% > age 64	8.7%	9.2%	9.6%	8.1%
Total households	190,011	293,675	377,589	477,505
Total housing units	198,954	316,611	430,291	508,999
Total occupied housing units	190,011	293,231	377,395	477,215
% occupied housing units	95.5%	92.6%	87.7%	93.8%
Average household income prior year	$9,975	$19,568	$36,554	$54,168

Source: U.S. Census Bureau, Census 1970–2000 Summary File 1; Geolytics, Neighborhood Change Database

In the 1980s, Luckingham (1983) wrote that Phoenicians had two core values: growth and quality of life. He observed that those values had finally come into severe conflict and that the city would have to choose between them. Perloff also studied Phoenix during the same period and criticized the city's planning efforts that failed to think about the possibility of economic decline and depopulation.

> The planners do not consider the possible changes in the region and in the national system of cities. These conditions are presently the source of Phoenix's good fortune. What kinds of changes, therefore, might alter the fortune of Phoenix in the future?
>
> (Perloff 1980, p. 71)

The resulting emphasis on growth over quality of life and a planning infrastructure that could not consider non-growth futures meant that by the early twenty-first century the city was on a path toward overbuilding and over-reliance on the real estate industry.

From 2002 to 2005, the city increased the number of single family permits issued by 69 percent from 6,629 in 2002 to 11,216 in 2005. Likewise, the total number of building permits issued increased by 53 percent during the same period, from 8,631 in 2002 to 13,221 in 2005 (see Table 8.2). This wild increase in new building was partially attributable to the growing economy of the region, but also driven by investors who never intended to live in the units they bought (Doom 2009).

As Phoenix sprawled toward its status as the next great American metropolis, there was some dissent. Not all Phoenicians sought a permanent expansion of the city into the desert and a small coalition of activists successfully created the Phoenix Mountains Preserve in 1973, an effort widely recognized as effective in managing growth and protecting important natural resources.[2]

In approaching the turn of the millennium, the spirit of the Phoenix Mountain Preserve initiative again grew within the region. Under the leadership of Arizona State University, a broad coalition of civic, private, governmental, and educational institutions came together to create a plan for Phoenix's next century. The Greater Phoenix 2010 plan used demographic projections to argue that the city's historic growth is likely to continue at a comparable pace, adding anywhere between 6 and 25 million new residents by 2050 (Arizona State University 2003). The plan called for a similar regionalist, New Urbanist development pattern as was developed at the same time in Fresno under the BluePrint project. The Greater Phoenix 2010 plan called for concentrated development in existing urban areas, open space preservation, and both pedestrian-oriented and transit-oriented development.

Contemporaneously with this massive planning project, the city reoriented its zoning and plan review processes to begin to incorporate these same ideas into its own processes and a new light rail system has begun operating. The result has been widely seen as successful, with the city being on the leading edge of large U.S. cities in managing growth.[3] When the foreclosure crisis hit Phoenix, beginning in 2006, all of this avant-garde planning and forward thinking was not so easy to adapt to a very new kind of problem: decline.

Table 8.2 Building permits issued, Phoenix, 2002–2009

	2002	2003	2004	2005	2006	2007	2008	2009*	ch 2002–2005	ch 2006–2009
Residential single-family	6,629	8,686	11,667	11,216	7,897	5,306	2,089	1,358	69%	–83%
Total permits	8,631	10,689	13,671	13,221	9,903	7,313	4,097	3,896	53%	–61%

* 2009 data was estimated based on an annual linear extrapolation of data from 1/1/09 to 10/17/09, 1FAM=1075, TotalPERM=3084
Source: City of Phoenix Building Department

A changing Phoenix, 2006–2009

The Greater Phoenix 2010 plan based its population projections on past growth. There is good reason, Phoenix has practically always grown—of late it has grown a lot. From 2000 to 2005 the city grew 11 percent from 1,327,375 to 1,473,223 persons. But a certain, indeterminate amount of that growth was the result of annexation and a big part of what fueled that growth was the homebuilding industry (host to 18 percent of Phoenix jobs[4]). When the housing market collapsed in early 2006, foreclosures skyrocketed and one of the region's economic legs began to fall. Foreclosure filings increased from a few hundred in 2005 to 8,000 in 2009, leaving the city with an estimated 3,801 bank-owned empty homes in 2009, with thousands more on their way.

Beyond foreclosures, several other city-collected indicators suggest that the population has fallen, including drops in the number of active city water accounts (5,600 fewer water users from fiscal years 2007–2008 to 2008–2009), and decline in garbage collection (2 percent fall from fiscal years 2006–2007 to 2007–2008) (Clancy and Newton 2009).

An examination of building permit data shows that from 2006 to 2008, single family permits issued dropped 83 percent from 7,897 to only 1,358. Total permits also eased dramatically from 9,903 in 2006 to 3,896 in 2009. As foreclosures mounted, prices plummeted, and the ordinary business of new construction collapsed.

City-wide, USPS data show a modest growth in occupied housing units from 2006 to 2009 in Phoenix (see Figure 8.1). But of the city's 43 zip codes, 23 (more than half) lost occupied housing units during the three-year period. Among those that lost units, the mean loss was 3 percent—not an insignificant amount of change for a city that has always been growing.

Like other formerly booming Sunbelt cities, there remains great uncertainty about the demographic future of Phoenix. Plenty of economists see the recent population and employment declines as both short term and cyclical in nature. Even if the city as a whole does manage to rebound and regrow, there remains much heterogeneity in how that growth will affect neighborhoods that are shrinking today. If economists are wrong and the city's decline continues for years, a new kind of planning that considers the changes afoot can be a powerful aid in maintaining high quality of life for the remaining residents of Phoenix.

Table 8.3 Housing occupancy patterns for Phoenix zip codes, 2006–2009

| Study neighborhood | Zip | LISC foreclosure score (Intrastate Foreclosure Component Score) * | Neighborhood name | 2000 Census | | |
				Total population	Total housing units	Land area (acres)
	85003	1		9,252	3,524	1,229
	85004	0.6		4,608	2,320	1,319
	85006	16		31,616	9,792	2,500
	85007	6.1		15,986	5,488	2,913
	85008	22.2		56,379	19,552	6,546
	85009	55.9		56,034	13,832	10,061
	85012	1.8		6,276	3,552	1,360
	85013	2.2		20,842	10,268	2,348
	85014	4.8		28,516	14,367	2,687
	85015	17.4		42,696	16,597	3,143
	85016	6.7		36,417	18,354	5,086
	85017	46.4		40,385	13,835	3,354
	85018	3.7		38,786	18,868	6,557
	85019	34		25,587	8,104	2,338
✓	85020	5.9	Sunnyslope	34,721	16,648	6,165
	85021	6		37,998	16,235	4,271
	85022	5.1		44,673	20,339	5,693
	85023	7.8		33,314	14,190	4,964
	85024	3.7		19,324	7,728	10,367
	85027	19.5		38,569	16,519	43,756
	85028	1.5		20,565	8,347	4,007
	85029	28.2		46,248	18,672	6,659
	85031	52		28,731	8,101	2,616
	85032	17.2		69,189	27,888	8,010
✓	85033	100	Maryvale	53,748	15,472	3,880
	85034	2.5		8,665	2,606	7,429
	85035	62.8		44,664	12,693	3,725
	85037	79.5		33,150	10,147	5,183
	85040	37.9		62,948	18,976	12,186
	85041	59.8		32,297	8,567	13,153
	85042	32.5		–	–	–
	85043	48.6		10,820	3,276	14,563
	85044	2.8		39,892	17,964	18,946
	85045	0.8		4,558	1,589	2,072
	85048	3.5		33,431	12,461	6,793
	85050	3		19,177	7,454	5,532
	85051	43.1		41,307	16,278	4,043
	85053	17.4		28,460	11,014	3,119
	85054	0.7		2,032	834	5,448
	85085	5.3		577	244	10,669
	85086	12.8		8,655	3,157	32,459
	85087	2.9		3,524	1,455	48,578
✓	85339	23.3	Laveen	6,346	1,987	65,192

* Local Initiative Support Corporation with Foreclosure Response project, Table 1: November 2008, http://www.housingpolicy.org/assets/foreclosure-response.

Adjusted occupied housing units per acre accounts for North Mt Preserve lands, roughly one-third of land area of the 85020. Unadjusted values are below.
Occupied housing units per acre – Feb '06 = 4.13   Occupied housing units per acre – Feb '09 = 3.92
% ch Feb '06–Feb '09 = –0.5%

USPS active residential delivery statistics

Occupied housing units – Feb '06	Occupied housing units – Feb '09	Change in occ. housing units Feb '06–Feb '09	Occupied housing units per acre – Feb '06	Occupied housing units per acre – Feb '09	% change Feb '06– Feb '09
3,638	3,620	−18	2.96	2.94	−0.5%
2,059	2,132	73	1.56	1.62	3.5%
9,041	8,856	−185	3.62	3.54	−2.0%
4,534	5,032	498	1.56	1.73	11.0%
20,607	20,402	−205	3.15	3.12	−1.0%
13,052	12,811	−241	1.3	1.27	−1.8%
3,339	3,361	22	2.45	2.47	0.7%
9,920	9,431	−489	4.22	4.02	−4.9%
12,996	12,228	−768	4.84	4.55	−5.9%
15,166	14,713	−453	4.83	4.68	−3.0%
16,755	16,460	−295	3.29	3.24	−1.8%
12,116	11,806	−310	3.61	3.52	−2.6%
17,920	17,525	−395	2.73	2.67	−2.2%
7,939	7,798	−141	3.4	3.33	−1.8%
16,805	15,951	−854	2.73	2.59	−5.1%
15,810	15,513	−297	3.7	3.63	−1.9%
21,381	20,944	−437	3.76	3.68	−2.0%
12,994	12,634	−360	2.62	2.54	−2.8%
8,163	9,537	1,374	0.79	0.92	16.8%
16,220	15,250	−970	0.37	0.35	−6.0%
8,150	8,198	48	2.03	2.05	0.6%
17,778	16,853	−925	2.67	2.53	−5.2%
8,184	7,848	−336	3.13	3	−4.1%
27,137	26,657	−480	3.39	3.33	−1.8%
15,655	14,901	−754	4.04	3.84	−4.8%
2,258	1,953	−305	0.3	0.26	−13.5%
12,925	13,054	129	3.47	3.5	1.0%
12,300	13,004	704	2.37	2.51	5.7%
8,636	8,935	299	0.71	0.73	3.5%
14,529	15,601	1,072	1.1	1.19	7.4%
13,242	13,185	−57	–	–	−0.4%
7,641	8,849	1,208	0.52	0.61	15.8%
17,780	17,490	−290	0.94	0.92	−1.6%
2,302	2,529	227	1.11	1.22	9.9%
12,638	12,595	−43	1.86	1.85	−0.3%
8,832	10,356	1,524	1.6	1.87	17.3%
15,445	15,344	−101	3.82	3.79	−0.7%
11,419	11,095	−324	3.66	3.56	−2.8%
1,562	2,273	711	0.29	0.42	45.5%
4,300	5,724	1,424	0.4	0.54	33.1%
12,521	13,853	1,332	0.39	0.43	10.6%
1,709	2,597	888	0.04	0.05	52.0%
5,499	10,535	5,036	0.08	0.16	91.6%

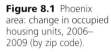

Figure 8.1 Phoenix area: change in occupied housing units, 2006–2009 (by zip code).

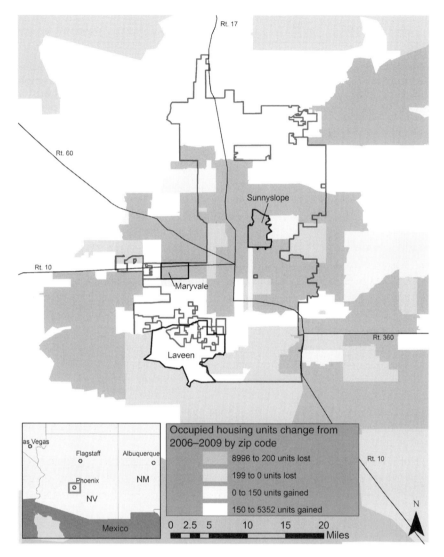

With the future uncertain, city officials charged with providing services to Phoenix neighborhoods have to face the problems of today and they say with unanimity that the biggest challenges they face are the abandoned pools— "with those mosquitos, all kinds of diseases can come from that," said one manager. The fear is palpable while walking the halls of City Hall and the streets of Phoenix's neighborhoods. One leader of a community organization estimated that there were 40,000 foreclosures in 2009, but he is expecting 100,000 in 2010.

Three neighborhoods in Phoenix

As with the Flint and Fresno case studies, I present here an in-depth examination of three of Phoenix's neighborhoods to better capture the changes afoot since the crash of the housing market in 2006. After examining the USPS data and consulting with several knowledgeable Phoenicians, I selected neighborhoods that have each suffered from the foreclosure crisis but represented the spectrum of the ecozone, from the high-density urban (Ecozone 5), to the medium-density suburban (Ecozone 4), to the rural/suburban (Ecozone 3). The urban neighborhood chosen here is Sunnyslope, perhaps the oldest and most historically significant neighborhood in Phoenix. The medium-density suburban neighborhood examined is Maryvale, which scored the highest possible rating in terms of foreclosure risk by the Local Initiatives Support Corporation (LISC), and was developed as one of the region's first planned communities in the 1950s. The rural/suburban neighborhood selected, Laveen, was highlighted over and over in my preliminary interviews as the epicenter of Phoenix's foreclosure crisis, but did not appear in the USPS data because it is classified by the USPS as outside the city's limits (see Table 8.3). The classification is a result of the fact that roughly half of Laveen is incorporated into the City of Phoenix, where the other half is unincorporated—but incorporated areas are sited squarely next to unincorporated areas making the distinction almost invisible.

Sunnyslope (85020)

Settled in 1927 by a small community of missionaries, doctors, the infirm, and their families as the Desert Mission of Sunnyslope, the neighborhood was a therapeutic refuge from the cold and harsh climates of the Northeast and Midwest (Gober and Trapido-Lurie 2006). John C. Lincoln, a philanthropist, came to the community to care for his wife's illness and upon her recovery established a hospital there. The community quickly made history, being the first in the nation to offer free dental care and blazing new ground in the integration of mind and body to address disease.

Figure 8.2 Restored historic homes along 4th Street in Sunnyslope near Townley Avenue (photo by Margaret Wagner-Smith, used with permission).

Figure 8.3 Newly constructed Mount Central Place gated community on the edge of Sunnyslope buts up against the Northern Mountain Reserve.

Nestled up against the mountains of the Phoenix Mountain Preserve, the neighborhood is perched high enough to have spectacular views of the city as well as breathtaking views of the mountains above. The vast majority of homes built in the first part of the twentieth century still remain, but many low quality multi-family homes were constructed in the 1970s and 1980s. Among the older homes, there is an unusual (for the Southwest) degree of historic architecture—a stroll through the neighborhood shows evidence of dozens of restored historic homes (see Figure 8.2). During the 1990s and 2000s, a small number of luxury, gated subdivisions were built on the edge of the neighborhood, creating a stark contrast against the largely poor population in the remainder of the neighborhood (see Figure 8.3).

Demographically speaking, the neighborhood was largely White (83 percent) and Latino (23 percent) according to 2000 Census data[1] (see Table 8.4). But my field research found that the Latino population is growing, as is the almost undetectable African American population in 2000. In addition, the neighborhood has a disproportionate share of residents older than 65 years, 13 percent as compared to 8 percent city-wide.

[1] In the 2000 Census, the identity category of Latino was not mutually exclusive to White or Black.

Table 8.4 Neighborhood-level demographic and housing data, Phoenix, 2000

Neighborhood	Total population	% White	% African American	% Latino	% < age 18	% > age 64	Total housing units	Total occupied housing units	% occupied housing units
85020 – Sunnyslope	34,721	82.5%	2.5%	23.4%	21.4%	13.3%	16,648	15,284	91.8%
85033 – Maryvale	53,748	55.4%	8.3%	56.3%	37.5%	4.8%	15,472	14,911	96.4%
85339 – Laveen	6,346	48.4%	1.5%	22.7%	23.1%	7.5%	1,987	1,865	93.9%

Source: U.S. Census Bureau, Census 2000 Summary File 1

Sunnyslope's long history as an organized, public health-driven community has ensured ongoing attention to the issue of the built environment and health issues. The John C. Lincoln Hospital sponsors a non-profit organization, the Desert Mission Neighborhood Renewal, which is dedicated to these very issues. As a veritable hub of community development activities, Desert Mission builds affordable housing and promotes business development in Sunnyslope.

From 2006 to 2009, the neighborhood lost 854 housing units—a particularly high figure, given the proliferation of so much new luxury, gated housing on the fringe of the area (see Table 8.3). In looking at changing occupied housing unit density, a problem appears in the data. According to Table 8.3, Sunnyslope has a relatively low housing density, but that is based on a total land area for the zip code where at least one-third of the zip code's land area includes protected open space in the Phoenix Mountain Preserve. Factoring in a smaller total acreage of the zip code, the adjusted occupied housing unit density for the neighborhood in 2006 was 4.13, and 3.92 in 2009, a drop of 5 percent.

A visual inspection of the neighborhood and interviews with long-time residents and community leaders confirmed these results. I personally witnessed scores of abandoned buildings and an even greater number of homes of indeterminate occupancy (see Figures 8.4 and 8.5). Among those homes that were clearly occupied, many were in poor condition and not well maintained.

Interviewees spoke often about the serious impacts on their neighborhood of the foreclosure and abandonment crisis. They described how the first wave of foreclosure was due to subprime lending, but the next wave had more to do with job loss. In Sunnyslope, when people leave they bring their fixtures with them. According to one community leader, "half of homeowners take appliances, ceiling fans, doors, and cabinets" when they are kicked out. And the problems range the "whole spectrum of values" as one resident explained, no matter whether the house is worth $150,000 or $1,000,000, "they are trashing them."

Figure 8.4 Boarded up single-family home on 1st street in Sunnyslope, with dead grass and unkempt appearance.

Figure 8.5 Abandoned multi-family housing complex called Mountain View in West Sunnyslope. A defaced "for sale" sign stands eerily in a patch of desert grass, a signal of the lack of care or attention by any property or mortgage holder.

Maryvale (85033)

John F. Long built Phoenix's first planned development in 1954 along the lines of the Long Island protypical suburb Levittown (Gober and Trapido-Lurie 2006). Maryvale, named after Long's wife Mary, was built outside Phoenix but was quickly annexed into the city—a pattern of incorporating suburban developments into the urban realm that defines Phoenix's built form. The notion of Phoenix as a city of suburbs was born in the cul-de-sacs and spacious backyards of Maryvale.

A contrast to the original public health and humanitarian orientation of the historic Sunnyslope, Maryvale had been lacking in any formal community organizations until the Maryvale Revitalization Corporation was founded in the 1990s. The relatively new organization had been active in fighting the challenges of a relatively older community. Most of the homes in Maryvale are between 40 and 50 years old, at a point where most require major renovations (see Figure 8.6). In order to make the deteriorating structures valuable, some investors have broken the single families into dupluxes and converted sheds into housing units. This is the same trend witnessed in Flint, where single-family houses were converted into multi-families and then, once the structures were either unsafe or unprofitable, "bulldozer or fires" would consume them. At this point, arson and demolition is rare in Maryvale, but the Flint case suggests that it might not be so far away.

While Maryvale's proximity to Downtown Phoenix is a real amenity, rising crime (some related to the foreclosure problem, some related to larger structural social and economic problems in the neighborhood) makes the neighborhood less than desirable for newcomers who can buy brand new homes 20–30 miles outside of Phoenix for the same price they might pay to buy and restore in Maryvale. This dilemma is faced by hundreds of similarly situated communities throughout the country and the way that Maryvale adapts to this change will offer valuable lessons to others.

To say foreclosures are the worst in Maryvale is no exaggeration; as indicated earlier, the national foreclosure risk scores compiled by LISC put Maryvale at the top with a 100 percent ranking. Likewise, in the Maricopa County's counts for total foreclosures from January 2006 to September 2008, Maryvale is ranked fifth among 135 zip codes at 1,090 foreclosures (Maricopa County 2009). For a neighborhood of only 15,000 homes it is an extraordinary statistic.

Figure 8.6 Example of a typical 1950s style ranch single-family home in Maryvale

Figure 8.7 When owners are forced out of their homes due to foreclosure, they often dump their trash and unwanted belongings in a heap in their front yard, as with this single-family home on Devonshire Avenue in Maryvale.

The USPS data shows a similar trend, with a loss of 754 occupied housing units from 2006 to 2009 and a drop in occupied housing unit density from 4.04 to 3.84 (nearly 5 percent). Data collected by one block watch association in Maryvale is even more striking. The Tomahawk Village Block Watch went door to door and identified every home in their roughly 1,000 unit development and found 345 that were vacant, as of March 2009. Among the vacant homes, association officers were most concerned about the ones they call "orphans" where no one is showing any real concern for the protection, maintenance, or reuse of the property. Among the 345 vacant homes, there are 137 of these orphans.

So far, the neighborhood has not adapted well. "We have some boarded up houses, kids vandalize and break into the houses," one resident described. Another went on to say, "Some move out in the middle of the night and take the front door with them." Without a front door, the desert environment quickly destroys anything that vandals do not. Often, when they move out they simply leave their trash in a pile in the front yard, causing an array of problems related to pests and vermin (see Figure 8.7). Despite the way that former owners leave these structures, some residents felt that there is still much value in these orphan properties, but the lack of buyers and the lack of income generation suggests otherwise.

Laveen (85339)

A dairy cow adorns the "Welcome to Laveen" sign that greets visitors to this sprawling rural–suburban enclave south of Phoenix. A rural heritage has characterized this stretch of agricultural lands only ten miles from downtown Phoenix, where cotton, watermelons, and grapes have been grown in abundance.

For decades, this area was entirely part of the unincorporated areas of Maricopa County. But since the 1980s, there has been a steady growth in new housing in the neighborhood. The county is known to disapprove of any new housing owing to lack of water supplies, so for a landowner to convert their property to a housing subdivision, annexation by the city is a requirement and then water flows from city sources. The only requirement by the City of Phoenix is that the land to be annexed must be contiguous with the city. This mandate has created a bizarre gerrymandering network of city properties, interspersed with unincorporated county properties (see Figure 8.1).

The early 2000s brought a massive assault of new building, both residential and commercial, into Laveen. Almost exclusively low density, automobile-oriented, conventional urban sprawl to date, Laveen planners have been working on employing the precepts of New Urbanism and the Transect Model in shaping new growth. During a tour, one community leader pointed out a new Wal-Mart shopping center and bragged about the architectural design elements that activist residents insisted upon. Hardly a victory against growth, the Laveen community simply needed to wait until 2006 to get any real relief.

The 2000 Census showed only 6,346 people and 1,987 housing units in the 65,192-acre neighborhood. The building boom continued through 2006 and shows up in the USPS data. Table 8.3 shows that the number of occupied housing units nearly doubled from 2006 to 2009 from 5,499 to 10,535. That astronomical growth is mitigated by Maricopa County data collected from January 2006 to September 2008 that lists 688 foreclosures, the twelfth highest count in the county.

A drive around the Laveen community confirms both statistics: at least half of the housing appears to be built since the mid-2000s and there is widespread vacancy throughout, between 25 and 30 percent of units look empty. The problem of studying changing land-use conditions in Laveen is highlighted by an example. During my field observations, I approached the Silva Mountain housing development. "For sale" signs had all collapsed or been removed, the brand new complex sat half-built, baking in the sun (see Figure 8.8). A smattering of homes appeared occupied, hundreds were empty and at least a hundred more buildable lots were empty. This complex, by and large would not appear in the USPS data because the vast majority of the empty homes have never been occupied and have never received mail. Across the street though sits a gleaming new housing complex that was completed in mid-2006. This development was fully occupied at some point, but "for sale" and "for rent" signs are everywhere and at least a few units are empty without signs (orphans, as Maryvale residents call them).

To take these two complexes together, the total additional occupied housing units for USPS purposes is only 10–15 for the half-built complex and roughly 750 units for the one with massive vacancy, minus those 50–75 vacant units. The net contribution of these developments in February 2006 would be zero, the net contribution in February 2009 would be around 800.

More valuable than interpreting the statistics is to talk to people who live or work in Laveen. Based on those interviews, I learned that the scores of unbuilt and half-built subdivisions that litter the neighborhood are causing severe problems for the residents left behind. "There are so many empty houses, they become crime magnets," explained one long-term resident. I asked him about breaking and entering. "It's just huge," he responded, "it's a daily occurrence."

Figure 8.8 Brand new housing like this sat unoccupied for more than three years in the Silva Mountain development in Laveen.

Home Owner Associations (HOAs) try to dissuade criminals by removing "for sale" and "for rent" signs at vacant homes. Entire hundred plus unit developments have no signs, when county data show more than a 10 percent foreclosure rate (see Figure 8.9). By keeping down the signs, the HOAs also may be compounding the problem by making the vacant units harder to sell or rent—keeping them vacant even longer.

Figure 8.9 Dobbins Corner condominium complex in Laveen where subtle signs of vacancy appear in the form of round-the-clock closed window blinds. The combination of an active homeowners' association and neighborhood watch signage are intended to deter criminal activity at the vacant buildings, but it does not help much.

HOAs attempted to keep their communities home-owner only by prohibiting investor purchasers in property deed covenants. But those covenants were never enforced. The frenzy of the mid-2000s was intense and investors were responsible for the rapid rise in prices (which property owners and housing developers were in full support of). A resident I spoke with told me about a new housing project where you needed to win a lottery in order to be able to buy one of the houses. For four months, he tried to win the lottery and lost each week. Finally, as the tide turned in the market in 2006, the developer called him and said that they decided to get rid of the lottery and invited him to come and make an offer—the slide in prices started there and prices are now half if not less than the peak the developer hit during the lottery.

Planning/policy response

The most remarkable thing about the City of Phoenix's response to the foreclosure crisis is its stalwart denial that the crisis is deep or enduring. The NSP, with its accompanying millions of dollars, has forced the city's hand to take some action. But, given the scope of the problem facing Phoenicians, the response has been anemic and wholly ineffective at the time of this writing. Rather than seeing the crisis as an opportunity for the city to address longstanding land-use, environmental, and development challenges, city leaders have instead buried their heads in the desert sands and responded with a mild NSP plan that does little to reshape neighborhoods devastated by physical blight and abandonment. The one exception to this is an initiative begun prior to the start of the housing crash to revitalize the Maryvale neighborhood.

Through the leadership of city and neighborhood leaders, the West Phoenix Revitalization Area covers Maryvale and adjacent neighborhoods in West Phoenix. Responding to persistent low income levels and high crime, the initiative seeks to systematically invest multiple-levels of city resources into the neighborhood in a coordinated fashion (not unlike what Fresno officials did in the Lowell neighborhood) (Dandekar *et al.* 2005). The West Phoenix area is one of several of the city's target areas for NSP funding, as well.

By most measures, the City of Phoenix received an astounding amount of NSP money, more than any other city in America besides Detroit and Chicago. A whopping $39 million was allocated in 2009, that is the equivalent of $70 per housing unit. But community development professionals in the field are skeptical. One activist said, "the problem is so enormous it doesn't matter that Phoenix got the most money, it's almost irrelevant." Another rejected the city's plans to renovate houses all over the city; he remarked, "let's not spread it like peanut butter."

Despite the energies devoted by city staff in the Department of Community and Economic Development, Phoenix's vast planning apparatus has been largely left out of any response to the city's changing fortunes. In fact, because the Planning Department's revenues come largely from real estate development applications and those have dried up, funding drops have caused the city to lay off scores of planners. Among those left behind, there is little attention to how Phoenix is changing, but instead to preparing for the "next wave of new growth" expected by one of the city's village planners.

This attitude toward depopulation appears to be embedded in the ideology of Phoenix planners. One planner responding to the foreclosure crisis said, "the efforts of planning are somewhat limited." Others feel that the crisis is good for their office, it gives them a chance to catch up on long-term growth planning, to think about the big picture in a way that the boom times do not allow for.

Since 1993, the city has engaged with the problem of depopulation in a few very narrow areas within the city, but their response is typical of big city planning in its economic development orientation. The initiative is ongoing and involves a heavy investment by the city in housing rehabilitation and redevelopment in zones they call Neighborhood Improvement Areas (NIAs). The six NIAs have been recognized as an effective strategy for concentrating federal block grant monies and were the subject of a recent evaluation conducted by Arizona State University researchers (Dantico *et al.* 2007). The NIAs are generally small, the largest is about five acres and there are only six of them throughout the entire city. But community leaders scoff at the effort, one commented that the "city is working in these areas, but that's not where the foreclosures are happening." In fact, the only overlap between the NIAs and the neighborhoods studied in this chapter is a half-acre zone within Sunnyslope and another half-acre zone within Maryvale.

In contrast to city-led efforts, the response of non-governmental organizations to abandonment and depopulation has been striking. Two examples of creativity and innovation at the NGO level are worth describing here: 1) the inventory efforts of a neighborhood block watch in Maryvale, and 2) the aggressive strategies of homeowners' associations in Laveen.

Earlier in the chapter, I presented data collected by the Tomahawk Village Block Watch (TVBW) an informal group of residents of a subzone within Maryvale. TVBW is one of the more active block watches in the city, but the effort involved to generate the data presented is nothing less than extraordinary. In February 2008, an officer of the block watch noticed that on her very own street of about a dozen homes, four had gone through foreclosure. She was worried and brought up her concerns at the next TVBW meeting. The board agreed to begin to coordinate volunteers to track every empty house and every house for sale for code violations and evidence of care and maintenance. Their monthly reports were shared with city officials and used to lobby property owners to take action. "Our block watch works under the broken windows theory," explained one resident.

Ultimately, like the neighborliness seen in Fresno in watering others' lawns, volunteer energy can eventually peter out and by July 2009 the TVBW stopped collecting data. Their last report was their longest, with 362 vacant addresses.

Finding non-profit organizations in Laveen is easy—every housing development built in the last two decades has one. Besides HOAs, there is little evidence of a third sector in this historically rural village.[5] With little formal government involvement here on the outskirts of Phoenix, the HOAs rule with an iron fist. And the single center of this HOA power is the Laveen Organization of Home Owner Associations (LOHOA). The power of these HOAs and the LOHOA comes from dues paid by homeowners; as abandonment rates grow, dues payments fall and thus the HOAs are in big trouble.

The tightly controlled design guidelines that HOAs uphold restrict the placement of "for sale" and "for rent" signs. In some, the signs may be placed in centrally located areas on certain weekend days and at certain times. In other developments, the signs are prohibited all together. HOAs are concerned that a slew of signs suggests their community is undesirable, they feel that if you can control the signage, you can control the market.

In Laveen, the HOAs are right to be scared of what all the signs mean. Board members of HOAs are running around their neighborhoods and taking down "for sale" and "for rent" signs by the dozens. While technically just enforcing their HOA covenants, the spirit and consistency with which the HOAs are prioritizing the sign removal suggests how dire conditions really are. Decreased dues collections combined with increased expenses related to caring for vacant units have stretched association budgets to the breaking point. HOAs are raising dues and, by doing so, further reducing the values of their units, flaming a cycle that increases foreclosures and further stresses HOAs' ability to perform their legal minimum duties as private government agencies.

Opportunities for smart decline

As Phoenix loses population, loses housing units, and faces an uncertain economic future, smart decline offers a framework for responding. Planning for anything but growth is heretical in this mountain desert region, but the inevitability of continued astronomical population growth can finally be challenged. For decades, planners told their publics here that growth was coming—the only question was how to respond. In calling for a New Urbanist-style smart growth response, the planners never gave population decline a chance. Now, with the city and its region in a state of decline, that chance to reconfigure the city for a smaller population is available and solving the biggest problems of environmental degradation, water and air pollution, low-density placeless sprawl, and affordable housing is seen to be within reach. In fact, the current economic crisis appears to be solving them on its own and the only question for planners is how to fit the new, slimmer, fitter Phoenix into the much larger pants of the older, bloated Phoenix.

The Village Planning Model described earlier in the chapter is a brilliant policy innovation for addressing the problems of a large growing city in a way that responds to neighborhood needs. When the brakes came on the city's growth juggernaut in 2006, the Village Planning Committee would have been an ideal place to re-conceive the physical fabric of the city—one village at a time.

Each Village Committee in Phoenix has diverse representation from political, community, and neighborhood actors, is relatively autonomous, and has a narrow enough geographic scope to be effective in generating a vision for smart decline and implementing it. The Village Committees are well positioned to develop grass-roots analysis and plans for reconfiguring the physical plant of their neighborhoods to match their smaller populations. While continuing their official role to plan for growth using smart growth strategies, the committees can also plan for depopulation simultaneously. Building on the Reverse Transect Model introduced in Chapter 5, the committee could link local planning and development regulations to the ecozone concept. Much of the way that this has been accomplished in growing areas is through form-based codes. These zoning requirements put a burden on builders to match certain physical forms most appropriate for the ecozone they are building in. The same requirements could be adapted for a declining neighborhood, but the burden should be placed on local governments working in partnership with community organizations and builders to find creative and innovative ways to devise successor land uses for abandoned buildings and vacant lots.

A second strategy available for Phoenix in adopting smart decline is through a current initiative led by Arizona State University urban planning professor Emily Talen. The Retrofitting Phoenix effort is seeking to identify, in a systematic manner, which neighborhoods within the city have the greatest potential for retrofitting into compact, mixed-use, transit-supportive, pedestrian-oriented urban spaces using the principles of New Urbanism. In Professor Talen's (2009) work, she examines indicators of walkability, urban morphology, and access to transit.

During a session of the Association of Collegiate Schools of Planning conference, where Professor Talen introduced the work, another urban planning expert, Professor Rachel Weber of the University of Illinois, Chicago suggested that Talen's work could be improved by the introduction of an additional variable in her model that accounts for depopulation. Weber argued that striving for effective urban spaces could be most promising if that redevelopment activity happened where land and buildings were actually available owing to abandonment.

The idea is a useful one and could aid Phoenix officials in trying to accomplish the stated goal of creating meaningful urban, vibrant places while also addressing the city's declining population and changing physical form. Taken together, these goals do not have to be mutually exclusive and, as Weber discovered, they may reinforce each other.

The third opportunity for Phoenix to embrace smart decline is in its scores of incomplete housing developments. These half-built projects are the blank slate in any creative smart decline strategy. While property ownership, mortgage, and tax lien issues provide plenty of complication, there is a need for local residents to reclaim their public sphere and take ownership for the planning and reuse of abandoned subdivisions.

Successor land uses for half-built housing developments could be wildlife refuges, parks, or even agriculture. Most of these plots of land were used for agriculture prior to their development, so such a use would be a logical state to return to. But for developments where some residents remain, community gardens or truck parking might make more sense. For others, cemeteries or ball fields would be a good reuse. The incomplete housing development is a canvas for creative ideas to be expressed, but where new structures need not be part of that expression. For too long, urban planning has wrapped a straightjacket around communities, telling them that they have to grow[6]—new structures are the only possible future for a piece of land. In fact, innovation and creativity harnessed through a neighborhood-based planning process can generate even better ideas than presented in these pages.

Final thoughts on Phoenix

In a city celebrated widely for its newness, its post-smokestack economy, and its modern infrastructure, it should be no surprise that historic preservation is a weak cause célèbre. One-hundred-year-old homes dot the streets of Sunnyslope, while the mid-century suburban homes of Maryvale help define a new kind of urbanization. The ravages of economic decline and depopulation have begun to shred the very urban fabric of these places, yet public policy and planning efforts do little to preserve them. The Phoenix attitude is to make way for the new, eliminate the old. The city's very founding was about building upon archeological ruins, not preserving them as relics. This attitude toward the past is widely seen in urban planning circles (as well as more generally in society) as heartless and un-American. However, destroying and rebuilding is what Phoenix has been doing for more than a century and may just be the secret to its success in managing depopulation.

Attachment to history and the past is at the very core of why places suffer so much when they lose jobs and people. The out-of-work steelworkers in Youngstown who want to be close to the graves of their deceased relatives, the preservationists intent on protecting the original structures that housed the very birth of the American automobile industry in Flint, are all admirable and noble, but interfere tremendously when a place looses population. It is their intransigence, their love of old buildings that make it difficult to implement smart decline. In Phoenix, that preservationist spirit is largely absent, removing a critical barrier to smart decline.

CHAPTER 9

Abandonment outside the magic kingdom

What went wrong in Orlando?

After living in Orlando's Englewood neighborhood for 32 years, Katherine and her husband Earl have had enough. When they moved into their brand new home on a brand new cul-de-sac in the booming suburban-style neighborhood just minutes from downtown, they felt like they were on top of the world. Suddenly, in 2006 that all began to change. As the "new" houses in the neighborhood passed the 30 year mark, their age began to show. Major renovations were needed on the vast majority of the 11,000 homes in Englewood. When the economy was roaring and housing values high, such investments were sensible for long-time homeowners. They could always recoup renovations costs by selling their homes for upwards of $300,000. But, beginning in 2006, home values took a precipitous fall and homeowners are now making the economic decision not to renovate their home—the result is a general down-grading of the neighborhood's housing stock.

For Katherine and Earl, their neighborhood's general decline in housing quality is worsened by the wave of foreclosures that have swept through leading to vacant homes, high crime, and "black" pools. They are fed up with the unkempt lawns and high weeds and, recently retired, they have decided to leave. They are not sure where they will go, but would like to be in a "newer" community, probably far outside Orlando into Lake County where half-built subdivisions line the county roads.

Katherine and Earl settled in Englewood just a few years after Walt Disney World broke ground in 1971. Their neighborhood was built to accommodate the population growth that Disney and other new industries brought to Orlando. Walt Disney himself was a utopian planner—sketching out a vision for a community that was modern in its attachment to the machine but traditional in form and aesthetics. While not exact, the Englewood neighborhood embodied many of Disney's own ideals for suburban-style development in the city, with relatively large lots and plenty of room for automobiles. But three decades later the shine has worn off Englewood, while Disney's other legacy—Walt Disney World, is as polished as ever.

In approaching depopulation and abandoned property, the case of Orlando screams to be told. The thrill rides of Disney World mimic the roller-coaster housing bubble that infected the region in the early 2000s. In a city that has not stopped growing since its early settlement in the nineteenth century, 2009 was a watershed year. Demographers estimate that the city lost 1,000 residents, while the Central Florida region lost 9,700 and the state as a whole lost 57,294 residents from April 2008 to April 2009 (Kunerth and Shrieves 2009). When this broader population shift is considered along with the foreclosure crisis (which has hit Florida hard) the impacts are seen as enormous on the physical form and quality of urban neighborhoods. This chapter explores the kinds of impacts this depopulation has had on Orlando and, as with the previous case study chapters, examines the ways in which government and non-governmental organizations have responded.

A brief history of planning and development in Orlando

By the late nineteenth century, the native populations of Central Florida had been largely dispersed by force. White Europeans began to settle in the Orlando area in the 1880s owing to the presence of an Army Fort and later owing to the establishment of the city as the county seat (Shofner 1984). For decades later, population steadily grew as the climate and natural resources proved to be well suited for citrus growing (Mormino 2005). But things began to change in the 1950s when city officials lobbied successfully to build a series of limited access highways directly through Orlando—putting the city squarely at the crossroads of Florida (Fogelson 2001). Shortly thereafter, the U.S. Missile Test Center was built 50 miles east of Orlando at Cape Canaveral bringing a whole bevy of high-tech industries to the city (Shofner 1984).

During this Cold War era, Orlando experienced growth and prosperity, but everything would be different once Walt Disney decided to locate his reprise of Disney Land just south of the city of Orlando. The theme park's opening in 1971 was met with open arms by local officials in the rural counties where the company bought thousands of acres of swampland. The Mayor of Orlando at the time, Carl T. Langford declared that the coming of Disney was "the greatest thing that's happened since the city got its charter" (Mormino 2005, p. 28).

Within just a few years, Disney quickly became the biggest commercial tourist attraction in the world with more than 30 million annual visitors (Fogelson 2001). To house and feed these guests and to run the sprawling 7,000-acre facility, the sleepy Orlando of 1970 was quickly transformed into a modern, booming metropolis. The city shot up in population from 99,006 to 185,951, while the metro area more than tripled between 1970 and 2000 (U.S. Census 2000) (see Table 9.1). Mormino (2005) called Orlando Florida's "most influential city"—with its world-class tourism industry the place would seem to be the envy of all other cities (p. 26).

The problem, as Fogelson (2001) sees it is that Orlando is stuck with too much reliance on tourism and all its faults. Despite the prosperity that came with Disney, the Mouse also brought an economy that is structurally deficient—the vast majority of workers are part-time, low-wage, and have few if any benefits (see Judd and Fainstein 1999). As in Fresno, the Orlando area is home to a permanent underclass of gainfully employed workers who cannot break through to higher-wage positions. Fogelson argues that the political models of path dependency apply in Orlando (see Putnam 1993). The ability of the city of Orlando to adjust its economy beyond tourism and to improve the quality of life and income of its residents is limited by the current path it is on.

Table 9.1 City-wide demographic and housing data, Orlando, 1970–2000

	1970	1980	1990	2000
Total population	171,129	212,876	266,321	307,293
% White	80.2%	76.4%	72.8%	65.0%
% African American	19.5%	21.6%	22.4%	25.7%
% Latino	1.9%	4.1%	8.8%	18.3%
Total population foreign born	3.0%	5.0%	6.9%	13.9%
% < age 18	32.3%	24.5%	22.5%	23.1%
% > age 64	11.3%	11.9%	11.3%	10.7%
Total households	57,237	79,313	104,007	123,740
Total housing units	61,742	84,554	115,292	134,276
Total occupied housing units	57,237	78,918	103,773	123,923
% occupied housing units	92.7%	93.3%	90.0%	92.3%
Average household income prior year	$8,799	$15,405	$34,003	$50,286

Source: U.S. Census Bureau, Census 1970–2000 Summary File 1; Geolytics, Neighborhood Change Database

The other challenge that Orlando's growth brought was related to land use and sprawl. The city's former mayor Langford retired from public life in the 1980s and moved to North Carolina. He was quoted as saying, "I spent 30 years of my life trying to get people to move down there [Orlando], and they all did" (Corliss 1989, quoted in Mormino 2005). With all those new people came new houses, new stores, and new roads. In fact, the State of Florida requires concurrency in its 1985 Growth Management Act. Local governments must provide infrastructure simultaneously with new growth. Instead of managing growth, the Act just made growth easier and low-density, placeless development spread across the Orlando area over the last 25 years, largely unabated. By 1998, the Sierra Club dubbed the Orlando metropolitan area the worst sprawling in America[1] and by 2006 the problems were even worse (Brown *et al.* 1998).

While the Orlando metro area was being skewered in the news, there was a slightly different development pattern in place within the city. While low-density, sprawling suburban-style housing had been built in the city since the mid-century, it was minor compared to the kind of exurban growth of concern to the Sierra Club and others. In fact, Orlando has a long history of promoting and creating traditional urban neighborhoods and the well-known sprawl is largely outside the city limits. "Orlando has been pretty good at smart growth, the benefits of mixed-uses, New Urbanism, generally the city gets it for the last 50–60 years," said one current city official. He went on to explain recent events: "There was not this crazy speculation and overdevelopment in the city. Much of it was logically done and consistent with a plan." My own field observations and interviews with community leaders and residents confirmed these statements.

Within the city, there have been few large-scale new housing developments that could be classified as sprawl—the major exception to this is the southeastern portion of the city. Also, strong efforts have been made to prevent isolated enclaves or gated communities from being built within Orlando. "We've only approved two gated communities in the last ten years," explained an official from the planning department.

Table 9.2 Building permits issued, Orlando, 2002–2009

	2002	2003	2004	2005	2006	2007	2008	2009*	ch 2002–2005	ch 2006–2008
Residential single-family	642	1,299	1,823	1,104	769	404	223	171	72%	–78%
Residential multi-family	3,590	2,697	2,299	4,273	4,239	1,516	1,932	66	19%	–98%
Total permits	6,234	5,999	6,126	7,382	7,014	3,927	4,163	6,264	18%	–11%

* 2009 data was estimated based on an annual linear extrapolation of data from 1/1/09 to 4/30/09, 1FAM=57, M-FAM=22, TotalPERM=2088

Source: City of Orlando Building Department

But overall, the 2000s were a period of major new housing construction in Orlando. From 2002 to 2005, the number of residential single-family permits issued per year grew from only 642 to 1,104—a jump of 72 percent (see Table 9.2). Multi-family permits were 3,590 in 2002 and climbed to an astonishing 4,273 in 2005. This was a time of major growth and expansion in Orlando and city officials understood that well.

Working together, Orlando and its neighboring cities and towns came together in 1999 to address growth from a regional perspective. myregion.org is similar in many ways to regional planning projects in metro Phoenix and the Central Valley. The central question asked in this regional planning exercise is "how shall we grow?" During this period of decline, the question may be the wrong one to ask.

As with Fresco and Pheonix, the forces of growth and sprawl disappeared in 2006 and since then the Orlando area has been fighting decline. Unfortunately, the myregion.org planning effort is not nimble enough to respond to recent demographic changes and the planners are incapable of refocusing their energies on a regional planning vision of managing depopulation and decline.

Few Floridians are native born—statewide in 2000, four in ten; only Nevada had a lower rate of natives, 28.2 percent (Mormino 2005, p. 356). Mormino says that it has "contributed to a weak civic bond" in the state. Commentator Michael Barone (1993) wrote, "a feeble public sector that extends from universities to environmental protection to criminal justice" (p. 356), perhaps accounting for a weak response to decline.

A changing Orlando, 2006–2009

When the real estate market crashed and the foreclosure crisis lit up in 2006, the number of building permits issued by the city fell, too. There was a drop of 78 percent from 2006 to 2009 in the number of single-family permits issued. The multi-family market crashed even harder, with permits falling a whopping 98 percent from 4,239 in 2006 to only 66 permits in 2009.

City-wide, USPS data showed net growth in occupied housing units from 2006 to 2009 in Orlando (see Table 9.3 and Figure 9.1). But almost one-third (10 of 31) of Orlando's neighborhoods had a net loss in occupied units—combined, those losing zip codes shed 2,721 units. The spatial distribution of the gaining and losing zips is presented in Figure 9.1. The zips that lost the most occupied units form nearly a perfect ring around the traditional core city of Orlando and include nearby county lands.

Table 9.3 Housing occupancy patterns for Orlando zip codes, 2006–2009

Study neighborhood	Zip	LISC foreclosure score (Intrastate Foreclosure Component Score) *	Neighborhood name	2000 Census		
				Total population	Total housing units	Land area (acres)
✓	32808		Pine Hill	48,886	17,489	7,799
✓	32807		Englewood Park	29,167	11,197	5,944
	32825			43,682	15,114	23,687
	32811			33,391	14,253	5,221
	32809			22,676	8,719	6,631
	32805			24,432	9,806	4,038
	32826			24,253	9,125	6,651
	32806			26,682	11,827	4,298
	32804			18,083	9,168	4,391
	32831			57	22	554
	32821			13,930	7,385	12,751
	32803			21,280	10,877	4,585
	32835			31,387	13,823	6,647
	32812			35,952	15,113	5,811
	32817			27,923	10,643	6,306
	32837			34,855	12,530	10,211
	32818			35,679	12,434	7,265
	32810			32,623	12,992	6,195
	32833			5,092	2,004	20,184
	32836			12,109	4,656	14,977
	32819			23,913	9,207	12,902
	32820			3,007	1,143	10,228
	32822			52,182	23,438	17,617
	32839			40,457	14,713	5,040
	32801			7,979	4,959	1,457
	32827			2,186	867	20,840
✓	32814		Baldwin Park	–	–	–
	32829			3,565	1,190	1,383
	32824			19,327	7,060	16,993
	32832			1,860	735	38,854
	32828			22,301	8,177	10,203

* Local Initiative Support Corporation with Foreclosure Response project, Table 1: November 2008, http://www.housingpolicy.org/assets/foreclosure-response.

USPS active residential delivery statistics					
Occupied housing units – Feb '06	Occupied housing units – Feb '09	Change in occ. housing units Feb '06–Feb '09	Occupied housing units per acre – Feb '06	Occupied housing units per acre – Feb '09	% change Feb '06–Feb '09
17,925	17,291	−634	2.30	2.22	−4%
12,657	12,065	−592	2.13	2.03	−5%
19,972	19,579	−393	0.84	0.83	−2%
14,827	14,520	−307	2.84	2.78	−2%
9,427	9,214	−213	1.42	1.39	−2%
8,775	8,562	−213	2.17	2.12	−2%
8,241	8,084	−157	1.24	1.22	−2%
11,238	11,093	−145	2.61	2.58	−1%
8,236	8,170	−66	1.88	1.86	−1%
99	92	−7	0.18	0.17	−8%
8,111	8,125	14	0.64	0.64	0%
9,541	9,647	106	2.08	2.10	1%
16,585	16,703	118	2.50	2.51	1%
13,702	13,826	124	2.36	2.38	1%
11,916	12,050	134	1.89	1.91	1%
17,659	17,824	165	1.73	1.75	1%
15,417	15,607	190	2.12	2.15	1%
12,284	12,533	249	1.98	2.02	2%
3,068	3,342	274	0.15	0.17	8%
6,254	6,591	337	0.42	0.44	5%
9,312	9,667	355	0.72	0.75	4%
2,325	2,748	423	0.23	0.27	15%
22,589	23,074	485	1.28	1.31	2%
17,293	18,125	832	3.43	3.60	5%
5,703	6,669	966	3.92	4.58	14%
1,449	2,463	1,014	0.07	0.12	41%
1,288	2,545	1,257	–	–	–
4,660	6,290	1,630	3.37	4.55	26%
10,104	11,872	1,768	0.59	0.70	15%
2,986	4,817	1,831	0.08	0.12	38%
16,731	20,439	3,708	1.64	2.00	18%

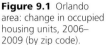

Figure 9.1 Orlando area: change in occupied housing units, 2006–2009 (by zip code).

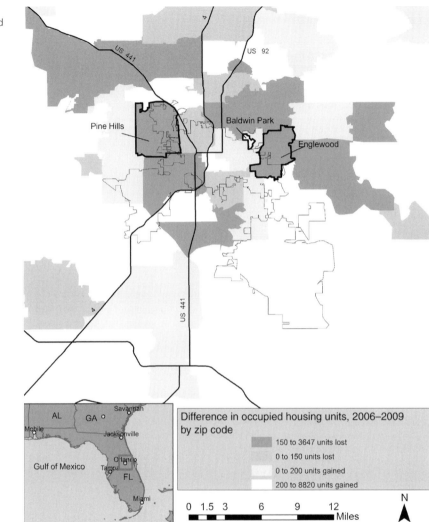

During this period of loss and abandonment, both Orlando and nearby Orange County have invested heavily in trying to protect and maintain abandoned homes. In describing the importance of mowing, a local official admitted:

> if you let [the grass] grow too high, it creates other issues with rodents and rats and other wildlife. A lot of foreclosures have pools, you have the green pool syndrome, becomes a breeding ground for mosquitos and its dangerous for children—under 12 [years old], drowning is the number one cause of death in Florida.

Orlando has an active code enforcement program, but, according to one resident, "they try to stay on top of them, but there are so many foreclosures in the area." Beyond a lack of adequate resources for the job, my own interviews with city officials shed a different kind of problem. Those charged with guiding the City of Orlando's efforts to address job loss, depopulation, and housing abandonment are in a state of denial. They have difficulty recognizing the severity of the current conditions and rely too heavily on past growth and prosperity in guiding government intervention. When confronted with documented declines in jobs, people, and occupied housing units, one city official remarked, "I sense we'll continue to grow."

Three neighborhoods in Orlando

As with the other case studies, I present here an in-depth examination of three of Orlando's neighborhoods to probe deeper into the impacts of depopulation and widespread foreclosure since 2006 (see Tables 9.3 and 9.4). After examining the USPS data and speaking to government and non-governmental officials, I selected neighborhoods that each suffered from the foreclosure crisis but had a range of different historical contexts and current policy attention.

The first neighborhood chosen is Pine Hills, a largely African American and Hispanic neighborhood that includes properties within the City of Orlando and properties within Orange County—a real patchwork of governmental authority, and a subject of major, ongoing redevelopment attention by City Hall. The next neighborhood is Englewood (profiled briefly in the beginning of the chapter)—currently one of the epicenters of foreclosure in Orlando, the city has been in the sights of NSP activities. The last neighborhood is Baldwin Hills, a new community built on a former military base in the city using the principles of New Urbanism—as one of the few new communities in Orlando, it has been hit hard by foreclosure.

Orlando's first distant suburb: Pine Hills (32808)

Orlando was a very urban place until the highway building era kicked off in the early 1950s. Slowly, new developments across the city appeared that were suburban in nature and in proximity to downtown. After Highway 50 was laid east–west across Orlando, Pine Hills was the first subdivision to be developed far outside of the core city (see Figure 9.1). Partially in Orange County, partly in the City of Orlando, Pine Hills was a community of choice when first built out.

Table 9.4 Neighborhood-level demographic and housing data, Orlando, 2000

Neighborhood	Total population	% White	% African American	% Latino	% < age 18	% > age 64	Total housing units	Total occupied housing units	% occupied housing units
32807 – Englewood Park	29,167	72.8%	6.9%	38.6%	24.8%	11.3%	11,197	10,772	96.2%
32808 – Pine Hills	48,886	33.8%	53.0%	12.2%	33.0%	8.3%	17,489	16,284	93.1%
32814 – Baldwin Park	–	–	–	–	–	–	–	–	–

Source: U.S. Census Bureau, Census 2000 Summary File 1

Today, Pine Hills is home to some of Orlando's poorest residents, but is also home to middle-class, working families. The neighborhood is diverse, with 53 percent African American, 12 percent Latino, and 34 percent White (U.S. Census 2000) (see Table 9.4). The under-18 years of age population is higher, on average, than the city as a whole with a median age of 30 (as compared to a median age of 33 for the entire city). The nearly 50,000 residents of Pine Hills live in a diverse set of housing, including single-family homes, duplexes, and scores of small, medium, and large apartment complexes. One city official described Pine Hills as "not the best place, there's a lot of crime out there, very low income." A local realtor was less sanguine, but admitted that home values had plummeted since 2006: "You can buy three bedroom homes all day long [in Pine Hills] in the $30,000s."

During the real estate boom of the early 2000s, investors honed their attention onto Pine Hills. According to interviews with residents and local officials, several large-scale redevelopment projects were under way when the real estate market crashed in 2006 and those projects are now all on hold. The slowdown in gentrification is seen with some ambivalence by many in the neighborhood. Residents "don't want to see [Pine Hills] go to pot, but they don't want it taken over by people who don't care," commented one long-time resident and community leader.

The USPS data indicate that Pine Hills lost 634 occupied housing units from 2006 through 2009. The relatively low-density neighborhood went from 2.3 occupied housing units per acre in 2006 to 2.22 in 2009, a 4 percent drop. Field observations and interviews with long-time residents and community leaders confirmed these results. There are hundreds if not thousands of unoccupied homes throughout Pine Hills. Roughly one-half appear to be either for sale or rent or orphans, where nobody appears to be taking responsibility for the property (see Figures 9.2, 9.3, 9.4, and 9.5).

Figure 9.2 A vacant home on Georgetown Drive in Pine Hills, either for sale or for rent.

Figure 9.3 An unmaintained, damaged, and empty home on Chantelle Road with an empty beer bottle in the front yard.

Figure 9.4 Arson is suspected in a fire at this Dardenelle Drive foreclosed home in Pine Hills.

Figure 9.5 Lack of lawn and tree maintenance has created a semi-forested environment in side and backyards like at this cinderblock home on Carousel Road in Pine Hills.

Crime is also on the rise in the neighborhood and according to one resident, "the reason is we have these empty houses." That resident went on to tell me: "Yesterday, I had to call 911, a guy was selling drugs in front of the [vacant] home [on my block]." A Pine Hills community leader said, "people are going inside those homes, you see them climbing in the windows." While Pine Hills has always had its difficulties with crime and gangs, the abandoned property problem has taken things to a new level. Despite all of its challenges, many residents in Pine Hills have a strong sense of connection to their community: "I wouldn't leave my little house here—I will give it to my children. Everyone says 'hi, have a drink of juice or whatever'. You look forward to coming home…These houses are usually passed down from generation to generation."

Englewood: suburban development in the city (32807)

After World War II, the military scene in Orlando settled quietly down as bases closed all over the country. But the Cold War meant the reactivation of several military installations in and around Orlando, leading to a mini-boom in the real estate economy. The Englewood development was built in several stages, beginning in the 1950s, largely completed by 1980. Typical of the time, the suburban-style development was low density, with winding roads, and plenty of grass (see Figure 9.6 for a typical home built during the 1960s period). Most of the housing was single-family, but a few subdivisions had duplex homes, where the owner could rent out the second unit.

Into the 1980s and early 1990s, higher-density condominiums were built, some even gated. By 2000, the nine-square-mile neighborhood was largely built out with nearly 30,000 residents living in just over 11,000 homes. The vast majority of those residents are White (73 percent in 2000) with growing Latino and African American populations. Age-wise, the Englewood neighborhood closely mirrors the city-wide profile, with a healthy mix of seniors and young people.

Figure 9.6 Typical home built in Englewood during the 1960s, this Andes Avenue unit is vacant.

Figure 9.7 "For sale" and "for rent" signs are a ubiquitous presence throughout Englewood.

Figure 9.8 Tall grass and an open door are indications of abandonment at this house on Shenandoah Way in Englewood.

From 2006 to 2009, the Englewood neighborhood lost 592 occupied housing units and dropped in occupied housing density from 2.13 to 2.03 units per acre (see Table 9.3). A 5 percent fall in housing density is recognizable in a casual stroll through Mackenzie Street or down Alder Avenue; for sale, for rent, and unkempt landscape is everywhere (see Figures 9.7, 9.8, and 9.9). Hardly a single street remains untouched—the foreclosure disease has spread across this once humble place and has turned a stable community upside down.

Figure 9.9 Desperation is apparent in this provocative sign placed on the lawn of a Mercado Avenue home in Englewood.

Among the many relatively new condominium complexes in the neighborhood, the biggest impact of foreclosures is a steep drop in dues collections. With fewer resources, associations in Englewood are cutting back on landscaping and preventative maintenance. In 2009, 11 percent of dues in one homeowners' association were more than six months delinquent (in a complex of 112 units)—"we're losing about $20,000 a year," according to an officer of the association. The drop in revenues is a real problem for associations; they can either cut services or raise dues.

When a home is foreclosed, state law in Florida restricts how much unpaid dues can be paid from the sale. For condominiums, the association can only collect six months in back dues, where a homeowners' association can collect 12 months. Foreclosed homes have generally been sitting empty for between one and two years in Englewood, meaning that even if the associations collect something at a foreclosure sale it's not enough.

The strain on associations is only part of how this crisis has impacted Englewood. For neighborhoods without associations, lawns are dying, weeds are growing, and what had been a minor graffiti and vandalism problem has reached epidemic proportions. "There's an awful lot of vacant homes here all of a sudden," said one long-time resident.

Crime is encroaching on neighborhoods that had never had any problems before; with the neighborhood changing, things are different in Englewood: one homeowner shockingly explained to me how his neighbor has "got two prostitutes sitting on the front porch right now!"

Baldwin Park: New Urbanism in action (32814)

When the Orlando Naval Training Center closed in 1997, city officials demanded that the site be reused in a manner consistent with New Urbanist principles. It was through a community-planning process that involved over 200 meetings that a Master Plan for the 1,100-acre site was devised that would be an antidote to the business-as-usual sprawl development that the region was famous for (Baldwin Park Development Company 2006).

While city officials were committed to the principles of New Urbanism for decades, it was the phenomenal financial success of the New Urbanist community celebration by the Disney Corporation that opened the door for nearby Orlando's leaders to consider a similar approach. Celebration was first announced as a project by Disney in 1991 and lot sales began in 1996. Promoted as an extension of Walt Disney's dreams of a utopian community, the mixed-use, pedestrian-oriented development was replete with pocket parks, traditional architecture, and high-quality urban design. Heralded as an alternative to conventional single-use, automobile-oriented subdivisions, Celebration sold quickly and by 2000 the first residential components were completely built out.

With the success of Celebration in mind, developers at Baldwin Park broke ground in 2003 with a clear vision: they would replicate the Celebration model by mimicking the traditional urban form of neighborhoods within Orlando and elsewhere, creating a pedestrian-oriented, mixed-use neighborhood with a true sense of place (see Figure 9.10). By the end of 2009, the housing component of Baldwin Park was substantially built out with 2,000 units and only a few commercial parcels remain vacant.

Figure 9.10 Downtown Baldwin Park supports pedestrian and bicycle uses, as well as public art and street furniture.

During the boom years, according to my interviews, Baldwin Park was the single most desirable neighborhood in Central Florida. "Every senator in the state has a home here," quipped one resident of Baldwin Park. At the peak of the market, developers were fetching upward of $2.5 million for the premier luxury homes and $700,000 for four-bedroom colonials. The condominiums and attached homes were also selling at levels well above the average for new construction in the region. The properties were so popular, at the peak you needed to win a lottery ticket in order to buy one—as was seen in Phoenix's Laveen neighborhood around the same time. The reasons for the high volume of sales were amenities, sense of place, and proximity to Downtown Orlando. The neighborhood is part of a highly rated school district and is served by top-quality fire and police services. In Orlando, as is common in the Sunbelt, there are regional school districts that have made living within the city limits more attractive than outside (a very different phenomenon than exists in Rustbelt cities such as Flint).

But the party could not last forever and by 2006 sales began to slow down in such a desirable neighborhood. By 2009, the developer was slashing prices and still holding on to empty homes—by one count the developer had over 100. According to the Baldwin Park Homeowners' Association (which all owners are obligated to join) among those units sold, not counting the developers' properties they are trying to sell, 13 percent are more than 45 days late on their monthly dues (260 of approximately 2,000 housing units). If all of those 260 units are empty, then combined with the unsold units the total vacancy rate could be as high as 17 percent (360 empty units divided by 2,100 total units). Also of note is the smattering of vacant lots throughout the development, most very well cared for but suggestive of an empty landscape waiting to be filled (see Figures 9.11 and 9.12).

Figure 9.11 Empty mansions dot the idyllic streetscapes of Baldwin Park. This new Spanish-style mansion on New Broad Street was constructed in 2006 with an asking price of over $3 million. At the time of the photograph (September 2009) the home had never been occupied and remains for sale.

Figure 9.12 Vacant lots are common throughout the Baldwin Park development, including this one on Lower Union Road.

USPS data for Baldwin Park is difficult to interpret because of all the new housing being built there. According to Table 9.3, the neighborhood nearly doubled from 1,288 to 2,545 occupied housing units from 2006 to 2009. The association dues statistics and my own direct observation and interviews appear to suggest that despite the net growth in occupied units, there is a major vacancy problem in this brand new community.

Where foreclosure and abandonment is associated with all flavors of visual blight in most neighborhoods, the powerful homeowners' association and continued presence of the master developer in Baldwin Park has meant that empty homes are generally being cared for, lawns and landscaping are usually being watered and weeded, and "for sale" signs are kept to a minimum (there are even design guidelines on what a "for sale" sign must look like). These extra duties tax the master developer and the homeowners' association, but as of this writing at the end of 2009 Baldwin Park has maintained an image of stability. Unfortunately, the debt is building on the master developer and the budget for the homeowners' association is significantly strained. Unless things change soon, cracks in the armor may soon appear and the visual signs of vacancy and abandonment may emerge.

Planning/policy response

The City of Orlando's primary strategy for responding to the foreclosure and abandonment crisis is through the NSP and through aggressive code enforcement. Also worthy of discussion is the city's longstanding adoption of New Urbanism as a framework for approaching growth and development.

With $6.7 million in hand, the City of Orlando is focusing much of its attention on the federally supported NSP (Schlueb 2008a; Schlueb 2008b). City officials began with their own analysis of what the traditional ingredient of neighborhood stability has been in Orlando and concluded that the answer was single-family homeownership. One city official elaborated on their approach: "Our own experience working in Orlando, particularly studying these [priority area] neighborhoods—they have a higher percentage of single-family homes." The city's work in a few select priority areas has led to some improvements in housing quality and neighborhood conditions. What the city has learned from these experiences is that the introduction of single-family owner-occupied units is the key causal variable in transforming places. The logic being used here is faulty.

Disentangling all of the complex socio-economic and political variables at work, not to mention the role of the private sector and the agency of individuals in the neighborhood is quite challenging and to then conclude that a single factor is the ingredient ignores the three requirements for causation developed by eighteenth-century philosopher David Hume: 1) correlation, 2) time order, and 3) non-spuriousness. City officials see a correlation between neighborhoods that have low crime and high property values with those with high percentages of single-family and owner-occupied residences. They also perceive that single-family homes are coming prior to the neighborhood transforming, suggesting a satisfying of the requirement of time order. But the final requirement is that no other explanation or alternative variable might be explaining the change in the neighborhood. Here they fail, where scores of other possible reasons can account for neighborhood change and, more importantly for this study, the notion that single-family is the answer as opposed to lower density is flawed.

A key idea in smart decline is that a depopulating neighborhood may simply demand fewer occupied housing units per acre, in some cases single-family housing units help a community get to that lower density. But there are numerous ways in which a neighborhood can achieve lower densities without rallying around the notion of single-family units. A neighborhood of triple-deckers could move toward duplexes, a neighborhood of low-rise apartment buildings could look to transform into a neighborhood of townhouses. The magic bullet of single-family owner-occupied housing is fallacious and could contribute to a policy response that does not address the policy problem.

Regardless of the intelligence of the single-family approach, the city adopted it in spending its NSP funds. Through a policy of buying foreclosed single-family homes, rehabbing them, and selling them to owner-occupiers, city officials hope to intervene in neighborhoods to increase the numbers of single-family owner-occupied units.

If the city successfully acquires and rehabilitates a foreclosed home using the federal funds, the next step is to find a buyer—preferably an owner-occupant. According to one official, "our biggest fear is: are we going to have buyers for these things when we finish rehabbing them?" If broader demographic and economic forces contributed to a sinking demand for housing, will that demand jump again owing to the city's efforts? At the time of this writing, the answer remains unknown.

Oddly, the NSP rules are written in such a way that city officials are given incentives to not acquire orphan homes or structures that are in derelict condition. Instead, the city's goal is to acquire homes as soon as they are foreclosed—in some cases attempting to beat out the commercial property. Focusing funds in this way means that the real problem properties are sitting idle.[2]

One potential explanation for this myopic perspective is the lack of the kind of long-term perspective that planners can bring to city government. The stovepipes between planning and community development (where the NSP program is being implemented) are enormous, a surprise given that they are both in the same Economic Development Department and even on the same floor. "NSP isn't a planning function per se because it's a program about existing housing stock," explained a community development official. This distinction between existing housing stock and planned housing stock is erroneous and feeds into the building of walls among city officials. Planners deal with existing housing stock in any master plan or redevelopment plan—their absence from the NSP discussions reflects the problems within city government more than anything else.

"On foreclosure stuff, it's more about how to get existing housing stock online and occupied," reported a senior city official. Again these comments reflect a basic lack of understanding about what land-use planning can offer to the challenge of depopulation and abandonment. All these officials can see is empty homes and all they can do to respond is to fill those homes with people. When the population falls, there are fewer people to fill those homes and even the best efforts of government are insufficient. At the end of the chapter, I return to this point in highlighting the potential for smart decline to help officials address all of the empty houses.

The structural forces that separate planners and planning from the NSP are significant. One Orlando planner embarrassedly told me that he lacked even basic knowledge about the extent of foreclosures and abandonment—"it's just not something I've been following closely." While other city departments are busily spending millions in federal aid through the NSP, the planning department has been left largely out of the debate. They are focused primarily on updating their rules and regulations and a few small-scale area plans.

For at least two decades, City of Orlando policies and planning have advanced the principles of New Urbanism. The city has been active in planning for the Baldwin Park project highlighted earlier in the chapter, as well as several other neo-traditional developments and redevelopments. And in 2009, the planning department began working on a neighborhood plan for the College Park section of Orlando—they are employing the Transect Model as a key organizing principle in the plan.

By constraining growth, concentrating new development, and creating neighborhoods with a sense of place, the city has limited the kind of low-density, placeless sprawling development that has generated some of the highest rates of foreclosure in the region.[3] One planner in Orlando said, "we're always trying to accommodate development when it's consistent with our vision." This vision of quality development according to the principles of New Urbanism has been a powerful one and the results are in clear contrast to surrounding cities and towns who do not have such a vision. For the half-dozen new housing development projects under way in Orlando in 2009, I found that none had more than 10 percent vacancy. Contrast that with the scores of entirely empty or largely empty housing projects just beyond the city boundaries in Orange, Osceola, Seminole, and Lake Counties.

Local officials are convinced that their planning strategies around New Urbanism are responsible for the city's relatively low foreclosure rates for new homes compared to outlying areas. "A lot of the overdevelopment—the huge tracts of subdivisions have not occurred in Orlando"—instead a city official contends they have occurred outside the city boundaries in Lake, Orange, and Seminole counties. What is indisputable is that traditional urban areas within the city have been impacted. For a place such as Baldwin Park, the city has done practically nothing to respond to abandonment and vacancy. With a real estate developer and a homeowners' association actively serving the role of a private government, there is ostensibly no reason for the city government to step in. That is, unless things get worse.

Opportunities for smart decline in Orlando

The political challenges of implementing smart decline are immense—in a city with such a rich history of growth such as Orlando it may be even harder. The research presented here provides a few clues to what might be effective strategies for making smart decline happen in Orlando, but as with anywhere, building the political will to do so is equally challenging.

I present three strategies worthy of consideration in thinking about Orlando as a smaller, better city. The first is a simple extension of the ongoing commitment of the city to the principles of New Urbanism—a formal adoption of the Transect model as a means to both manage depopulation and prepare for growth if and when it returns. The second strategy is to open up stovepipes. The city could reorganize itself to bring the innovative, creative energies of the planning department to be a force for addressing the abandonment problem. The third strategy is for the city to partner with condominium and homeowners' associations, those agents of private government, to retrofit vacant land (in the case of new developments) and empty housing units for new, non-intensive uses.

The language of the Transect is familiar within the halls of City Hall—moving from T3 ecozone to T4 ecozone is a routine exercise in planning for neighborhood change in a growing Orlando. In a shrinking Orlando, the Reverse Transect can work just as well. Preserving the integrity of each ecozone, the city can systematically manage the physical changes occurring in neighborhoods to respond to depopulation—just as described in Chapter 5. For example, portions of Englewood are bursting with duplexes. On one street, more than half the duplexes had "for rent" signs hanging. Depopulation has meant lower demand in Englewood for housing and owners of duplexes are having difficulty finding tenants for their rental units.

An easy way to address this problem is for the city to work with property owners to convert the structures into single-family homes or convert the rental units into another, alternative use. Through city incentives, grants, and loans, Englewood could quite easily transition to a lower density of occupied housing units while preserving the physical integrity of the neighborhood. Fewer rental units will mean a smaller population, potentially leading to a less congested community for those who stay behind.

In the earlier discussion about the NSP, I demonstrated the city's mindset that homes must be occupied. Using smart decline, the problem of abandonment can be solved not by occupying every home that's been abandoned, but through creative land-use planning that takes some homes out of use for residences and identifies successor land uses.

Figure 9.13 The sidewalk ends along Snow Road where two vacant lots sit across the street from the formal and permanent Union Park (on the right) in Baldwin Park.

Lastly, an opportunity is available for the city government to partner with its friendly private government agencies to find successor land uses for abandoned buildings and vacant lots. For example, vacant land that is slotted for new housing in Baldwin Park could be re-imagined as an extension of a nearby park (see Figure 9.13). Such a change in use does not have to be permanent. In fact, this is happening to some extent on its own. While developers wait out the economy, a parcel of land zoned for commercial use in Baldwin Park was converted to an interim use as a parking lot.

The city can play an active role in Orlando's private realms to facilitate more of these interim uses and to support lower housing densities. During a time when associations are facing steep increases in dues or even bankruptcy, the city can support them by helping to reduce the footprint of these developments. In the short term, such moves will mean reduced property tax revenues to the city, but in time city services should also be reduced in serving a smaller city. Often, seeing this longer term view is hard, particularly so for politicians.

Final thoughts on Orlando

It has been said that Orlando was forever changed when Walt Disney's plane flew over the teeming swamps just south of the city and he remarked "that's it" effectively choosing the city (Fogelson 2001, p. 15). Much more subtly, the city began to change again in 2006 as the unstoppable growth machine that was Orlando and the rest of Florida finally began to slow down and shift into reverse. Orlando will never be the same again now that growth is not a given.

In early 2007, City Hall celebrated boisterously their supposed achievement of attracting the Burnham Institute for Medical Research to build a satellite campus in the southern part of the city and bring 303 jobs (Ping 2007). In competing against other locations considered by the Institute, Orlando and Orange County put together an incentive package comprised of $367.2 million in cash and in-kind donations (Ping 2007). At a price tag of $1.2 million per employee, it may just be the most expensive firm recruitment in the history of economic development.[4] Facing the prospect of population decline, city officials are eager to bring in new jobs and new residents to turn the tide back. An investment of $367.2 million in retrofitting and reconfiguring Orlando's neighborhoods might just be a wiser choice than in "buying" jobs at the Burnham Institute.

The history of economic development policy was marked heavily by the 2005 Supreme Court case that held in favor of the City of New London's economic development strategy to accommodate what they viewed as their most important employer, pharmaceutical company Pfizer (*Kelo v. City of New London*, 545 U.S. 469 (2005)). At the end of 2009, Pfizer announced that it would close the plant at the very center of the court dispute over economic development policy and lay off 1,400 employees (McGeehan 2009). When will cities learn? Investing in job growth can be costly and the benefits are often illusory, where investing in right-sizing shrinking neighborhoods to improve the quality of life for remaining residents can not be taken away or shuttered.

Table 9.5 Comparison of housing restrictions between City of Orlando and Orange County

City of Orlando	Heavy restrictions on new development	→	Little new growth, that which did happen in 2000s was New Urbanist with a strong sense of place
Orange County	Light restrictions on new development	→	A lot of new growth, all conventional low-density sprawl with little sense of place.*

* The one exception in the Orlando region is the Celebration new town development in Osceola County.

New real estate development does not always generate the best outcomes for places. A quick comparison between the city and Orange County's experiences is useful here. Table 9.5 highlights how the City of Orlando put much greater restrictions on new development within its boundaries than Orange County. As a result, the city had far fewer new homes built, but the ones that were built were integrated into the city's fabric and had a strong sense of place. The high rate of foreclosure in Orange County further supports the Lucy and Phillips' (2000) theory of suburban decline, where they argue that new suburban areas with little sense of place will experience the greatest decline. While further research is needed to better test these findings, the research here supports the notion that the City of Orlando's investment in tight controls on development over the last ten to 20 years, along with their strict focus on creating neighborhoods with a sense of place (by implementing the principles of New Urbanism[5]), has resulted in far less new development within the city, but also far fewer foreclosed and abandoned properties than surrounding counties that took a different tack.

CHAPTER 10

Toward a new kind of city planning

I began this book by contrasting two families who have experienced the decline of their neighborhoods differently. Leroy and his wife and children struggle in a contracting Detroit neighborhood, surrounded by vacancy and abandonment; while Deborah and Hank hold their ground among vacant half-built homes in economically ravaged coastal Florida. Stories of shrinking Rustbelt neighborhoods are common, but in this book I have added a twist: decreased population means decreased housing density and can, in some places, mean *smaller, better* neighborhoods. The review of Census data shows that Rustbelt-wide, there are statistically significant relationships between a neighborhood's population decline and the decline in the number of occupied homes. The investigation into how such a relationships plays out in Flint, Michigan paves the way for a new kind of hope about what shrinking means for urban neighborhoods: if done well, depopulation can mean more room to breathe, more space for pets to run, space for gardens, and less congestion.

The Reverse Transect model points toward a conceptual framework for implementing such a neighborhood reconfiguration—extending smart decline from theory to practice. For the dozens of Sunbelt cities that experienced net housing decline from 2006 through 2009, this new model offers hope and one step further: guidance. The three case studies of shrinking Sunbelt cities shows how each might embrace smart decline to adapt their neighborhoods to match smaller populations. While each city has active economic development programs in place, cities ought to plan for decline at the same time. Invest in firm recruitment (if politically necessary), provide tax incentives and grants (if state and federal officials say you must), but city governments must be aware of the consequences of not preparing for a less rosy future. The lesson of the Flint case study is that not all neighborhoods manage decline as well as others. There is, in fact, a role for local governments (with the support of regional, state, and federal agencies) to manage that decline—even if fighting against it at the same time.

For the three Sunburnt Cities profiled here, confronting decline was far from natural. Those interviewed from Phoenix and Orlando could not have conceived of a future without population growth, while many in Fresno could imagine the tide turning toward shrinkage. This difference is partially explained by the history of each city, Fresno having already faced population decline and disinvestment in the middle of the twentieth century. Likewise, Fresno was most prepared to address the changes it was experiencing through aggressive code enforcement and abandoned building registration and tracking—tools that were less developed and less adroitly employed in Phoenix and Orlando.

For each of the three cities, it was easy enough to find neighborhoods at urban, suburban, and rural scales within city borders. While each city had at least one neighborhood that thrived during the period of study, an interesting finding here was that all had neighborhoods at each of the three scales that suffered drastically. Population decline and housing abandonment is manifested differently at each scale, but it is hard to say it is better or worse for each. Depopulation in the high-density (urban) Sunnyslope neighborhood of Phoenix meant a lot of semi-empty apartment buildings and some of the highest vacancy levels of the entire study. Depopulation in the medium-density (suburban) Englewood neighborhood of Orlando meant scores of "for rent" signs on two-family homes, high grass and weeds on nearly every block, and a growing crime problem. And turning to the West of 99 low-density (rural) neighborhood of Fresno the change was manifested in empty subdivisions, increased gang graffiti, and a plummeting of real estate values.

Across density levels, across these Sunburnt Cities, decline has meant different things to different places, but it is the Reverse Transect that connects them all. The Reverse Transect provides a common framework to help each neighborhood, in each city, reconfigure and redesign themselves as they move up or down along the transect; up or down because growth may come down the road and cities ought to be ready for it.

Perloff's (1980) work on planning for uncertainty is key here. If city officials do not know where population and employment levels are heading, for sure, then they will likely make huge mistakes in their policies and planning. Of course, it is impossible to know the future for certain, but Perloff argues that if we consider the risks of each possible future and create policy tools that are nimble enough, we can address change. It is not unlike Wiechmann's (2008) call for strategic flexibility to address the unknowns of population decline and growth. Through a case study of Dresden's population growth and decline from 1990 to 2007, Wiechmann concludes that neither planning for growth nor decline is the answer. Rather he argues that "Preparedness, robustness, and resilience displace to a certain extent rational analysis and error prevention as key qualifications of planning in shrinking cities" (Wiechmann 2008, p. 444). For Sunbelt cities only accustomed to rapid growth and now, many for the first time facing decline, there is much allure to the notion of strategic flexibility.

To some extent, strategic flexibility fits well into the model developed here for a Reverse Transect. Using the tools of smart growth and smart decline, cities can be strategic about managing changes along the metropolitan transect but be flexible about which direction a neighborhood might move in. While today a neighborhood may be in transition from ecozone 4 to 3, tomorrow it might move back to 4—cities can develop the appropriate policy tools to be ready for that, to be both strategic about how their community changes, while being flexible to handle change in either direction.

A number of very specific policy recommendations emerge from the research presented in this book. Below I outline recommendations for improved planning and public policy at the local, state, and federal levels. Next, I review some limitations of this research and offer suggestions for future research.

For local officials, the scope of what they can do is limited. As Peterson (1981) wrote about in *City Limits*, the ability for cities to address their problems is limited by exogenous state and federal control. Given those limits, cities can control their vision for the future and can align some regulations and policies in support of that vision. Crafting a vision that comports with reasonable demographic projections is the first task for any shrinking city. Overcoming the political challenges of growth-obsessed cultures is not insignificant, but if accomplished, then cities can begin to view themselves as *smaller* and *better*. This vision can be accomplished through a master planning process or through a scaled-back visioning process that includes a reasonable level of background research. Either way, the end product should express a common future that does not depend upon unlikely growth scenarios, but rather is grounded in the likely and less pleasant future of decline.

For local officials, the next step is to develop regulatory, policy, and planning tools and techniques to manage decline. I suggest the following:

1) Discourage new housing construction in already high vacancy residential districts

There are numerous actions routinely taken by local governments that promote new housing construction, whether local officials realize it or not. Setting up their zoning ordinances to allow new construction by right increases the ease and quantity of new construction. Instead, cities should routinely require that builders obtain special permits for construction in zones deemed to have an excess supply of housing. A special permit process allows for consideration by local officials of the costs and benefits of new construction and provides a forum for public debate. For many shrinking cities, the bulk of new construction is in the form of low-income tax credit housing—subsidized by the federal government. Local governments can work with HUD and affordable housing developers to steer new units away from those neighborhoods with an excess supply of housing. The same is true for the often admirable work of Habitat for Humanity. Local officials can tap the spirit and energy of Habitat leaders to build new housing only where demand remains high and instead focus their efforts on deconstruction and demolition of derelict structures. The Saginaw, Michigan affiliate of Habitat did just that in 2009 and 2010 when they demolished over 200 abandoned homes, and about 100 other Habitat affiliates are also in the deconstruction business (Davey 2009).

2) Require property or mortgage owners to protect and maintain vacant buildings

Building construction and renovation codes are standard practice in municipalities throughout the U.S. and much of the developed world. What is less common are property maintenance codes that municipalities adopt in the same way as building codes, but allow them to require lawn and landscaping care and other building exterior maintenance. The International Property Maintenance Code of 2006 provides standard, adoptable language for cities and towns to lay out minimum maintenance standards and then collect fines and penalties for property owners (or banks in the case of foreclosures) who do not meet those standards. Local governments should also adopt the techniques employed in Fresno through its abandoned buildings and foreclosed building registration ordinances. These measures help a municipality track and monitor abandoned and foreclosed properties so that they can be proactive in code enforcement.

3) Expedite the process of placing tax-reverted properties into public ownership through a land bank

The Genesee County Land Bank in Michigan has been widely heralded as an effective model for addressing widespread abandonment. Sunburnt Cities can learn from the Flint example and adopt land banking practices that quickly get tax delinquent properties that are blighting their neighborhoods into the hands of a centralized government agency with planning authority. While not always ideal, in a shrinking city a centralized agency can use strategic planning processes to consider the reuse of such land and buildings, improving the equilibrium of the housing market.

4) Offer these tax-reverted properties to abutters at low cost

The blotting process described earlier in the book allows the density levels of shrinking places to decline gradually as one homeowner after another adds abutting lots to their property. Some of this blotting happens as part of the legal property transfer process, but some occurs through old-fashioned squatting. Either way, local governments ought to facilitate a process of reducing density in shrinking places in order to meet the needs of those residents who stay behind for larger house lots. Transit advocates tend to reject any redesign or reconfiguration of urban environments that would decrease density for fears that transit would become harder to financially support. These are valid concerns and transit planners should use shrinkage as an opportunity to challenge density requirements and to rethink what a fair and equitable transit system should look like in the face of depopulation.

5) Quickly rehabilitate or demolish publicly owned abandoned buildings

While local governments may encounter difficulties demolishing or forcing the rehabilitation of privately owned property, they exert much greater power when it comes to publicly owned buildings. Political concerns might constrict the ability of a mayor to demolish a local school or redevelop a local library for warehousing purposes, but depopulation almost always means decreased tax revenues for municipalities and the need to reduce public services. These are tough choices for elected leaders to make, but a smaller city means a smaller government footprint, too. Consequently, rehabbing or demolishing empty or semi-abandoned publicly owned buildings need to be a priority for local governments trying to manage decline.

6) Provide subsidies to assist in the rehabilitation or demolition of privately owned abandoned buildings

While much harder than fixing up or demolishing publicly owned structures, local governments can influence how the private building stock of their community shrinks. Through tax incentive and direct subsidies, local governments can help property owners raze derelict structures or rehabilitate them for alternative uses (where demand might be present). Local governments can achieve an economy of scale by hiring a demolition contractor at a low per housing unit rate and pass those savings on to property owners looking to demolish their units.

7) Invest in the protection and maintenance of publicly owned vacant lots

Too few cities and towns are aggressive in caring for and protecting their own vacant lots. An investment in low-mow grasses and low maintenance landscaping on these lots can go far in keeping government costs down. Kent State University (2009) urban designers developed a guide for low cost and easy care of vacant lots. With attention to these kinds of details and an effective crime management strategy, cities and towns can keep their vacant lots out of trouble and help to contribute to stable, healthy neighborhoods.

8) Provide grants and low-cost loans to encourage property owners to convert active residential lands into recreational or agricultural lands

While it is difficult for local governments to force a property owner to change the use of her property, it is possible to provide incentives through grants and low-cost loans to do so. The most politically feasible successor land use to residential in most shrinking places is either recreational or agricultural.[1] Therefore, specific and detailed plans should be drawn up by local governments to invest strategically in helping that to happen through incentive mechanisms.

9) Implement Relaxed Zoning codes that provide for a trigger when neighborhoods experience decline to allow for a broader range of uses than are typically allowed in residential neighborhoods

Returning to the idea presented in Chapter 2, Relaxed Zoning can be adopted widely as an overlay zone in areas of a community expected to see future population decline. The overlay zone will only be triggered when a neighborhood reaches a certain level of vacancy, whereby a much broader range of uses beyond residential would be allowed. This kind of zoning overlay could be adopted in a range of cities and towns, customizable to meet the needs of cities facing shrinkage.

10) Assist residents in shrinking areas to help them relocate to places with better employment prospects

Perhaps the most controversial of these recommendations, the idea of moving people, is seen by many as draconian and mean-spirited. In fact, I have found in this research that most people who can leave an area when faced with poor employment prospects, do leave. It is largely the people who do not have the financial resources to make a move who stay behind. The effect for many shrinking cities is a growing concentration of poorer and poorer residents as a city loses its population. Financial incentives to facilitate relocation help to address this cycle of escalating poverty rates.

It smooths out the economists' Tiebolt model introduced in Chapter 2 that suggests that people will follow job opportunities. If a person is so desperately poor and cannot move, it does not matter how good the employment prospects might be elsewhere.

At the state level, funds can be made available to assist local governments in implementing the above policies and when they exist, barriers can be removed. For example, in Ohio state law was changed in February 2009 to allow local governments to create land banks (S.B. 353, 127th General Assembly).

At the federal level, the same is true. Many federal grant programs could more effectively be channeled to bolster the ability of local governments to effectively address depopulation, as recommended in the Brookings Institution report described in Chapter 2 (Mallach 2010). At present, most federal grants designed to support neighborhood and community development require that new jobs be created to qualify for the funding. This burden is quite a harsh one for shrinking cities looking to retrofit their footprint to be smaller. Additionally, much of the "entitlement" funding that cities receive from the federal government for education, health, and community development are tied to population levels—the more people, the more money. These formulas are particularly injurious to those cities that are losing population. These formulas are the very meat behind the political demands for growth; adjustments to favor cities working toward improved quality of life (in spite of lower population levels) could do much to shift the tide toward better smart decline practices.

There are a number of important limitations to the research presented here. In any scholarly endeavor, there are restrictions on time and resources and compromises are always made with the hope of maintaining validity and reliability. The first limitation is in how I defined the Sunbelt. With a keen interest in understanding and analyzing large city policymaking and planning, I restricted the empirical analysis primarily to within large city boundaries. But, undoubtedly, the Sunbelt as a region comprises those vast suburban and exurban territories surrounding major Sunbelt cities. Their omission from this research is defensible, but much can be learned from the broader patterns of growth and decline outside of large cities. For future research, I suggest others examine these suburbs and outlying areas to understand how they were affected by the Great Recession and how those local governments responded. The larger question of smart decline could also be better understood within a broader metropolitan context: can the Reverse Transect operate in far flung suburbs?

Within the investigation of Sunbelt Cities, my decision to focus on residential land-use change and residential density was a very intentional one, but an important limitation to the broader generalizability of the research. Future research could look more generally at how commercial, institutional, and industrial land uses and densities shift in depopulating neighborhoods and how local governments can and should respond. I began such an inquiry with my first book *Polluted and Dangerous: America's Worst Abandoned Properties and What Can Be Done About Them* (2009) where I studied the impacts of depopulation and economic decline on large commercial and industrial properties in major U.S. cities. There is much more room for further examination of these topics in understanding how traditional downtowns can more successfully adapt to lower demand for retail and office uses, how religious and educational institutions can reinvent themselves during periods of decreased membership and attendance, how university campuses facing declining enrollments can adapt to smaller sizes, and what role public policy and planning can play in supporting this restructuring through smart decline.

Another limitation of the research is the choice to only examine in close detail four cities. To look at more cities offers the opportunity for more diversity of housing, economic, and geographical characteristics among the cases. However, doing so limits the depth in which each case can be explored—the essential trade-off in all questions of research design between increasing sample size and increasing the quality of the sample. Future research could complement this study with less in-depth studies of a larger number of Sunbelt cities, in order to determine which unique factors might be most influential in contributing to neighborhood change and determining policy and planning responses.

While these limitations are important to note, in general, the findings here are both valid and reliable and contribute to our broader understanding of the problems of depopulation, how cities respond, and how smart decline can help. Cities are often so eager to step into the fray and *combat* the problems of depopulation and job loss, the findings presented here suggest that doing so might not be so prudent. Instead, local officials should be attuned to the larger demographic and economic forces at work in their community, in their region, and in their country to be able to craft sensible and realistic policies and plans to respond to those changes. As Wiechman (2008) explained, those responses must be drawn up in a flexible way so that when change happens again, those cities will be ready.

One of the biggest incentives for a city to embrace smart decline is that if it works for them and they create *smaller*, *better* neighborhoods and improve the overall quality of life for residents, people will be attracted to that city and the population will rise. Cleverly designed policy and planning tools will allow quick and easy responses to that change so that neighborhoods can move effortlessly along the Reverse Transect.

Buddhist philosopher Mingyur Rinpoche was quoted as saying "make friends with the problem" in a recent Phoenix newspaper editorial mulling the foreclosure-related problems facing Phoenix (Valdez 2009). For Phoenicians and all those in the Sunbelt affected by foreclosure and housing abandonment that is just the kind of optimism that is needed. Cities that experienced unprecedented growth for decades are facing a new kind of challenge and are largely turning to growth to fix it. The $1 million per employee firm recruitment strategy in Orlando is probably the worst example of this.

The lessons of history are critical here, in Rust's (1975) review he found that the cities with the biggest population losses were the ones that boomed the most earlier. These constant shifts in boom and bust are a result of the regular waxing and waning of locational advantage. By looking from the 1800s to 1970s Rust showed that you may have locational advantages one decade, but not another (near a canal one decade, near a rail crossing another; in the desert with sun and fun one decade, in a climate insensitive and environmentally stressed area another). Rather than invest heavy resources into reshaping advantage, cities can learn from the lessons in this book and focus on improving the quality of life of the people left behind, to retrofit the physical environment of cities to match smaller populations, and most important of all: to prepare for future changes and be flexible.

Appendices

Appendix A

1980 cities

Minneapolis

Units	Acreage	Density (units/ acre)	Change in population	Change in occupied units	New number of units	New density	% change in density
300	100	3.0	−100	51	351	3.51	16.95%
250	100	2.5	−100	51	301	3.01	20.34%
200	100	2.0	−100	51	251	2.51	25.43%
150	100	1.5	−100	51	201	2.01	33.91%
100	100	1.0	−100	51	151	1.51	50.86%

Reading

Units	Acreage	Density (units/ acre)	Change in population	Change in occupied units	New number of units	New density	% change in density
300	100	3.0	−100	−84	216	2.16	−28.11%
250	100	2.5	−100	−84	166	1.66	−33.73%
200	100	2.0	−100	−84	116	1.16	−42.16%
150	100	1.5	−100	−84	66	0.66	−56.22%
100	100	1.0	−100	−84	16	0.16	−84.33%

Rochester

Units	Acreage	Density (units/ acre)	Change in population	Change in occupied units	New number of units	New density	% change in density
300	100	3.0	−100	−21	279	2.79	−7.12%
250	100	2.5	−100	−21	229	2.29	−8.55%
200	100	2.0	−100	−21	179	1.79	−10.68%
150	100	1.5	−100	−21	129	1.29	−14.25%
100	100	1.0	−100	−21	79	0.79	−21.37%

Scranton

Units	Acreage	Density (units/acre)	Change in population	Change in occupied units	New number of units	New density	% change in density
300	100	3.0	−100	−107	193	1.93	−35.83%
250	100	2.5	−100	−107	143	1.43	−43.00%
200	100	2.0	−100	−107	93	0.93	−53.74%
150	100	1.5	−100	−107	43	0.43	−71.66%
100	100	1.0	−100	−107	−7	−0.07	−107.49%

St. Louis

Units	Acreage	Density (units/acre)	Change in population	Change in occupied units	New number of units	New density	% change in density
300	100	3.0	−100	−191	109	1.09	−63.73%
250	100	2.5	−100	−191	59	0.59	−76.48%
200	100	2.0	−100	−191	9	0.09	−95.60%
150	100	1.5	−100	−191	−41	−0.41	−127.46%
100	100	1.0	−100	−191	−91	−0.91	−191.19%

Syracuse

Units	Acreage	Density (units/acre)	Change in population	Change in occupied units	New number of units	New density	% change in density
300	100	3.0	−100	−113	187	1.87	−37.69%
250	100	2.5	−100	−113	363	3.63	−45.22%
200	100	2.0	−100	−113	313	3.13	−56.53%
150	100	1.5	−100	−113	263	2.63	−75.37%
100	100	1.0	−100	−113	213	2.13	−113.06%

Trenton

Units	Acreage	Density (units/acre)	Change in population	Change in occupied units	New number of units	New density	% change in density
300	100	3.0	−100	35	335	3.35	11.60%
250	100	2.5	−100	35	285	2.85	13.91%
200	100	2.0	−100	35	235	2.35	17.39%
150	100	1.5	−100	35	185	1.85	23.19%
100	100	1.0	−100	35	135	1.35	34.79%

Youngstown

Units	Acreage	Density (units/ acre)	Change in population	Change in occupied units	New number of units	New density	% change in density
300	100	3.0	−100	−126	174	1.74	−42.15%
250	100	2.5	−100	−126	124	1.24	−50.58%
200	100	2.0	−100	−126	74	0.74	−63.22%
150	100	1.5	−100	−126	24	0.24	−84.30%
100	100	1.0	−100	−126	−26	−0.26	−126.44%

Boston

Units	Acreage	Density (units/ acre)	Change in population	Change in occupied units	New number of units	New density	% change in density
300	100	3.0	−100	88	388	3.88	29.17%
250	100	2.5	−100	88	338	3.38	35.01%
200	100	2.0	−100	88	288	2.88	43.76%
150	100	1.5	−100	88	238	2.38	58.35%
100	100	1.0	−100	88	188	1.88	87.52%

Buffalo

Units	Acreage	Density (units/ acre)	Change in population	Change in occupied units	New number of units	New density	% change in density
300	100	3.0	−100	−26	274	2.74	−8.52%
250	100	2.5	−100	−26	224	2.24	−10.22%
200	100	2.0	−100	−26	174	1.74	−12.77%
150	100	1.5	−100	−26	124	1.24	−17.03%
100	100	1.0	−100	−26	74	0.74	−25.55%

Camden

Units	Acreage	Density (units/ acre)	Change in population	Change in occupied units	New number of units	New density	% change in density
300	100	3.0	−100	−147	153	1.53	−49.13%
250	100	2.5	−100	−147	397	3.97	−58.95%
200	100	2.0	−100	−147	347	3.47	−73.69%
150	100	1.5	−100	−147	297	2.97	−98.25%
100	100	1.0	−100	−147	247	2.47	−147.38%

Canton

Units	Acreage	Density (units/acre)	Change in population	Change in occupied units	New number of units	New density	% change in density
300	100	3.0	−100	−75	225	2.25	−25.01%
250	100	2.5	−100	−75	325	3.25	−30.02%
200	100	2.0	−100	−75	275	2.75	−37.52%
150	100	1.5	−100	−75	225	2.25	−50.03%
100	100	1.0	−100	−75	175	1.75	−75.04%

Cleveland

Units	Acreage	Density (units/acre)	Change in population	Change in occupied units	New number of units	New density	% change in density
300	100	3.0	−100	−116	184	1.84	−38.76%
250	100	2.5	−100	−116	366	3.66	−46.51%
200	100	2.0	−100	−116	316	3.16	−58.14%
150	100	1.5	−100	−116	266	2.66	−77.52%
100	100	1.0	−100	−116	216	2.16	−116.28%

Dayton

Units	Acreage	Density (units/acre)	Change in population	Change in occupied units	New number of units	New density	% change in density
300	100	3.0	−100	−66	234	2.34	−22.16%
250	100	2.5	−100	−66	316	3.16	−26.60%
200	100	2.0	−100	−66	266	2.66	−33.25%
150	100	1.5	−100	−66	216	2.16	−44.33%
100	100	1.0	−100	−66	166	1.66	−66.49%

Detroit

Units	Acreage	Density (units/acre)	Change in population	Change in occupied units	New number of units	New density	% change in density
300	100	3.0	−100	−103	197	1.97	−34.45%
250	100	2.5	−100	−103	353	3.53	−41.34%
200	100	2.0	−100	−103	303	3.03	−51.68%
150	100	1.5	−100	−103	253	2.53	−68.91%
100	100	1.0	−100	−103	203	2.03	−103.36%

Flint

Units	Acreage	Density (units/ acre)	Change in population	Change in occupied units	New number of units	New density	% change in density
300	100	3.0	−100	−127	173	1.73	−42.20%
250	100	2.5	−100	−127	377	3.77	−50.64%
200	100	2.0	−100	−127	327	3.27	−63.30%
150	100	1.5	−100	−127	277	2.77	−84.39%
100	100	1.0	−100	−127	227	2.27	−126.59%

Gary

Units	Acreage	Density (units/ acre)	Change in population	Change in occupied units	New number of units	New density	% change in density
300	100	3.0	−100	−116	184	1.84	−38.76%
250	100	2.5	−100	−116	366	3.66	−46.51%
200	100	2.0	−100	−116	316	3.16	−58.13%
150	100	1.5	−100	−116	266	2.66	−77.51%
100	100	1.0	−100	−116	216	2.16	−116.27%

Hartford

Units	Acreage	Density (units/ acre)	Change in population	Change in occupied units	New number of units	New density	% change in density
300	100	3.0	−100	−104	196	1.96	−34.79%
250	100	2.5	−100	−104	354	3.54	−41.75%
200	100	2.0	−100	−104	304	3.04	−52.18%
150	100	1.5	−100	−104	254	2.54	−69.58%
100	100	1.0	−100	−104	204	2.04	−104.37%

Newark

Units	Acreage	Density (units/ acre)	Change in population	Change in occupied units	New number of units	New density	% change in density
300	100	3.0	−100	−139	161	1.61	−46.47%
250	100	2.5	−100	−139	389	3.89	−55.76%
200	100	2.0	−100	−139	339	3.39	−69.70%
150	100	1.5	−100	−139	289	2.89	−92.94%
100	100	1.0	−100	−139	239	2.39	−139.40%

Philadelphia

Units	Acreage	Density (units/acre)	Change in population	Change in occupied units	New number of units	New density	% change in density
300	100	3.0	−100	−148	152	1.52	−49.42%
250	100	2.5	−100	−148	398	3.98	−59.30%
200	100	2.0	−100	−148	348	3.48	−74.13%
150	100	1.5	−100	−148	298	2.98	−98.84%
100	100	1.0	−100	−148	248	2.48	−148.26%

Pittsburg

Units	Acreage	Density (units/acre)	Change in population	Change in occupied units	New number of units	New density	% change in density
300	100	3.0	−100	−124	176	1.76	−41.22%
250	100	2.5	−100	−124	374	3.74	−49.46%
200	100	2.0	−100	−124	324	3.24	−61.82%
150	100	1.5	−100	−124	274	2.74	−82.43%
100	100	1.0	−100	−124	224	2.24	−123.65%

Providence

Units	Acreage	Density (units/acre)	Change in population	Change in occupied units	New number of units	New density	% change in density
300	100	3.0	−100	−236	64	0.64	−78.78%
250	100	2.5	−100	−236	486	4.86	−94.54%
200	100	2.0	−100	−236	436	4.36	−118.17%
150	100	1.5	−100	−236	386	3.86	−157.56%
100	100	1.0	−100	−236	336	3.36	−236.34%

1990 cities

Minneapolis

Units	Acreage	Density (units/ acre)	Change in population	Change in occupied units	New number of units	New density	% change in density
300	100	3.0	−100	−170	130	1.30	−56.60%
250	100	2.5	−100	−170	80	0.80	−67.92%
200	100	2.0	−100	−170	30	0.30	−84.90%
150	100	1.5	−100	−170	−20	−0.20	−113.19%
100	100	1.0	−100	−170	−70	−0.70	−169.79%

Reading

Units	Acreage	Density (units/ acre)	Change in population	Change in occupied units	New number of units	New density	% change in density
300	100	3.0	−100	39	339	3.39	13.10%
250	100	2.5	−100	39	289	2.89	15.72%
200	100	2.0	−100	39	239	2.39	19.65%
150	100	1.5	−100	39	189	1.89	26.21%
100	100	1.0	−100	39	139	1.39	39.31%

Rochester

Units	Acreage	Density (units/ acre)	Change in population	Change in occupied units	New number of units	New density	% change in density
300	100	3.0	−100	−81	219	2.19	−27.13%
250	100	2.5	−100	−81	169	1.69	−32.55%
200	100	2.0	−100	−81	119	1.19	−40.69%
150	100	1.5	−100	−81	69	0.69	−54.25%
100	100	1.0	−100	−81	19	0.19	−81.38%

Scranton

Units	Acreage	Density (units/ acre)	Change in population	Change in occupied units	New number of units	New density	% change in density
300	100	3.0	−100	−104	196	1.96	−34.62%
250	100	2.5	−100	−104	146	1.46	−41.55%
200	100	2.0	−100	−104	96	0.96	−51.93%
150	100	1.5	−100	−104	46	0.46	−69.24%
100	100	1.0	−100	−104	−4	−0.04	−103.87%

St. Louis

Units	Acreage	Density (units/acre)	Change in population	Change in occupied units	New number of units	New density	% change in density
300	100	3.0	−100	−19	281	2.81	−6.30%
250	100	2.5	−100	−19	231	2.31	−7.56%
200	100	2.0	−100	−19	181	1.81	−9.45%
150	100	1.5	−100	−19	131	1.31	−12.61%
100	100	1.0	−100	−19	81	0.81	−18.91%

Syracuse

Units	Acreage	Density (units/acre)	Change in population	Change in occupied units	New number of units	New density	% change in density
300	100	3.0	−100	−131	169	1.69	−43.75%
250	100	2.5	−100	−131	119	1.19	−52.49%
200	100	2.0	−100	−131	69	0.69	−65.62%
150	100	1.5	−100	−131	19	0.19	−87.49%
100	100	1.0	−100	−131	−31	−0.31	−131.24%

Trenton

Units	Acreage	Density (units/acre)	Change in population	Change in occupied units	New number of units	New density	% change in density
300	100	3.0	−100	−219	81	0.81	−73.00%
250	100	2.5	−100	−219	31	0.31	−87.60%
200	100	2.0	−100	−219	−19	−0.19	−109.51%
150	100	1.5	−100	−219	−69	−0.69	−146.01%
100	100	1.0	−100	−219	−119	−1.19	−219.01%

Youngstown

Units	Acreage	Density (units/acre)	Change in population	Change in occupied units	New number of units	New density	% change in density
300	100	3.0	−100	−149	151	1.51	−49.77%
250	100	2.5	−100	−149	101	1.01	−59.72%
200	100	2.0	−100	−149	51	0.51	−74.65%
150	100	1.5	−100	−149	1	0.01	−99.54%
100	100	1.0	−100	−149	−49	−0.49	−149.30%

Boston

Units	Acreage	Density (units/ acre)	Change in population	Change in occupied units	New number of units	New density	% change in density
300	100	3.0	−100	−110	190	1.90	−36.67%
250	100	2.5	−100	−110	140	1.40	−44.00%
200	100	2.0	−100	−110	90	0.90	−55.00%
150	100	1.5	−100	−110	40	0.40	−73.33%
100	100	1.0	−100	−110	−10	−0.10	−110.00%

Buffalo

Units	Acreage	Density (units/ acre)	Change in population	Change in occupied units	New number of units	New density	% change in density
300	100	3.0	−100	−120	180	1.80	−39.86%
250	100	2.5	−100	−120	130	1.30	−47.83%
200	100	2.0	−100	−120	80	0.80	−59.79%
150	100	1.5	−100	−120	30	0.30	−79.72%
100	100	1.0	−100	−120	−20	−0.20	−119.58%

Camden

Units	Acreage	Density (units/ acre)	Change in population	Change in occupied units	New number of units	New density	% change in density
300	100	3.0	−100	−117	183	1.83	−38.86%
250	100	2.5	−100	−117	133	1.33	−46.63%
200	100	2.0	−100	−117	83	0.83	−58.29%
150	100	1.5	−100	−117	33	0.33	−77.72%
100	100	1.0	−100	−117	−17	−0.17	−116.58%

Canton

Units	Acreage	Density (units/ acre)	Change in population	Change in occupied units	New number of units	New density	% change in density
300	100	3.0	−100	−124	176	1.76	−41.25%
250	100	2.5	−100	−124	126	1.26	−49.50%
200	100	2.0	−100	−124	76	0.76	−61.87%
150	100	1.5	−100	−124	26	0.26	−82.50%
100	100	1.0	−100	−124	−24	−0.24	−123.74%

Cleveland

Units	Acreage	Density (units/ acre)	Change in population	Change in occupied units	New number of units	New density	% change in density
300	100	3.0	−100	−131	169	1.69	−43.57%
250	100	2.5	−100	−131	119	1.19	−52.28%
200	100	2.0	−100	−131	69	0.69	−65.35%
150	100	1.5	−100	−131	19	0.19	−87.13%
100	100	1.0	−100	−131	−31	−0.31	−130.70%

Dayton

Units	Acreage	Density (units/ acre)	Change in population	Change in occupied units	New number of units	New density	% change in density
300	100	3.0	−100	−131	169	1.69	−43.68%
250	100	2.5	−100	−131	119	1.19	−52.41%
200	100	2.0	−100	−131	69	0.69	−65.51%
150	100	1.5	−100	−131	19	0.19	−87.35%
100	100	1.0	−100	−131	−31	−0.31	−131.03%

Detroit

Units	Acreage	Density (units/ acre)	Change in population	Change in occupied units	New number of units	New density	% change in Density
300	100	3.0	−100	−237	63	0.63	−78.90%
250	100	2.5	−100	−237	13	0.13	−94.68%
200	100	2.0	−100	−237	−37	−0.37	−118.35%
150	100	1.5	−100	−237	−87	−0.87	−157.80%
100	100	1.0	−100	−237	−137	−1.37	−236.69%

Flint

Units	Acreage	Density (units/ acre)	Change in population	Change in occupied units	New number of units	New Density	% change in Density
300	100	3.0	−100	−146	154	1.54	−48.74%
250	100	2.5	−100	−146	104	1.04	−58.49%
200	100	2.0	−100	−146	54	0.54	−73.11%
150	100	1.5	−100	−146	4	0.04	−97.48%
100	100	1.0	−100	−146	−46	−0.46	−146.23%

Gary

Units	Acreage	Density (units/ acre)	Change in population	Change in occupied units	New number of units	New density	% change in density
300	100	3.0	−100	−115	185	1.85	−38.30%
250	100	2.5	−100	−115	135	1.35	−45.96%
200	100	2.0	−100	−115	85	0.85	−57.45%
150	100	1.5	−100	−115	35	0.35	−76.60%
100	100	1.0	−100	−115	−15	−0.15	−114.89%

Hartford

Units	Acreage	Density (units/ acre)	Change in population	Change in occupied units	New number of units	New density	% change in density
300	100	3.0	−100	−153	147	1.47	−50.86%
250	100	2.5	−100	−153	97	0.97	−61.03%
200	100	2.0	−100	−153	47	0.47	−76.29%
150	100	1.5	−100	−153	−3	−0.03	−101.71%
100	100	1.0	−100	−153	−53	−0.53	−152.57%

Newark

Units	Acreage	Density (units/ acre)	Change in population	Change in occupied units	New number of units	New density	% change in density
300	100	3.0	−100	−135	165	1.65	−45.05%
250	100	2.5	−100	−135	115	1.15	−54.06%
200	100	2.0	−100	−135	65	0.65	−67.57%
150	100	1.5	−100	−135	15	0.15	−90.10%
100	100	1.0	−100	−135	−35	−0.35	−135.14%

Philadelphia

Units	Acreage	Density (units/ acre)	Change in population	Change in occupied units	New number of units	New density	% change in density
300	100	3.0	−100	−92	208	2.08	−30.78%
250	100	2.5	−100	−92	158	1.58	−36.94%
200	100	2.0	−100	−92	108	1.08	−46.18%
150	100	1.5	−100	−92	58	0.58	−61.57%
100	100	1.0	−100	−92	8	0.08	−92.35%

Pittsburg

Units	Acreage	Density (units/ acre)	Change in population	Change in occupied units	New number of units	New density	% change in density
300	100	3.0	−100	−95	205	2.05	−31.83%
250	100	2.5	−100	−95	155	1.55	−38.20%
200	100	2.0	−100	−95	105	1.05	−47.74%
150	100	1.5	−100	−95	55	0.55	−63.66%
100	100	1.0	−100	−95	5	0.05	−95.49%

Providence

Units	Acreage	Density (units/ acre)	Change in population	Change in occupied units	New number of units	New density	% change in density
300	100	3.0	−100	−308	−8	−0.08	−102.57%
250	100	2.5	−100	−308	−58	−0.58	−123.09%
200	100	2.0	−100	−308	−108	−1.08	−153.86%
150	100	1.5	−100	−308	−158	−1.58	−205.14%
100	100	1.0	−100	−308	−208	−2.08	−307.71%

2000 cities

Minneapolis

Units	Acreage	Density (units/ acre)	Lost people	Lost units	New number of units	New density	% decline in density
300	100	3.0	−100	−50	250	2.50	−16.61%
250	100	2.5	−100	−50	200	2.00	−19.93%
200	100	2.0	−100	−50	150	1.50	−24.91%
150	100	1.5	−100	−50	100	1.00	−33.21%
100	100	1.0	−100	−50	50	0.50	−49.82%

Reading

Units	Acreage	Density (units/ acre)	Lost people	Lost units	New number of units	New density	% decline in density
300	100	3.0	−100	−163	137	1.37	−54.18%
250	100	2.5	−100	−163	87	0.87	−65.02%
200	100	2.0	−100	−163	37	0.37	−81.27%
150	100	1.5	−100	−163	−13	−0.13	−108.36%
100	100	1.0	−100	−163	−63	−0.63	−162.54%

Rochester

Units	Acreage	Density (units/ acre)	Lost people	Lost units	New number of units	New density	% decline in density
300	100	3.0	−100	−92	208	2.08	−30.65%
250	100	2.5	−100	−92	158	1.58	−36.77%
200	100	2.0	−100	−92	108	1.08	−45.97%
150	100	1.5	−100	−92	58	0.58	−61.29%
100	100	1.0	−100	−92	8	0.08	−91.94%

Scranton

Units	Acreage	Density (units/ acre)	Lost people	Lost units	New number of units	New density	% decline in density
300	100	3.0	−100	−25	275	2.75	−8.27%
250	100	2.5	−100	−25	225	2.25	−9.92%
200	100	2.0	−100	−25	175	1.75	−12.41%
150	100	1.5	−100	−25	125	1.25	−16.54%
100	100	1.0	−100	−25	75	0.75	−24.81%

St. Louis

Units	Acreage	Density (units/ acre)	Lost people	Lost units	New number of units	New density	% decline in density
300	100	3.0	−100	−121	179	1.79	−40.18%
250	100	2.5	−100	−121	129	1.29	−48.22%
200	100	2.0	−100	−121	79	0.79	−60.27%
150	100	1.5	−100	−121	29	0.29	−80.36%
100	100	1.0	−100	−121	−21	−0.21	−120.54%

Syracuse

Units	Acreage	Density (units/ acre)	Lost people	Lost units	New number of units	New density	% decline in density
300	100	3.0	−100	−52	248	2.48	−17.30%
250	100	2.5	−100	−52	198	1.98	−20.77%
200	100	2.0	−100	−52	148	1.48	−25.96%
150	100	1.5	−100	−52	98	0.98	−34.61%
100	100	1.0	−100	−52	48	0.48	−51.91%

Trenton

Units	Acreage	Density (units/ acre)	Lost people	Lost units	New number of units	New density	% decline in density
300	100	3.0	−100	−39	261	2.61	−13.10%
250	100	2.5	−100	−39	211	2.11	−15.72%
200	100	2.0	−100	−39	161	1.61	−19.64%
150	100	1.5	−100	−39	111	1.11	−26.19%
100	100	1.0	−100	−39	61	0.61	−39.29%

Youngstown

Units	Acreage	Density (units/ acre)	Lost people	Lost units	New number of units	New density	% decline in density
300	100	3.0	−100	−58	242	2.42	−19.26%
250	100	2.5	−100	−58	192	1.92	−23.11%
200	100	2.0	−100	−58	142	1.42	−28.89%
150	100	1.5	−100	−58	92	0.92	−38.52%
100	100	1.0	−100	−58	42	0.42	−57.78%

Boston

Units	Acreage	Density (units/ acre)	Lost people	Lost units	New number of units	New density	% decline in density
300	100	3.0	−100	−68	232	2.32	−22.62%
250	100	2.5	−100	−68	182	1.82	−27.14%
200	100	2.0	−100	−68	132	1.32	−33.93%
150	100	1.5	−100	−68	82	0.82	−45.23%
100	100	1.0	−100	−68	32	0.32	−67.85%

Buffalo

Units	Acreage	Density (units/ acre)	Lost people	Lost units	New number of units	New density	% decline in density
300	100	3.0	−100	−79	221	2.21	−26.22%
250	100	2.5	−100	−79	171	1.71	−31.46%
200	100	2.0	−100	−79	121	1.21	−39.33%
150	100	1.5	−100	−79	71	0.71	−52.44%
100	100	1.0	−100	−79	21	0.21	−78.66%

Camden

Units	Acreage	Density (units/ acre)	Lost people	Lost units	New number of units	New density	% decline in density
300	100	3.0	−100	−53	247	2.47	−17.67%
250	100	2.5	−100	−53	197	1.97	−21.20%
200	100	2.0	−100	−53	147	1.47	−26.50%
150	100	1.5	−100	−53	97	0.97	−35.33%
100	100	1.0	−100	−53	47	0.47	−53.00%

Canton

Units	Acreage	Density (units/ acre)	Lost people	Lost units	New number of units	New density	% decline in density
300	100	3.0	−100	−55	245	2.45	−18.39%
250	100	2.5	−100	−55	195	1.95	−22.06%
200	100	2.0	−100	−55	145	1.45	−27.58%
150	100	1.5	−100	−55	95	0.95	−36.77%
100	100	1.0	−100	−55	45	0.45	−55.16%

Cleveland

Units	Acreage	Density (units/ acre)	Lost people	Lost units	New number of units	New density	% decline in density
300	100	3.0	−100	−74	226	2.26	−24.59%
250	100	2.5	−100	−74	176	1.76	−29.50%
200	100	2.0	−100	−74	126	1.26	−36.88%
150	100	1.5	−100	−74	76	0.76	−49.17%
100	100	1.0	−100	−74	26	0.26	−73.76%

Dayton

Units	Acreage	Density (units/ acre)	Lost people	Lost units	New number of units	New density	% decline in density
300	100	3.0	−100	−31	269	2.69	−10.25%
250	100	2.5	−100	−31	219	2.19	−12.29%
200	100	2.0	−100	−31	169	1.69	−15.37%
150	100	1.5	−100	−31	119	1.19	−20.49%
100	100	1.0	−100	−31	69	0.69	−30.74%

Detroit

Units	Acreage	Density (units/ acre)	Lost people	Lost units	New number of units	New density	% decline in density
300	100	3.0	−100	−89	211	2.11	−29.61%
250	100	2.5	−100	−89	161	1.61	−35.54%
200	100	2.0	−100	−89	111	1.11	−44.42%
150	100	1.5	−100	−89	61	0.61	−59.23%
100	100	1.0	−100	−89	11	0.11	−88.84%

Flint

Units	Acreage	Density (units/ acre)	Lost people	Lost units	New number of units	New density	% decline in density
300	100	3.0	−100	−74	226	2.26	−24.74%
250	100	2.5	−100	−74	176	1.76	−29.68%
200	100	2.0	−100	−74	126	1.26	−37.10%
150	100	1.5	−100	−74	76	0.76	−49.47%
100	100	1.0	−100	−74	26	0.26	−74.21%

Gary

Units	Acreage	Density (units/ acre)	Lost people	Lost units	New number of units	New density	% decline in density
300	100	3.0	−100	−130	170	1.70	−43.31%
250	100	2.5	−100	−130	120	1.20	−51.97%
200	100	2.0	−100	−130	70	0.70	−64.96%
150	100	1.5	−100	−130	20	0.20	−86.61%
100	100	1.0	−100	−130	−30	−0.30	−129.92%

Hartford

Units	Acreage	Density (units/ acre)	Lost people	Lost units	New number of units	New density	% decline in density
300	100	3.0	−100	−45	255	2.55	−15.05%
250	100	2.5	−100	−45	205	2.05	−18.05%
200	100	2.0	−100	−45	155	1.55	−22.57%
150	100	1.5	−100	−45	105	1.05	−30.09%
100	100	1.0	−100	−45	55	0.55	−45.14%

Newark

Units	Acreage	Density (units/ acre)	Lost people	Lost units	New number of units	New density	% decline in density
300	100	3.0	−100	−100	200	2.00	−33.45%
250	100	2.5	−100	−100	150	1.50	−40.14%
200	100	2.0	−100	−100	100	1.00	−50.18%
150	100	1.5	−100	−100	50	0.50	−66.90%
100	100	1.0	−100	−100	0	0.00	−100.35%

Philadelphia

Units	Acreage	Density (units/ acre)	Lost people	Lost units	New number of units	New density	% decline in density
300	100	3.0	−100	−64	236	2.36	−21.47%
250	100	2.5	−100	−64	186	1.86	−25.77%
200	100	2.0	−100	−64	136	1.36	−32.21%
150	100	1.5	−100	−64	86	0.86	−42.94%
100	100	1.0	−100	−64	36	0.36	−64.42%

Pittsburg

Units	Acreage	Density (units/ acre)	Lost people	Lost units	New number of units	New density	% decline in density
300	100	3.0	−100	−54	246	2.46	−18.08%
250	100	2.5	−100	−54	196	1.96	−21.70%
200	100	2.0	−100	−54	146	1.46	−27.12%
150	100	1.5	−100	−54	96	0.96	−36.16%
100	100	1.0	−100	−54	46	0.46	−54.24%

Providence

Units	Acreage	Density (units/ acre)	Lost people	Lost units	New number of units	New density	% decline in density
300	100	3.0	−100	−61	239	2.39	−20.29%
250	100	2.5	−100	−61	189	1.89	−24.35%
200	100	2.0	−100	−61	139	1.39	−30.43%
150	100	1.5	−100	−61	89	0.89	−40.58%
100	100	1.0	−100	−61	39	0.39	−60.87%

1980

Dependent variable: change in occupied housing unit

	Beta	Mean
Constant	80.57	–
Living in poverty	0.14	–59.1224
High school graduates	0.40	–39.4161
Foreign born	0.22	–87.2751
Unemployed	0.36	78.7844
African American	0.05	–479.3054
% receiving public assistance	–0.25	146.7436
Older than 65 years	0.75	–88.3625
Change in population since prior decade	0.17	–1,416.8147
Dummy – Minneapolis	129.62	–
Dummy – Reading	–5.57	–
Dummy – Rochester	57.39	–
Dummy – Scranton	–28.73	–
Dummy – St. Louis	–112.43	–
Dummy – Syracuse	–34.30	–
Dummy – Trent	113.55	–
Dummy – Youngstown	–47.68	–
Dummy – Boston	166.28	–
Dummy – Buffalo	53.21	–
Camd_DUM	–68.62	–
Cant_DUM	3.72	–
Dummy – Cleveland	–37.52	–
Dummy – Dayton	12.27	–
Dummy – Detroit	–24.60	–
Dummy – Flint	–47.83	–
Dummy – Gary	–37.51	–
Dummy – Hartford	–25.61	–
Dummy – Minneapolis	129.62	–
Dummy – Newark	–60.64	–
Dummy – Philadelphia	–69.50	–
Dummy – Pittsburg	–44.89	–
Dummy – Providence	–157.58	–

1990

Dependent variable: change in occupied housing unit

	Beta	Mean
Constant	50.14	–
Living in poverty	–0.01	–41.5431
High school graduates	0.16	–62.1608
Foreign born	0.31	–39.2005
Unemployed	0.16	–20.1538
African American	0.12	–291.7016
% receiving public assistance	0.32	–36.6946
Older than 65 years	0.62	–25.4382
Change in population since prior decade	0.09	–568.4184
Dummy – Reading	84.80	–
Dummy – Rochester	–35.88	–
Dummy – Scranton	–58.37	–
Dummy – St. Louis	26.59	–
Dummy – Syracuse	–85.74	–
Dummy – Trent	–173.52	–
Dummy – Youngstown	–103.81	–
Dummy – Boston	–64.51	–
Dummy – Buffalo	–74.08	–
Camd_DUM	–71.08	–
Cant_DUM	–78.25	–
Dummy – Cleveland	–85.20	–
Dummy – Dayton	–85.53	–
Dummy – Detroit	–150.02	–
Dummy – Flint	–59.55	–
Dummy – Gary	–69.40	–
Dummy – Hartford	–107.08	–
Dummy – Minneapolis	–124.30	–
Dummy – Newark	–89.65	–
Dummy – Philadelphia	–46.86	–
Dummy – Pittsburg	–50.00	–
Dummy – Providence	–262.22	–

2000

Dependent variable: change in occupied housing unit

	Beta	Mean
Constant	32.01	–
Living in poverty	0.07	−226.6445
High school graduates	0.08	−52.3077
Foreign born	0.05	11.3112
Unemployed	−0.05	−51.9918
African American	0.00	−217.1585
% receiving public assistance	0.34	−55.5291
Older than 65 years	0.36	−67.3193
Change in population since prior decade	0.17	−446.1585
Dummy – Reading	−118.33	–
Dummy – Rochester	−47.73	–
Dummy – Scranton	19.39	–
Dummy – St. Louis	−76.34	–
Dummy – Syracuse	−7.71	–
Dummy – Trent	4.92	–
Dummy – Youngstown	−13.58	–
Dummy – Boston	−23.65	–
Dummy – Buffalo	−34.45	–
Camd_DUM	−8.80	–
Cant_DUM	−10.95	–
Dummy – Cleveland	−29.55	–
Dummy – Dayton	13.47	–
Dummy – Detroit	−44.64	–
Dummy – Flint	−30.00	–
Dummy – Gary	−85.71	–
Dummy – Hartford	−0.93	–
Dummy – Minneapolis	−5.61	–
Dummy – Newark	−56.15	–
Dummy – Philadelphia	−20.21	–
Dummy – Pittsburg	−10.03	–
Dummy – Providence	−16.67	–

Appendix B

City	State	Combined acreage of all ZCTAs within city boundaries	Feb '06 occupied housing units (OHU)
New Orleans city	Louisiana	105,163	217,451
Chandler city	Arizona	81,478	96,992
Scottsdale city	Arizona	536,280	150,482
Gilbert town	Arizona	25,309	44,307
Glendale city	Arizona	52,078	106,098
Reno city	Nevada	1,036,474	80,775
Clearwater city	Florida	36,098	91,022
St. Petersburg city	Florida	55,359	176,961
Pompano Beach city	Florida	58,839	182,880
Fort Lauderdale city	Florida	125,086	334,285
Pembroke Pines city	Florida	14,007	43,999
San Bernardino city	California	106,139	69,207
Mesa city	Arizona	173,988	182,805
Hollywood city	Florida	11,620	50,581
Downey city	California	8,008	34,662
Norwalk city	California	6,268	27,436
Santa Ana city	California	27,450	102,039
Long Beach city	California	44,603	196,119
Modesto city	California	136,310	87,614
Richmond city	California	24,191	58,551
Pomona city	California	27,439	55,712
Lakewood city	Colorado	7,695	30,495
Fullerton city	California	13,572	46,615
Arlington city	Texas	–	33,949
Tempe city	Arizona	27,344	66,584
Huntington Beach city	California	18,435	76,965
Dallas city	Texas	213,619	464,845
Jackson city	Mississippi	127,386	41,107
Glendale city	California	21,281	77,252
Hayward city	California	63,765	79,146
Charleston city	South Carolina	141,130	106,455
Stockton city	California	251,218	114,188
West Covina city	California	10,410	32,717
Fairfield city	California	27,357	24,880
Riverside city	California	105,810	122,281
Salinas city	California	186,428	52,438
Tucson city	Arizona	1,130,516	317,096
Anaheim city	California	33,470	103,376
Escondido city	California	98,890	55,355
Phoenix city	Arizona	345,732	464,156
Costa Mesa city	California	11,229	40,760
Garden Grove city	California	11,407	47,245
Concord city	California	30,385	60,785
Gainesville city	Florida	49,312	38,800
Pasadena city	Texas	26,351	50,098
Burbank city	California	11,366	44,296

Feb '09 occupied housing units (OHU)	Difference in OHU '06–'09		OHU density Feb '06	OHU density Feb '09	Number of zip codes that lost OHUs
	No.	%			
165,198	−52,253	−24%	2.1	1.6	16
87,241	−9,751	−10%	1.2	1.1	5
144,325	−6,157	−4%	0.3	0.3	9
42,539	−1,768	−4%	1.8	1.7	2
101,951	−4,147	−4%	2.0	2.0	7
78,745	−2,030	−3%	0.1	0.1	2
89,264	−1,758	−2%	2.5	2.5	9
173,839	−3,122	−2%	3.2	3.1	13
179,833	−3,047	−2%	3.1	3.1	10
328,744	−5,541	−2%	2.7	2.6	21
43,353	−646	−1%	3.1	3.1	3
68,331	−876	−1%	0.7	0.6	5
180,895	−1,910	−1%	1.1	1.0	9
50,137	−444	−1%	4.4	4.3	2
34,372	−290	−1%	4.3	4.3	3
27,226	−210	−1%	4.4	4.3	1
101,296	−743	−1%	3.7	3.7	5
195,045	−1,074	−1%	4.4	4.4	11
87,192	−422	0%	0.6	0.6	5
58,297	−254	0%	2.4	2.4	3
55,498	−214	0%	2.0	2.0	2
30,379	−116	0%	4.0	3.9	3
46,452	−163	0%	3.4	3.4	3
33,833	−116	0%	–	–	1
66,407	−177	0%	2.4	2.4	2
76,822	−143	0%	4.2	4.2	3
464,409	−436	0%	2.2	2.2	19
41,095	−12	0%	0.3	0.3	2
77,259	7	0%	3.6	3.6	3
79,157	11	0%	1.2	1.2	2
106,523	68	0%	0.8	0.8	2
114,317	129	0%	0.5	0.5	6
32,776	59	0%	3.1	3.1	1
24,931	51	0%	0.9	0.9	1
122,551	270	0%	1.2	1.2	5
52,557	119	0%	0.3	0.3	1
317,970	874	0%	0.3	0.3	13
103,700	324	0%	3.1	3.1	3
55,540	185	0%	0.6	0.6	1
465,713	1,557	0%	1.3	1.3	25
40,930	170	0%	3.6	3.6	1
47,496	251	1%	4.1	4.2	0
61,122	337	1%	2.0	2.0	2
39,050	250	1%	0.8	0.8	1
50,426	328	1%	1.9	1.9	1
44,623	327	1%	3.9	3.9	1

City	State	Combined acreage of all ZCTAs within city boundaries	Feb '06 occupied housing units (OHU)
El Paso city	New Mexico	1,472	2,960
Daly City city	California	7,588	32,855
Birmingham city	Alabama	227,995	209,591
Vallejo city	California	43,363	44,246
Thousand Oaks city	California	58,797	51,911
Inglewood city	California	6,870	43,568
Los Angeles city	California	133,798	842,230
Torrance city	California	15,038	63,760
Oakland city	California	40,265	165,625
Sacramento city	California	140,429	294,396
Hialeah city	Florida	37,474	109,462
Montgomery city	Alabama	208,798	84,367
Fremont city	California	50,505	70,978
Peoria city	Arizona	55,455	45,611
El Monte city	California	9,721	32,216
Ontario city	California	28,485	45,359
Fresno city	California	197,120	138,693
Miramar city	Florida	32,401	77,809
Berkeley city	California	9,900	56,456
Las Vegas city	Nevada	1,435,019	897,070
Mesquite city	Texas	46,773	57,725
Garland city	Texas	41,600	82,618
San Jose city	California	218,960	306,281
Ventura	California	92,027	42,540
Pasadena city	California	18,488	65,585
Salt Lake City city	Utah	211,527	152,404
San Francisco city	California	29,739	336,535
San Diego city	California	190,917	477,343
Oxnard city	California	42,901	42,037
Chula Vista city	California	34,739	73,287
Beaumont city	Texas	236,635	52,894
Sunnyvale city	California	15,369	45,915
Orange city	California	17,403	46,296
Henderson city	Nevada	121,374	47,699
Carrollton city	Texas	24,318	43,521
Mobile city	Alabama	179,613	111,639
Tampa city	Florida	159,304	264,806
Little Rock city	Arkansas	182,318	93,878
Santa Clara city	California	11,770	42,231
Simi Valley city	California	48,703	41,629
Miami city	Florida	390,504	688,328
Abilene city	Texas	282,868	47,022
Irving city	Texas	43,992	84,635
Shreveport city	Louisiana	273,075	92,449
Santa Clarita city	California	261,535	66,115
Fontana city	California	33,048	53,356
Lubbock city	Texas	272,905	94,906
Columbus city	Georgia	83,652	75,230
Albuquerque city	New Mexico	264,826	225,384

Feb '09 occupied housing units (OHU)	Difference in OHU '06–'09		OHU density Feb '06	OHU density Feb '09	Number of zip codes that lost OHUs
	No.	%			
2,987	27	1%	2.0	2.0	0
33,160	305	1%	4.3	4.4	0
211,779	2,188	1%	0.9	0.9	16
44,712	466	1%	1.0	1.0	1
52,477	566	1%	0.9	0.9	1
44,065	497	1%	6.3	6.4	2
851,986	9,756	1%	6.3	6.4	24
64,514	754	1%	4.2	4.3	0
167,694	2,069	1%	4.1	4.2	5
298,213	3,817	1%	2.1	2.1	14
110,932	1,470	1%	2.9	3.0	2
85,595	1,228	1%	0.4	0.4	6
72,024	1,046	1%	1.4	1.4	0
46,297	686	2%	0.8	0.8	1
32,705	489	2%	3.3	3.4	0
46,091	732	2%	1.6	1.6	2
140,983	2,290	2%	0.7	0.7	8
79,097	1,288	2%	2.4	2.4	1
57,402	946	2%	5.7	5.8	1
912,178	15,108	2%	0.6	0.6	44
58,720	995	2%	1.2	1.3	1
84,078	1,460	2%	2.0	2.0	2
311,791	5,510	2%	1.4	1.4	9
43,310	770	2%	0.5	0.5	1
66,842	1,257	2%	3.5	3.6	2
155,334	2,930	2%	0.7	0.7	3
343,010	6,475	2%	11.3	11.5	12
487,011	9,668	2%	2.5	2.6	13
42,908	871	2%	1.0	1.0	0
74,887	1,600	2%	2.1	2.2	2
54,104	1,210	2%	0.2	0.2	3
46,981	1,066	2%	3.0	3.1	0
47,402	1,106	2%	2.7	2.7	1
48,858	1,159	2%	0.4	0.4	1
44,610	1,089	3%	1.8	1.8	0
114,480	2,841	3%	0.6	0.6	6
271,765	6,959	3%	1.7	1.7	8
96,390	2,512	3%	0.5	0.5	4
43,376	1,145	3%	3.6	3.7	0
42,796	1,167	3%	0.9	0.9	0
708,726	20,398	3%	1.8	1.8	18
48,448	1,426	3%	0.2	0.2	1
87,218	2,583	3%	1.9	2.0	2
95,322	2,873	3%	0.3	0.3	3
68,228	2,113	3%	0.3	0.3	2
55,077	1,721	3%	1.6	1.7	1
98,072	3,166	3%	0.3	0.4	6
77,801	2,571	3%	0.9	0.9	2
233,306	7,922	4%	0.9	0.9	3

City	State	Combined acreage of all ZCTAs within city boundaries	Feb '06 occupied housing units (OHU)
Houston city	Texas	534,509	1069,387
Santa Rosa city	California	117,779	76,818
Huntsville city	Alabama	145,247	76,826
Waco city	Texas	205,100	65,501
Orlando city	Florida	299,662	319,086
Provo city	Utah	74,294	31,138
Savannah city	Georgia	236,468	92,861
Corpus Christi city	Texas	179,191	109,521
Baton Rouge city	Louisiana	150,307	152,517
North Las Vegas city	Nevada	26,563	46,970
Amarillo city	Texas	395,380	80,903
Atlanta city	Georgia	60,394	136,497
El Paso city	Texas	613,128	218,348
Moreno Valley city	California	67,962	49,118
Winston-Salem city	North Carolina	111,742	82,593
Tallahassee city	Florida	359,835	83,788
Roseville city	California	53,922	52,133
Fayetteville city	North Carolina	241,335	92,356
Elk Grove city	California	85,872	37,771
McAllen city	Texas	36,591	43,201
Rancho Cucamonga city	California	40,424	51,872
Palmdale city	California	170,699	48,103
Lafayette city	Louisiana	61,290	59,247
Plano city	Texas	48,599	100,156
Durham city	North Carolina	116,318	84,716
Jacksonville city	Florida	540,694	364,701
Columbia city	South Carolina	183,605	126,260
Aurora city	Colorado	225,211	379,624
Brownsville city	Texas	96,047	54,253
Austin city	Texas	336,906	367,634
Bakersfield city	California	722,742	151,097
Cary town	North Carolina	11,424	15,502
Fort Worth city	Texas	294,938	299,478
Lancaster city	California	336,987	54,948
Grand Prairie city	Texas	40,427	51,560
Laredo city	Texas	475,341	62,229
Charlotte city	North Carolina	256,750	301,666
San Antonio city	Texas	565,540	539,495
Visalia city	California	145,766	43,253
Denton city	Texas	59,790	26,996
Cape Coral city	Florida	65,487	64,684
Corona city	California	89,479	60,585
Irvine city	California	38,958	60,112
Killeen city	Texas	299,745	59,516
Port St. Lucie city	Florida	122,840	65,075
Net for all cities			
Mean		**155,172**	

Source: U.S. Postal Service, Active Residential Deliveries (March 2009)

Feb '09 occupied housing units (OHU)	Difference in OHU '06–'09		OHU density Feb '06	OHU density Feb '09	Number of zip codes that lost OHUs
	No.	%			
1107,185	37,798	4%	2.0	2.1	31
79,585	2,767	4%	0.7	0.7	0
79,657	2,831	4%	0.5	0.5	1
67,926	2,425	4%	0.3	0.3	2
331,082	11,996	4%	1.1	1.1	10
32,329	1,191	4%	0.4	0.4	0
96,414	3,553	4%	0.4	0.4	2
113,948	4,427	4%	0.6	0.6	4
158,689	6,172	4%	1.0	1.1	2
49,044	2,074	4%	1.8	1.8	1
84,497	3,594	4%	0.2	0.2	4
142,587	6,090	4%	2.3	2.4	1
228,100	9,752	4%	0.4	0.4	4
51,370	2,252	5%	0.7	0.8	2
86,508	3,915	5%	0.7	0.8	0
87,884	4,096	5%	0.2	0.2	0
54,750	2,617	5%	1.0	1.0	0
97,087	4,731	5%	0.4	0.4	1
39,745	1,974	5%	0.4	0.5	0
45,561	2,360	5%	1.2	1.2	0
54,721	2,849	5%	1.3	1.4	1
50,817	2,714	6%	0.3	0.3	1
62,703	3,456	6%	1.0	1.0	0
106,002	5,846	6%	2.1	2.2	0
89,690	4,974	6%	0.7	0.8	0
386,134	21,433	6%	0.7	0.7	8
133,729	7,469	6%	0.7	0.7	2
403,793	24,169	6%	1.7	1.8	6
57,836	3,583	7%	0.6	0.6	0
392,277	24,643	7%	1.1	1.2	4
161,232	10,135	7%	0.2	0.2	3
16,566	1,064	7%	1.4	1.5	0
320,181	20,703	7%	1.0	1.1	8
58,814	3,866	7%	0.2	0.2	1
55,399	3,839	7%	1.3	1.4	0
66,936	4,707	8%	0.1	0.1	1
324,921	23,255	8%	1.2	1.3	4
581,678	42,183	8%	1.0	1.0	14
46,678	3,425	8%	0.3	0.3	0
29,155	2,159	8%	0.5	0.5	0
70,462	5,778	9%	1.0	1.1	2
66,110	5,525	9%	0.7	0.7	1
66,824	6,712	11%	1.5	1.7	0
66,320	6,804	11%	0.2	0.2	1
72,584	7,509	12%	0.5	0.6	0
	415,203				
	2,965.7				

Notes

1 Introduction

1 Both here and throughout the book, pseudonyms are used in place of real names to protect the anonymity of research participants.

2 Ways to think about decline

1 Despite the small set of tools available to cities, some have had success in changing their basic economic structure to effectively increase employment and population levels through expensive firm recruitment strategies (Wilmington, Delaware), arts and cultural investments (San Francisco), and an asset-based approach that builds on existing strengths (Boston). The problem is that most cities have not been able to do so and no evidence exists to suggest that current strategies that have worked *can* be transferred to other locales.

2 This problem of "underwater" properties is a major fixture of the real estate bust that began in 2006. In 2009, 23 percent of homeowners were estimated to be underwater, with even higher rates in Sunbelt states (Simon and Hagerty 2009).

3 For a detailed review of this debate, see Abbott (1981) and Bernard and Bradley (1983).

4 Shrinking to greatness is an expression coined by Edward Glaeser (2007) in his essay about what should become of the perennially declining city of Buffalo, New York.

3 The shrinking Rustbelt: a pattern of decline

1 It is important to note that I only looked at occupied housing per acre as a land-use measure. As described in Chapter 2, vacant and abandoned homes are a major physical feature of depopulated neighborhoods. The statistic "occupied housing units per acre" allows for multi-year comparisons of the same neighborhoods and can reveal much about their changing physical form.

2 The Geolytics software includes 1970–2000 Census data normalized to 2000 Census boundaries to allow for comparison across years.

3 The number of tracts used in the analysis was 858, which excludes those tracts in Cincinnati (Ohio) that were due to persistent data errors discovered in the Geolytics database.

4 Only those tracts that lost population since the prior decade were selected for each regression. While all tracts lost population from 1970–2000, some gained population slightly during the study period. In order to isolate the way in which land use changes in depopulating neighborhoods, those that grew in population were filtered out of the analysis for the period in which they grew.

5 These correlations were conducted using Pearson's r. For both growing and declining tracts, for all time periods the relationship between change in population and change in occupied housing units was statistically significant at the 0.01 level.

6 While multi-collinearity might be a problem when working with closely related variables, I ran collinearity diagnostics for all regressions and found no evidence of multi-collinearity. Standard statistical practice suggests that multicollinearity is a problem when Eigenvalues are close to zero and when a condition index exceeds 30 (Belsley *et al.* 1980). In this analysis, Eigenvalues for each run were well above zero and condition indices did not exceed 17 for any regression (most were well below 15), indicating the absence of multi-collinearity in the data.

5 A new model for neighborhood change in shrinking cities

1 The primary means by which New Urbanists have advanced the transect concept is through form-based zoning. For more information, check out www.formbasedcodes.org.

2 Research assistants Sarah Spicer and Michelle Moon assisted in the creation of Figure 5.2.

3 In the burgeoning field of smart decline, a number of authors have speculated on what those strategies should be (Hollander and Popper 2007; Schwarz and Rugare 2008; Schilling and Logan 2008).

6 Unfamiliar patterns in the sun: what postal workers already know

1 The Northeastern cities included in the survey were, on average, larger and their per capita number of abandoned buildings (7.47 abandoned buildings per 1,000 inhabitants) was still dramatically higher than in the South (2.98) and West (0.62).

2 Three states below the 37th parallel were excluded because Sunbelt literature generally does not consider them as part of the region: Oklahoma, Missouri, and Tennessee.

3 Cities removed were: Athens-Clarke, Augusta-Richmond, Greensboro city, Raleigh city, Wichita Falls city, Oceanside, and Coral Springs.

4 Baton Rouge has continued to bleed population since being hit by Hurricane Gustav in 2008. But, interestingly, New Orleans was losing between 5,000

and 10,000 people annually from 2000 to 2005, when it was hit by Hurricane Katrina. In that one year, the city lost 245,000 people and has been growing steadily since.

5 It is worth noting that just as I was beginning to acquire the Postal Service data, the U.S. Department of Housing and Urban Development was starting to publish their own adapted version of vacancy data. Unfortunately, that data was not presented in a format that could be used in this study. I am currently undertaking a separate research project using the HUD/USPS data and it is proving to be valuable.

6 That is, the zip code boundaries did not change during the time period, according to records reviewed from the *Postal Gazette*. In addition, I excluded 42 zip codes from the analysis where there was no Census equivalent zip code listed from the 2000 Census.

7 Facing change in the Central Valley: a declining Fresno

1 Fresno County is one of eight counties that comprise the San Joaquin Valley which were the subject of the BluePrint Planning Process.

2 Continued population growth is likely owing to the city's policy of land annexation. For several years, the city has had a policy to annex county lands that are surrounded entirely by city lands (so-called islands) (Benjamin 2009).

3 Census 2000 data shows the neighborhood had 3,943 total housing units—the disparity could be due to some loss of housing units during the six year gap in time or more likely reflects the variation in how the data was collected among Census and USPS. However, a close analysis of 2000 housing unit data from the Census was compared to 2000 housing unit data from the USPS and the datasets were 99 percent correlated using Pearson's r.

4 Oddly, much of the new development that likely contributed to USPS's alteration of their zip code boundaries has not yet been occupied.

5 This body of literature includes scores of books including, to name a few, Newman (1972), Bright (2000), Greenstein and Sungu-Eryilmaz (2004); Byrum (1992) and hundreds of articles in journals such as *Urban Studies*, *Urban Affairs Review*, *Journal of Urban Affairs*, *Journal of the American Planning Association*, *Journal of Planning Education and Research*, and *Urban Geography*.

6 Another relevant exception is Nemeth's (2006) study of skateboarder's controversial use of public space in Philadelphia's Love Park.

8 Endless growth in the desert? The fall of Phoenix

1 Swilling named the settlement Pumpkinville, but it was soon renamed Phoenix to help make the metaphor of rebirth more complete.

2 The American Planning Association recognized the extraordinary achievement of the Mountain Preserve effort in 2008 by designating it as a National Planning Landmark.

3 The U.S. Environmental Protection Agency's Office of Smart Growth highlights Phoenix's investment in light rail on its website as exemplary of smart growth, see www.epa.gov/dced/sgia_communities.htm#az. Also, the National Center for Appropriate Technology's Smart Communities Network profiled Phoenix as a success story on its website, see www.smartcommunities.ncat.org/success/phoenix.shtml.

4 Construction and finance fields accounted for 18 percent of metropolitan Phoenix employment in the fall 2008, according to a report by real estate investment firm Cushman & Wakefield (2008).

5 The "Laveen citizens real estate development" is a loose group of environmental activists and Nimbys who have been major players in fighting new development; they have had no substantive role in addressing the foreclosure and abandonment problem to date.

6 Always with the few exceptions of park or conservation land scattered about a city or town.

9 Abandonment outside the magic kingdom: what went wrong in Orlando?

1 Among metro areas with populations between 500,000 and 1,000,000.

2 The problem with local governments targeting the low-hanging fruit was the subject of an earlier book of mine *Polluted and Dangerous: America's Worst Abandoned Properties and What Can Be Done About Them* (2009, University of Vermont Press).

3 For example, Tangelo Park in suburban Orange County was flagged by LISC as being a high foreclosure risk census tract due to 92.3 percent of all first mortgages issued being high-cost.

4 When multiplier-effects are considered, the development will likely create more than just 303 jobs, but the per employee incentive costs are still extraordinary.

5 New Urbanism is not the only design style that would guide developers in trying to create a sense of place in new or redeveloped neighborhoods—it is simply the most popular today.

10 Toward a new kind of city planning

1 In certain locales, a much broader range of industrial and commercial uses might be politically feasible, as well.

References

ABC News. 2009. Riding the foreclosure wave. *Nightline*. January 28.

Abbott, Carl. 1981. *The New Urban America: Growth and Politics in Sunbelt Cities*. Chapel Hill, NC: University of North Carolina Press.

Accordino, John and Gary T. Johnson. 2000. Addressing the vacant and abandoned property problem. *Journal of Urban Affairs* 22 (3): 301–315.

American Planning Association. 2000. *APA Policy Guide on Planning for Sustainability*. January 8, 1998, revised January 10, 2000.

Arizona Department of Commerce, Research Administration. 2010. Phoenix-Mesa-Scottsdale metropolitan area. Labor force and nonfarm employment. Available at www.workforce.az.gov/?PAGEID=67&SUBID=142 (accessed February 1, 2010).

Arizona Republic. 1955. Editorial. *The Arizona Republic*. December 8.

Arizona State University. 2003. *Greater Phoenix Regional Atlas: A Preview of the Region's 50-Year Future*. Tempe, AZ: Arizona State University.

Armborst, Tobias, Daniel D'Oca, and Georgeen Theodore. 2005. However unspectacular. In Philipp Oswalt (ed.) *Shrinking Cities. Volume 2: Interventions*. Ostfildern, Germany: Hatje Cantz.

Associated Press. 2009. Worst foreclosure rates found in 4 states. *Newswire*. April 23.

Baldwin Park Development Company. 2006. *Navy Base to Neighborhood: The Baldwin Park Story*. Baldwin Park, FL: Baldwin Park Development Company.

Barone, Michael. 1993. Snares of a lost paradise. *U.S. News and World Report*. October 11. p. 53.

Beauregard, Robert A. 2003. *Voices of Decline: The Postwar Fate of U.S. Cities*. 2nd edn. New York: Routledge.

Beauregard, Robert A. 2009. Urban population loss in historical perspective: United States, 1820–2000. *Environment and Planning A* 41: 514–528.

Belsley, David A, Edwin Kuh, and Roy E. Welsch. 1980. *Regression Diagnostics: Identifying Influential Data and Sources of Collinearity*. New York: John Wiley and Sons.

Benjamin, Marc. 2009. Fresno will add 94 county acres: Commission votes to annex land, 1,425 residents. *The Fresno Bee*. March 12.

Berg, Leo van den. 1982. *A Study of Growth and Decline*. Urban Europe/European Coordination Centre for Research and Documentation in Social Sciences. Oxford, Vol. 1.

Bernard, Richard M., and Rice R. Bradley (eds). 1983. *Sunbelt Cities: Politics and Growth since World War II*. Austin: University of Texas Press.

Bluestone, Barry and Bennett Harrison. 1982. *The Deindustrialization of America*. New York: Basic Books.

Bowman, Ann O'M. and Michael A. Pagano. 2004. *Terra Incognita: Vacant Land and Urban Strategies*. Washington, DC: Georgetown University Press.

Boyer, M.C. 1983. *Dreaming the Rational City*. Cambridge, MA: MIT Press.

Bradbury, Katherine, Anthony Downs and Kenneth A. Small. 1981. *Futures for a declining city: Simulations for the Cleveland area*. New York: Academic Press.

Bradbury, Katherine, Anthony Downs and Kenneth A. Small. 1982. *Urban Decline and the Future of American Cities*. Washington, DC: Brookings Institution.

Bright, Elise M. 2000. *Reviving America's Forgotten Neighborhoods: An Investigation of Inner City Revitalization Efforts*. New York: Garland Publishing.

Burchell, Robert W., Anthony Downs, David Listokin, Hilary Phillips, and Naveed A. Shad. 1998. *The Costs of Sprawl—Revisited*. Report/Transit Cooperative Research Program, 39. Washington, DC: National Academy Press.

Byrum, Oliver. 1992. *Old Problems in New Times: Urban Strategies for the 1990s*. Chicago, IL: American Planning Association.

Calthorpe, Peter. 1993. *The Next American Metropolis: Ecology, Community, and the American Dream*. New York, NY: Princeton Architectural Press.

Calthorpe, Peter and William Fulton. 2001. *The Regional City: Planning for the End of Sprawl*. Washington, DC: Island Press.

Cauchon, Dennis. 2008. Why home values may take decades to recover. *USA Today*. December 15.

Cave, Damien. 2009. After century of growth, tide turns in Florida. *New York Times*, August 30, A1.

Choldin, Harvey M. and Claudine Hanson. 1981. Subcommunity change in a changing metropolis. *The Sociological Quarterly* 22: 549–564.

Clancy, Michael and Casey Newton. 2009. Phoenix may be losing people: Population dip would further strain budget. *The Arizona Republic*. January 12.

Clark, D. 1989. *Urban Decline: The British Experience*. London: Routledge.

Clemings, Russell. 2009. Fresno faces $27.8 million budget gap. *The Fresno Bee*. October 22. Available at www.fresnobee.com/local/story/1682982.html (accessed October 23, 2009).

Cushman and Wakefield. 2008. Metro Phoenix office vacancies rise as national economy struggles. October 20. Available at www.cushwake.com (accessed December 1, 2009).

Dandekar, Hemalata, Carlos Balsas, Jacob Fisher, Justin Skay, and Nicholas Labadie. 2005. *A Plan for Planning the West Phoenix Revitalization Area*. School of Planning, Arizona State University, September 15.

Dantico, Marilyn, Subhrajit Guhathakurta, and Alvin Mushkatel. 2007. Housing quality and neighborhood redevelopment: A study of neighborhood initiatives in Phoenix, Arizona. *International Journal of Public Administration* 30 (1): 23–45. Available at www.informaworld.com/10.1080/01900690601050062 (accessed January 18, 2010).

Davey, Monica. 2009. Habitat Adds Demolition to its Mission. *The New York Times*. March 19, p. A19.

Dewar, Margaret E. 1998. Why State and Local Economic Development Programs Cause so Little Economic Development. *Economic Development Quarterly*, 12 (1): 68–87.

Doom, Justin. 2009. West-side story: A changing housing market. *The Arizona Republic*. April 13.

Doyle, Rodger. 2001. By the numbers: Sprawling into the third millennium. *Scientific American* 284 (3): 25. *Scientific American Archive Online*, EBSCOhost (accessed January 13, 2010).

Duany, Andres and Emily Talen. 2002. Transect Planning. *Journal of the American Planning Association* 68 (3): 245–266.

Edsforth, Ronald William. 1982. A second industrial revolution: The transformation of class, culture, and society in twentieth-century Flint. Unpublished Ph.D. dissertation. Michigan: Michigan State University.

Finkler, Earl, William J. Toner, and Frank J. Popper. 1976. *Urban Nongrowth: City Planning for People*. Praeger special studies in U.S. economic, social, and political issues. New York: Praeger.

Fletcher, Michael A. 2008. Housing crisis casts a cloud over Sun Belt. *The Washington Post*. February 5.

Fogelson, Robert M. 2001. *Downtown: Its Rise and Fall, 1880–1950*. New Haven, CT: Yale University Press.

Forester, J. 1999. *The Deliberative Practitioner: Encouraging Participatory Planning Processes*. Cambridge, MA: MIT Press.

Fresno Unified School District. 2009. Facilities Master Plan—Final Report. Fresno, CA.

Genesee County. 2007. *2005 Base Year Population Data; 2035 Population Projections; Methodology Report*. Genesee County Metropolitan Planning Commission. December.

Gilman, Theodore J. 1997. Urban redevelopment in Omuta, Japan and Flint, Michigan: A comparison. In P. P. Karan and K. Stapleton (eds) *The Japanese City*. Lexington, KY: University Press of Kentucky.

Glaeser, Edward L. 2007. Can Buffalo ever come back? Available at http://www.city-journal.org/html/17_4_buffalo_ny.html (accessed June 1, 2009).

Glaeser, Edward L. and Joseph Gyourko. 2005. Urban decline and durable housing. *Journal of Political Economy* 133 (2): 345–375.

Gober, Patricia and Barbara Trapido-Lurie. 2006. *Metropolitan Phoenix: Place Making and Community Building in the Desert*. Metropolitan portraits. Philadelphia, PA: University of Pennsylvania Press.

Goodman, Peter S. 2007. This is the sound of a bubble bursting. *New York Times*, December 23.

Gottlieb, Robert. 2007. *Reinventing Los Angeles: Nature and Community in the Global City*. Cambridge, MA: MIT Press.

Great Valley Center. 2007. *Our Valley, Our Choice: Building a Livable Future for the San Joaquin Valley*. Berkeley, CA: Heyday Books.

Greenstein, Rosalind and Yesim Sungu-Eryilmaz (eds). 2004. *Recycling the City: The Use and Reuse of Urban Land*. Cambridge, MA: Lincoln Institute of Land Policy.

Greenwald, Carol and Dorie Krauss. 1984. *Shout Youngstown*. New York: Cinema Guild (distributor).

Guralnik, D.B. (ed.) 1986. *Webster's New World Dictionary of the American Language*. New York: Prentice-Hall.

Hall, Peter. 1997. Modeling the post-industrial city. *Futures* 29 (4/5): 311–322.

Hempel, Lamont C. 1999. Conceptual and analytical challenges in building sustainable communities. In Daniel A. Mazmanian and Michale E. Kraft (eds) *Towards Sustainable Communities: Transition and Transformations in Environmental Policy*. Cambridge, MA: MIT Press.

Hillier, Amy E., Dennis P. Culhane, Tony E. Smith, and C. Dana Tomlin. 2003. Predicting Housing Abandonment with the Philadelphia Neighborhood Information System. *Journal of Urban Affairs* 25 (1): 91–105.

Hollander, Justin B. 2009. *Polluted and Dangerous: America's Worst Abandoned Properties and What Can Be Done About Them*. Burlington, VT: University of Vermont Press.

Hollander, Justin B. and Frank J. Popper. 2007. Planning practice and the shrinking city: reversing the land use allocation model. *Plan Canada* 47 (2): 38–40.

Hollander, Justin B., Karina Pallagst, Terry Schwarz, and Frank J. Popper. 2009. Planning shrinking cities. *Progress in Planning* 72 (4): 223–232.

Hoyt, Homer. 1933. *One Hundred Years of Land Values in Chicago: The Relationship of the Growth of Chicago to the Rise in its Land Values, 1830–1933*. Chicago, IL: University of Chicago Press.

Hughes, Mark Alan and Rebekah Cook-Mack. 1999. Vacancy Reassessed. *Public/Private Venture*. October 30. Available at www.issuelab.org/research/vacancy_reassessed (accessed June 19, 2010).

Immergluck, Daniel. 2009. *Foreclosed: High-risk Lending, Deregulation and the Undermining of America's Mortgage Market*. Ithaca: Cornell University Press.

Jackson, Kenneth T. 1985. *Crabgrass Frontier: The Suburbanization of the United States*. New York: Oxford University Press.

Johnson, Stephen, Gerald W. Haslam, and Robert Dawson. 1993. *The Great Central Valley: California's Heartland*. Berkeley, CA: University of California Press.

Judd, Dennis R. and Susan S. Fainstein. 1999. *The Tourist City*. New Haven, CT: Yale University Press.

Katz, Bruce. 2006. Revitalizing Weak Market Cities in the U.S.: Presentation to The Council on Foundations, May 8. Available at www.brookings.edu/speeches/2006/0508cities_katz.aspx (accessed October 10, 2010).

Keenan P., S. Lowe, and S. Spencer. 1999. Housing abandonment in inner cities: The politics of low demand for housing. *Housing Studies* 14 (5): 703–716.

Kent State University. 2009. *Vacant Land Re-Use Pattern Book*. Cleveland Urban Design Collaborative. April.

Kobrin, Frances E. 1976. The fall in household size and the rise of the primary individual in the United States. *Demography* 13 (1): 127–138.

Krueckeberg, Donald A. and A. Silvers. 1974. *Urban Planning Analysis: Methods and Models*. New York: John Wiley and Sons.

Kunerth, Jeff and Linda Shrieves. 2009. Central Florida is shrinking. Orlando, Orange County and the state saw populations dip for the first time in decades. *Orlando Sentinel*. August 20.

Landis, J. 2001. CUF, CUF II, and CURBA: a family of spatially explicit urban growth and land use policy simulation models. In R. Brail and R. Klosterman (eds) *Planning Support Systems*. Redlands, CA: ESRI.

Leigh, Nancy Green and Sharah L. Coffin. 2005. Modeling the relationship among brownfields, property values, and community revitalization. *Fannie Mae Foundation: Housing Policy Debate*, 16 (2): 257–280.

Leland, John. 2007. Officials say they are falling behind on mortgage fraud cases. *New York Times*, December 25.

Logan, J.R. and H.L. Molotch. 1987. *Urban Fortunes: The Political Economy of Place*. Berkeley, CA: University of California Press.

Logan, Michael F. 2006. *Desert Cities: The Environmental History of Phoenix and Tucson*. Pittsburgh, PA: University of Pittsburgh Press.

Luckingham, Bradford. 1983. Phoenix: The desert metropolis. In Richard M. Bernard and Rice R. Bradley (eds) *Sunbelt Cities: Politics and Growth since World War II*. Austin, TX: University of Texas Press.

Lucy, William H. and David L. Phillips. 2000. *Confronting Suburban Decline: Strategic Planning for Metropolitan Renewal*. Chicago, IL: Island Press.

McDonald, John F. 2008. *Urban America: Growth, Crisis, and Rebirth*. Armonk, NY: M.E. Sharpe.

McGeehan, Patrick. 2009. Pfizer to leave city that won land-use suit. *New York Times*, November 13, sec A; Metropolitan Desk.

McKinley, Jesse and Malia Wollan. 2008. Skaters jump in as foreclosures in U.S. drain the pool. *New York Times*. December 29.

Mallach, Alan. 2010. *Facing the Urban Challenge: Reimagining Land Use in America's Distressed Older Cities: The Federal Policy Role*. Washington, DC: Brookings Institution Press.

Mallach, Alan and Lavea Brachman. 2010. *Ohio's Cities at a Turning Point: Finding the Way Forward*. Washington, DC: Brookings Institution Press.

Maricopa County (Arizona). 2009. Foreclosure TD—status count 1/1/06 thru 9/29/08. Report.

Massey, Douglas S. and Nancy A. Denton. 1993. *American Apartheid: Segregation and the Making of the Underclass*. Cambridge, MA: Harvard University Press.

Matthews, Anne. 2002. *Where the Buffalo Roam: Restoring America's Great Plains*. Chicago, IL: University of Chicago Press.

Matthews, Rick Arnold. 1997. What's good for GM…: Deindustrialization and crime in four Michigan cities, 1975–1993. Unpublished PhD dissertation. Kalamazoo, MI: Western Michigan University.

May, George S. 1965. *Michigan: A History of the Wolverine State*. Grand Rapids, MI: William B. Eerdmans Publishing Company.

Meck, Stuart. 2002. *Growing Smart Legislative Guidebook Model Statutes for Planning and the Management of Change*. Chicago, IL: American Planning Association.

Miller, Thaddeus. 2009. CSU shrinks enrollment. *The Collegian Online*. October 7. Available at http://collegian.csufresno.edu/2009/10/07/csu-shrinks-enrollment/ (accessed October 19, 2009).

Mitchell, T. 2002. *Rule of experts: Egypt, techno-politics, modernity*. Berkeley, CA: University of California Press.

Mormino, Gary Ross. 2005. *Land of Sunshine, State of Dreams: A Social History of Modern Florida*. Gainesville, FL: University Press of Florida.

Mullins, Luke. 2008. Making a business of foreclosures. *U.S. News and World Reports*. February 5.

Nash, Linda. 2000. Transforming the Central Valley: Body, identity, and environment in California, 1850–1970. Unpublished PhD dissertation. University of Washington.

Nemeth, Jeremy. 2006. Conflict, exclusion, relocation: Skateboarding and public space. *Journal of Urban Design* 11 (3): 297–318.

New Jersey Department of Community Affairs. 2003. Office of Smart Growth: Greyfields Task Force web site. Available at www.nj.gov/dca/osg/commissions/gtf.shtml (accessed October 30, 2009).

Newman, Oscar. 1972. *Defensible Space; Crime Prevention through Urban Design*. New York: Macmillan.

Ophuls, William. 1996. Unsustainable liberty, sustainable freedom. In D. Pirages (ed.) *Building Sustainable Societies: A Blueprint for a Post-Industrial World*. New York: M.E. Sharpe.

Oswalt, Philipp (ed.). 2006. *Shrinking Cities, volume 2: Interventions*. Ostfildern, Germany: Hatje Cantz.

Pack, Janet Rothenberg (ed.). 2005. *Sunbelt/Frostbelt Public Policies and Market Forces in Metropolitan Development*. Washington, DC: Brookings Institution Press.

Pallagst, Karina J.A., Ivonne Audirac, Emmanuele Cunningham-Sabot, Sylvie Fol, Cristina Martinez-Fernandez, Sergio Moraes, Helen Mulligan, Jose Vargas-Hernandez, Thorsten Wiechmann, and Tong Wu. 2009. *The Future of Shrinking Cities—Problems, Patterns and Strategies of Urban Transformation in a Global Context*. Institute of Urban and Regional Development, Center for Global Metropolitan Studies, and the Shrinking Cities International Research Monograph Series. MG-2009-01. Berkeley, CA: University of California.

Perloff, Harvey S. 1980. *Planning the Post-Industrial City*. Washington, DC: Planners Press.

Perry, David C. and Alfred Watkins. 1977. *The Rise of the Sunbelt Cities*. Beverley Hills, CA: Sage.

Peterson, Paul. 1981. *City Limits*. Chicago, IL: University of Chicago Press.

Phillips, Kevin. 1969. *The Emerging Republican Majority*. New Rochelle, NY: Arlington House.

Pinderhughes, Raquel. 2004. *Alternative Urban Futures: Planning for Sustainable Development in Cities throughout the World*. Lanham, MD: Rowman & Littlefield Publishers.

Ping, Dan. 2007. Burnham deal includes free house, exhibit. *Orlando Business Journal*. March 9. Available at http://orlando.bizjournals.com/orlando/stories/2007/03/12 (accessed December 4, 2009).

Popper, Deborah E. and Frank J. Popper. 1987. The Great Plains: From dust to dust. *Planning* December. p. 12–18.

Popper, Deborah E. and Frank J. Popper. 2002. Small can be beautiful: Coming to terms with decline. *Planning* 68 (7): 20–23.

Popper, Deborah E. and Frank J. Popper. 2004. The great plains and the buffalo commons. In B. Warf, D. Janelle and K. Hansen (eds) *WorldMinds: Geographical Perspectives on 100 Problems*. Washington, DC: Association of American Geographers.

Portney, Kent E. 2002. *Taking Sustainable Cities Seriously: Economic Development, the Environment, and Quality of Life in American Cities*. Cambridge, MA: MIT Press.

Putnam, Robert D. 1993. *Making Democracy Work: Civic Traditions in Modern Italy*. Princeton, NJ: Princeton University Press.

Real Estate Research Corporation. 1974. The Costs of Sprawl: Detailed Cost Analysis. Prepared by the Council on Environmental Quality; the Office of Policy Development and Research, Department of Housing and Urban Development; the Office of Planning and Management, Environmental Protection Agency.

Rusk, D. 1995. *Cities Without Suburbs*. 2nd edn. Washington, DC: The Woodrow Wilson Center Press.

Rust, Edgar. 1975. *No Growth: Impacts on Metropolitan Areas*. Lexington, MA: Lexington Books.

Rybczynski, Witold. 1995. Downsizing cities: To make cities work better, make them smaller. *The Atlantic Monthly*, October, 36–47.

Ryznar, Rhonda M. and Thomas W. Wagner. 2001. Using remotely sensed imagery to detect urban change: viewing Detroit from space. *Journal of the American Planning Association* 67 (3): 327–336.

Sandercock, Leonie. 2003. *Cosmopolis II: Mongrel Cities of the 21st Century*. London: Continuum.

Sassen, Saskia. 1991. *The Global City: New York, London, Tokyo*. Princeton, NJ: Princeton University Press.

Sawers, Larry and William K. Tabb (eds). 1984. *Sunbelt/Snowbelt: Urban Development and Regional Restructuring*. New York: Oxford University Press.

Schilling, Joseph and Jonathan Logan. 2008. Greening the rust belt: A green infrastructure model for right sizing America's shrinking cities. *Journal of the American Planning Association* 74 (4): 451–466. Available at www.informaworld.com/10.1080/01944360802354956 (accessed January 13, 2010).

Schlueb, Mark. 2008a. Orlando to use $6.7 million to buy, revamp homes to protect neighborhoods. *Orlando Sentinel*. November 18.

Schlueb, Mark. 2008b. Line grows quickly for $35 million to fix housing in Central Florida. *Orlando Sentinel*. November 28. Available at orlandosentinel.com/news/custom/growth/orl-housing2808nov28,0,6860907.story (accessed November 8, 2009).

Schulman, Bruce J. 1994. *From Cotton Belt to Sunbelt: Federal Policy, Economic Development, and the Transformation of the South, 1938–1980*. Durham, NC: Duke University Press.

Schumacher, E.F. 1975. *Small is Beautiful: Economics as if People Mattered*. New York: Harper & Row.

Schumpeter, Joseph Alois. 1983. *The Theory of Economic Development: An Inquiry into Profits, Capital, Credit, Interest, and the Business Cycle*. Social science classics series. New Brunswick, NJ: Transaction Books.

Schwarz, Terry and Steve Rugare (eds). 2008. *Cities Growing Smaller*. Vol. 1, Urban-Infill. Cleveland, OH: Kent State University Cleveland Urban Design Collaborative.

Scott, James C. 1998. *Seeing Like a State: How Certain Schemes to Improve the Human Condition Have Failed*. New Haven, CT: Yale University Press.

Setencich, Eli. 1993. *Fresno: California's Heartland*. Memphis, TN: Towery Pub.

Shofner, Jerrell H. 1984. *Orlando: The City Beautiful*. American Portrait Series. Tulsa, OK: Continental Heritage Press.

Simon, Ruth and James R. Hagerty. 2009. One in four borrowers is underwater. *Wall Street Journal*, November 24.

Sobel, Lee S., Steven Bodzin, and Ellen Greenberg. 2002. *Greyfields into Goldfields: Dead Malls Become Living Neighborhoods*. San Francisco, CA: Congress for the New Urbanism.

Sugrue, T.J. 1996. *The Origins of the Urban Crisis: Race and Inequality in Postwar Detroit*. Princeton, NJ: Princeton University Press.

Talen, Emily. 2009. *Urban Design Reclaimed: Tools, Techniques, and Strategies for Planners*. Chicago, IL: American Planning Association, Planners Press.

Taylor, Robert W. and Justin B. Hollander. 2003. The new environmentalism: Challenges for urban-environmental management. In R. Domanski (ed.) *Recent Advances in Urban and Regional Studies, Studia Regionalia*, Vol. 12. Warsaw: Polish Academy of Sciences.

Temkin, Kenneth and William Rohe. 1996. Neighborhood change and urban policy. *Journal of Planning Education and Research* 15 (3) (April 1): 159–170.

Thomas, June M. 1997. *Redevelopment and Race: Planning a Finer City in Postwar Detroit*. Baltimore: Johns Hopkins University Press.

Thomas, June M. and J. Eugene Grigsby, III. 2000. Community development. In C.E. Hoch (ed.) *The Practice or Local Government Planning*, Washington, DC: International City/County Management Association.

U.N. World Commission on Environment and Development. 1987. *Our Common Future*. Oxford: Oxford University Press.

U.S. Census. 2000. Census website. Available at www.census.gov (accessed August 10, 2010).

U.S. Census. 2008. Census website. Available at www.census.gov (accessed August 10, 2009).

U.S. Census. 2009. Census website, population estimates. Available at www.census.gov (accessed August 10, 2010).

Valdez, Linda. 2009. Recession offers us a chance at positive changes. *The Arizona Republic*. April 26. Available at www.azcentral.com/arizonarepublic/viewpoints/articles/2009/04/25/20090425valdez26-vip.html (accessed December 1, 2009).

Vale, Lawrence J. and Thomas J. Campanella. 2005. *The Resilient City: How Modern Cities Recover from Disaster*. New York: Oxford University Press.

Vergara, Camilo José. 1999. *American Ruins*. New York: Monacelli Press.

Wallace, R. 1989. "Homelessness," contagious destruction of housing, and municipal service cuts in New York City: 1. Demographics of a housing deficit. *Environment and Planning A* 21 (12): 1585–1602.

Wiechmann, T. 2008. Errors expected—aligning urban strategy with demographic uncertainty in shrinking cities. *International Planning Studies* 13 (4): 431–446.

Wilson, David and Harry Margulis (1994) Spatial aspects of housing abandonment in the 1990s. *Housing Studies* 9 (4): 493–511.

Wilson, William J. 1987. *The Truly Disadvantaged: The Inner City, the Underclass, and Public Policy*. Chicago, IL: University of Chicago Press.

Weinstein, Bernard L. and Robert E. Firestine. 1978. *Regional Growth and Decline in the United States : The Rise of the Sunbelt and the Decline of the Northeast*. New York: Praeger.

White, C. Langdon, Edwin J. Foscue, and Tom L. McKnight. 1964. *Regional Geography of Anglo-America*. Englewood Cliffs, NJ: Prentice-Hall.

Worster, Donald. 1985. *Rivers of Empire: Water, Aridity, and the Growth of the American West*. New York: Pantheon Books.

Youngstown, City of. 2005. Youngstown 2010 citywide plan. Youngstown, OH.

Zumbrun, Joshua. 2008. America's Fastest-Dying Cities. *Forbes*. August 5. Available at http://www.forbes.com/2008/08/04/economy-ohio-michigan-biz_cx_jz_0805 dying.html (accessed June 16, 2010).

Index

JAPA

American Planning Association

Journal of the American Planning Association

Editor: David S. Sawicki, FAICP, *Georgia Institute of Technology, USA*
Managing Editor: Amy Helling, AICP, *USA*

2008 Impact Factor: 2.250
Ranking: 1/32 (Urban Studies),
2/43 (Planning & Development)
© 2009 Thomson Reuters, *2008 Journal Citation Reports®*

For more than 70 years, the quarterly *Journal of the American Planning Association* (*JAPA*) has published research, commentaries, and book reviews useful to practicing planners, policymakers, scholars, students, and citizens of urban, suburban, and rural areas. *JAPA* publishes only peer-reviewed, original research and analysis. It aspires to bring insight to planning the future, to air a variety of perspectives, to publish the highest quality work, and to engage readers.

JAPA is interested in manuscripts that examine historical or contemporary planning experience, broadly defined, in domestic or global contexts, and that do at least one of the following:
- contribute to the theoretical and conceptual foundation of planning;
- improve the link between planning and successful policy implementation;
- advance the methods used in planning practice and planning research;
- explain empirical relationships important to planning;
- interpret noteworthy physical, economic, and social phenomena that have spatial dimensions; or
- analyze significant consequences of planning approaches, processes, and contexts.

Recent articles include:

- **Overcoming the Barriers to Manufactured Housing Placement in Metropolitan Communities**
  Casey J. Dawkins and C. Theodore Koebel

- **Using Watered Landscapes to Manipulate Urban Heat Island Effects: How Much Water Will It Take to Cool Phoenix?**
  Patricia Gober, Anthony Brazel, Ray Quay, Soe Myint, Susanne Grossman-Clarke, Adam Miller and Steve Rossi

View selected free articles at:
www.tandf.co.uk/journals/rjpa

Routledge
Taylor & Francis Group

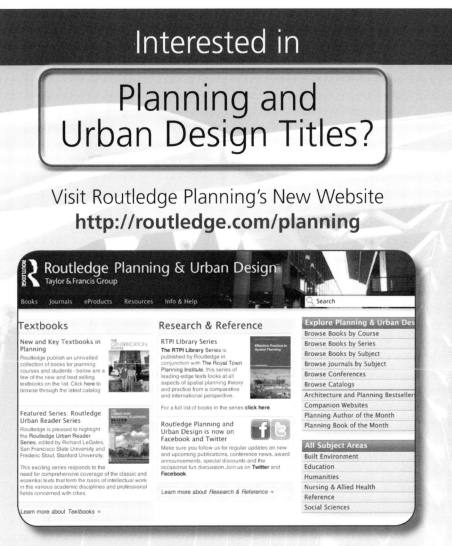